CASTE

*The Emergence of the
South Asian Social System*

CASTE

The Emergence of the
South Asian Social System

Morton Klass

A Publication of the
Institute for the Study of Human Issues
Philadelphia

Manufactured in the United States of America

Library of Congress Cataloging in Publication Data:

Klass, Morton, 1927–
    Caste: the emergence of the South Asian social system.

    Bibliography: p.
    Includes index.
    1. Caste—South Asia. I. Institute for the Study of Human Issues. II. Title.
HT725.S63K56   301.44′0954   79–26012
ISBN 0–915980–97–5

For information, write:

Director of Publications
ISHI
3401 Science Center
Philadelphia, Pennsylvania 19104
U.S.A.

For Phil,
who took the blame
and deserves the credit

The search for origins, like the quest of the Sangreal, possesses endless fascination, and if it does not yield any very tangible results, it at least has the merit of encouraging research.

Sir Herbert H. Risley—*The People of India*

Contents

Preface

I really enjoyed writing this book. Most of my other anthropological writings have derived from my own field notes. However fascinating these may be—and I bow to no one in my admiration of my own research—they can hold few surprises for me. In this work, however, I have had a wonderful opportunity to read extensively in the literature of my discipline. It has been a voyage of discovery and high adventure: here, I sailed between the Scylla and Charybdis of current theoretical dispute; there, I picked my way through the quagmire of nineteenth century views on the origin of caste. Like all good travelers, I am eager now to show you the places I have visited.

Forgive the inconsistencies you will note, at least those of orthography. Until comparatively recently, European writers have had little interest in achieving any uniform representation of words deriving from Sanskrit and other Indian languages. Writers I have cited refer to the priestly caste of India, for example, as Brahman, Brāhman, Bráhman, and Brahmin. Citations will refer to Sudra, Shudra, Shūdra, Vaishya, Vaiśya, and so on.

Nor is the problem only with words of foreign derivation. The English-speaking world has not as yet reached a consensus about whether we are to spell "labor" with a "u" or "colour" without one. "Archeology" is "archaeology" to some, and opinions are sharply divided about which words end in "ize" and which in "ise." Since this book contains extensive quotations from writers on both sides of the Atlantic, my sole effort has been to quote them correctly, and I wish the typesetter all the luck and patience in the world. I did try, whenever I took the floor myself, to maintain a consistency of spelling. This was occasionally difficult, particularly when there was a need to refer back to someone else's point—and term.

I did at times quote at considerable length. Some readers might have preferred summaries, but I considered it important, for a work such as this, that views be conveyed exactly—and how better than in the author's own words?

When one ranges over an extensive span of time, as I have done here, it is often important to note the order in which intellectual contributions were made. This is sometimes difficult because we often work with recent editions of books. Where I thought it advisable, I have indicated the original edition in the bibliographic citation. If the matter of date seemed to have no bearing on the question under consideration, the citation indicates only the particular edition I consulted.

The book was four intermittent years in the writing, but it reflects about two decades of reading, thinking, arguing, and teaching. As a graduate student I first became uneasy because the search for the origins of the caste system had been abandoned. As a teacher, perceiving the problems this abandonment precipitated in the minds of my students, I became even more uneasy. There were questions, I found, I was required to address.

For most of my professional life, too, I have been debating with colleagues, students—and myself—the advantages and disadvantages of various current theoretical approaches in anthropology . . . of *all* of them . . . of *none* of them. Nevertheless, as far as I know, the main points in this book are my own—anyway, I assume full responsibility for what I have written. I have, however, been stimulated and influenced by teachers, colleagues, and students, and I am immeasurably grateful to them all.

I am grateful to Barnard College for a small grant to defray some of the costs of typing and reproduction. I also wish to express my deep gratitude to Ainslie T. Embree, Theodore Riccardi, Jr., Stephen A. Rittenberg, and other members of the staff of the Southern Asian Institute of Columbia University for so generously providing me with a place to work in peace and solitude. Without that assistance, this book would have required months, perhaps years, more.

Joan Vincent was kind enough to read and criticize an early version of this manuscript. Phyllis Dain, Morton Fried, Creighton Peet, Herbert Lewis, Sidney Greenfield, and Conrad Arensberg offered valuable suggestions. I listened carefully, and I am grateful to them.

I have benefited greatly from the erudite advice of those who gather around the ISHI round table: Karen Kerner, David Feingold, Betty and Joel Jutkowitz, Douglas Gordon, and Janet Greenwood. Truly, these are the advisors and editors one dreams of in the darkness of the academic night. My abiding gratitude to all.

Work on this manuscript actually began during the summer of 1974 at Whitefish Lake, Minnesota. I mention this because it gives me an opportunity to thank Dan and Aurea Keyes, not only for their hospitality on that occasion, but also for many years of good friendship.

My children—Perri, David, and Judy—contributed to the completion of this manuscript with encouragement and suggestions, but especially with patience and forbearance. And I thank my wife, Sheila Solomon Klass, without whom this book could never have been written, nor anything else of note accomplished by me.

Leonia, July 1979

I

An Argument for Eclecticism

The ancients did not attempt to solve the ultimate problems confronting man by a single and coherent theory. . . . Ancient thought . . . admitted side by side certain limited insights, which were held to be simultaneously valid, each in its own proper context, each corresponding to a definite avenue of approach.

Henri Frankfort—*Ancient Egyptian Religion*

The primary purpose of this book is to present a reasonable explanation, in terms of contemporary anthropological knowledge and theories, of the coming into existence of that South Asian behavioral complex known as the "caste system."

I use the word "reasonable" because I think the explanation I am proposing is exactly that, and I would be delighted to be able to turn to my argument immediately, ignoring all the other issues that are going to take up a major portion of this work. I cannot; these other issues must be addressed first or all my arguments will drown in confusion and misunderstanding.

Broadly speaking, these issues may all be grouped under two headings, *caste* and *evolution*, both matters of passionate disagreement and debate within the discipline of anthropology. Undoubtedly, my arguments will not convince all of my colleagues, but I do want to make my positions on the various issues as clear as possible, and I want to be certain that the stranger to a particular issue understands what the debate is about. To accomplish all that, I must review the definitions, assumptions, and arguments of others, and where necessary put forth my own.

The topic of *caste* requires particularly careful delineation and

1

definition. Fortunately, in some ways, it is a topic of seemingly endless fascination for Western readers, and speculation on the subject reaches back two thousand years and more. Most of my readers are therefore likely to be familiar with the term "caste" and with the construct "caste system." The difficulty is that the term means such different things to different scholars—from a subdivision of a social insect society to a subdivision of a human society. Even for those who would use the term only as a human category, there are fundamental disagreements about the defining features of a caste, and even more about whether the caste system is best understood as a social, an economic, or a religious phenomenon. Such differences in definition obviously affect one's views on whether the caste system is unique. Are variations on "caste" found throughout the world, or is "caste" something peculiar to the Indian subcontinent?

Furthermore, the definition one subscribes to inevitably affects one's perception of how and why the caste system came into existence. This brings us to the second major concern of this book, *evolution*. As we shall see, we will have to review a number of crucial disputes among anthropological theorists, ones that will seem to take us far from the Indian subcontinent and its social system. My concern in this book, however, is with the emergence of the South Asian caste system, and so whatever the wider theoretical disputes about evolution, my problems are made additionally complicated by the fact that most contemporary writers on the nature of caste belong to schools of anthropological thought that tend to avoid the question of origins almost entirely. On the other hand, those modern anthropologists who *are* interested in origin and emergence (such as those commonly called "evolutionists" or "neoevolutionists") have not noticeably applied their theoretical perceptions to the issue of the South Asian caste system. In fact, many of them seem to have ignored the caste system entirely, as if it were somehow offensive to them, or in bad taste.

We are therefore left with a situation in which discussions about the nature of caste have progressed admirably in penetration and subtlety, as well as in the use of contemporary knowledge and theory, while explanations of its origin remained locked, *faute de mieux*, in a web of notions discredited over half a century ago. In other words, while contemporary theorists never express an acceptance of views on the nature of caste as dubious as, say, that of Sir Herbert Risley (namely that caste originated as an effort to prevent racial miscegenation), they no longer bother to challenge such explanations either, in effect leaving the field to Risley, or to the others with equally improbable explanations who are the only ones to tilt with Risley.

Part of the problem, we may begin to perceive, can be laid to a kind of theoretical straitjacket; if the attempt to reconstruct origins is immediately dismissed as "pseudohistory" then it becomes bad form to discuss the subject, even when the intent is only to rule out totally invalid explanations. In recent years, however, amid much swirling controversy, the issue of origins has been reopened for other regions and circumstances. Outmoded explanations have been exploded and swept away and more reasonable ones put forth and made the basis for continuing critical debate. This has not been the case for India and the caste system, and so in this work we will have to review and refute theories that should have long since been laid to rest, and it will be necessary to be very explicit about the theoretical building blocks upon which our edifice is constructed.

I am, as it happens, an eclectic. This means that I am in principle interested in understanding *all* theoretical approaches put forth in my discipline. There are, of course, many I have never been able to make use of, but when I can utilize a theoretical approach I am not particularly troubled by the fact that its proponents loudly proclaim the worthlessness of some other approach, which, quite often, I can also employ. Are you a "structuralist," a "cultural ecologist," or a "diffusionist"? Supposedly, if you are one of these, you cannot in good conscience subscribe to the tenets of either of the others. You may be interested in symbolism, or in techno-environmental determinism, or in personality-and-culture, but surely not in all three together, you say? Well, I am an eclectic, and I will use whatever methodological or ideological approach—or combination of them—allows me the best grasp of the problem at hand.

It seems to me that the eclectic approach is a rather humble get-about-your-business one, but it tends to get a bad press, particularly from those who think to advance one school by attempting to discredit all the others. Such people must (and do) find it infuriating to be told: "You're both right." Marvin Harris has expressed the classic attitude toward the eclectic:[1]

Eclecticism is certainly the path of least resistance through the frequently strident polemics of the system-mongers. Most anthropologists simply want to be left in peace to pursue the study of their "people." If one keeps technological, economic, social, political, and ideational factors "in mind," why should one have to get embroiled in the brouhaha of theoretical disputation?

Because of the strong logical affinity between an eclectic and an inductive approach, many Boasians have reacted with bewilderment and impatience to the critical evaluation of Boas' influence. The frequent assertion that Boas "founded no school" went along with the belief that the only thing that Boas insisted on was higher standards of proof; as long as it was responsible to the data, any theoretical interest was compatible with the attempt to preserve the vanishing fragments of primitive languages and cultures. . . .

Eclecticism, however, abounds with hidden dangers. In practice, it is often little more than a euphemism for confusion, the muddled acceptance of contradictory theories, the bankruptcy of creative thought, and the cloak of mediocrity. It bestows upon its practitioners a false sense of security and an unearned reputation for scientific acumen. Science consists of more than responsibility to the data; the data must be made responsible to theory. Neither one without the other suffices. It is impossible to be faithful to the facts and at the same time indifferent to theory.

The history of the Boasian period suggests that the problem of causality in culture can never be solved through a well-rounded eclectic approach. It seems likely that in practice eclecticism will always end by amplifying one's initial impression of randomness and unpredictability. The very idea of a scientific statement demands that some balance be struck among the relevant variables, that they be assigned different weights and values, and that they be segregated into dependent and independent relationships. To say that everything is equally important in every situation is to propose in effect that all situations should be the same (Harris 1968: 284–5).

As I interpret Harris' position, he sees eclectics in anthropology as those who wish, somewhat naively, to do field work and to

---

[1]See also Fried (1972: 156–7), and Geertz (1973: 4–5).

4

avoid disputation about theory. Harris sympathizes with their desire, but notes that it is in the end an unwise one, leading inevitably to confusion, inadequate explanation, contradiction and an impression of "randomness and unpredictability" hardly conducive to scientific inquiry.

And, if I follow him, he goes further: eclecticism is often little more than "the bankruptcy of creative thought and the cloak of mediocrity." In this he echoes the opinion of philosophers, particularly theological philosophers, since the early years of Christian theological disputation. The authoritative eleventh edition of the *Encyclopaedia Britannica* sums up the customary attitude by noting that "eclecticism" is:

a term used especially in philosophy and theology for a composite system of thought made up of views borrowed from various other systems. . . . Eclecticism always tends to spring up after a period of vigorous constructive speculation, especially in the latter stages of a controversy between thinkers of pre-eminent ability. Their respective followers, and more especially cultured laymen, lacking the capacity for original work, seeking for a solution in some kind of compromise, and possibly failing to grasp the essentials of the controversy, take refuge in a combination of those elements in the opposing systems which seem to afford a sound practical theory. Since these combinations have often been as illogical as facile, "eclecticism" has generally acquired a somewhat contemptuous significance ("Eclecticism" 1910: 887).

Though written half a century earlier, the quotation reflects views essentially similar to those of Harris. The article continues, however:

At the same time, the essence of eclecticism is the refusal to follow blindly one set of formulae and conventions, coupled with a determination to recognize and select from all sources those elements which are good or true in the abstract, or in practical affairs most useful *ad hoc* (*Ibid.*).

Here, it seems to me, an important dimension is added, one missing in Harris' commentary. For no one wants to defend, or be associated with, the fools, ignoramuses, connivers and deceivers in one's discipline, whatever their theoretical orientation or lack of it.

If our colleague be "muddled" or "unoriginal" or "illogical" we turn away from him in righteous contempt whether he be a structuralist or a techno-environmental determinist. The issue, clearly, is not whether *some* eclectics have been found intellectually or morally wanting, but whether the approach itself is worthless, or, in Harris' words, beset with "hidden dangers."

The distaste for the individual eclectic to be observed in both references is an interesting phenomenon, worth passing consideration. My own suspicion is that it originates in those aforementioned days of impassioned religious controversy. The controversy was impassioned because each school sought—and each thinker was convinced that he alone had found—God's own *Truth*, the only road to salvation.

Now if that is what we are seeking, if you and I have each constructed a system setting forth the meaning of the universe and the will of a demanding and remorseless divinity, and if we disagree with each other, then it is manifest (if I *know* the Truth) that you are immersed in sin and error. At best you are a misguided soul headed for hell; at worst you are an agent of the very devil, seeking to corrupt the innocent. And so you and I may call each other heretic, may seek to turn our followers against each other; we may even seek to burn each other at the stake. But at least we understand each other; we complement each other. Each of us has sought the Truth, each has a complete system of that Truth, and only one of us can be right. On all that we jointly agree.

Then along comes the eclectic, who listens to us both and suggests that we are *both* right, setting up a system that incorporates elements from both our systems, as well as elements from other systems that to both of us are clearly iniquitous. Such a person is obviously either a fool (unable to comprehend what the whole debate was about) or a charlatan (who understands the debate but, unable to construct an original system of his own, fools the unknowing public by faking one out of bits and pieces of other systems).

Personally, were I a theologian, or even a philosopher interested in the ultimate order and meaning of the universe, I think I would hold the eclectic in as much contempt as anyone. Theology and that kind of philosophic inquiry are not my concerns, however, as I should imagine they are not Harris', and in scientific research (including that of anthropology) it seems to me the issues are entirely different. I seek no ultimate Truth; in fact, unlike Harris, I even have difficulty with the term *causality*, and not only for cultural phenomena. After all, the term derives from prescientific modes of inquiry, and I try to stay in my own bailiwick.

We scientists observe, accumulate and assemble data, under strict rules of accountability. We must order the data without imposing extraneous and distorting categories, and that alone is more than enough, if we can do it well. It is so easy all unintentionally to cut, stretch, weight—and so distort—that I for one tremble at dicta such as Harris': "Science consists of more than responsibility to the data; the data must be made responsible to theory." Down that road lies many a Procrustean bed.

But of course we do seek to do more than order the data; we seek to isolate and weigh variables, to determine correlations and correspondences and so ultimately to reconstruct and to predict—to find, in other words, convincing explanations for past events and, by far the best of all, statements as to the nature of future events that will stand the tests of time. We acknowledge order and regularity, and attempt to formulate rules and laws as tersely and elegantly as we can. All this we try to do—or as much of it as we are individually able to do, and as the maturity of our discipline permits. Our discipline, like all scholarly disciplines, must inevitably exhibit a degree of distortion to the outside observer: we have our special areas of preoccupation and traditional concern, our jargon, our particular strengths and our abiding ignorance of the findings of other disciplines.

Ideally, of course, we hope eventually to be able to put all of our insights and findings together in one overarching system of explanation and prediction. In the end, we are all synthesists, or would like to be, and that is one reason I have not characterized myself as a "synthesist" despite some pressure by friends who find the term more comfortable than the usually pejorative "eclectic." The issue I am trying to raise here, however, is the need to avoid the shoals of dogmatism, the rocks of mono-theory. We would all be delighted to have one single synthetic approach capable of encompassing all the problems of interest to our discipline. But until that day arrives—and as far as I can see it is still some distance

7

away for anthropology—we have to cope as best as we can with seemingly unrelated problems, choosing as wisely as we can among the various proposals for dealing with such problems. And if the theologian abhors and castigates eclecticism, the scientist must fear and avoid dogmatism.

While it may be bad theology, I submit that it is perfectly good scientific methodology, to employ the explanatory system that appears to be most useful for the particular problem at hand, even when it is clear that the approach is useless for another order of problem. Emerson's eclectic squirrel put the issue most pointedly to a dogmatic mountain: "If I cannot carry mountains on my back, neither can you crack a nut."

There is no conflict, of course, between eclecticism and synthesis. The eclectic student is neither surprised nor disconcerted to discover that for some problems two or more seemingly unconnected—even contradictory—approaches may serve, if properly amalgamated, where no single one does, and this despite the fury of contending theorists.

And, since it is this last and particularly opprobrious variety of eclectic behavior that will occur repeatedly in this essay, I shall end my polemic and embark upon the substance with an example of two contending theoretical positions which, I hope, will be utilized in tandem in the effort to unravel the fundamental problem of this work: How and why did the caste system come into existence in South Asia?

One position is that of Harry Pearson, an economist, as set forth in a paper called "The Economy has no Surplus; Critique of a Theory of Development" (1957). The other position, in direct and immediate opposition to that of Pearson, was set forth in a paper significantly entitled "The Economy has no Surplus?" (1959). It was written by the anthropologist Marvin Harris.

Pearson's work constitutes a chapter of a book, *Trade and Market in the Early Empires: Economies in History and Theory*, edited by Karl Polanyi, Conrad M. Arensberg, and Harry Pearson himself (1957). Some of the arguments advanced in their book will be discussed in depth later on; let us note here only that it is a work challenging certain basic assumptions of economics, particularly that the human is a rational, economizing creature, and that eco-

nomic behavior may be approached and indeed understood primarily in terms of the interplay of scarce goods and multiple needs.
Pearson, in his paper, carries this argument further:

there is a concept of widely current use in anthropology, prehistory, and
economic history which bears a relationship to the analysis of economic
development similar to that between the scarcity postulate and economic
analysis. This is the concept of surplus employed in a way which makes
the appearance of a "surplus" over bare subsistence needs the critical deter-
minant in the evolution of complex social and economic institutions from
simple beginnings. Thus an oversufficiency of means is said to bring on
the development of economic institutions just as an insufficiency of means
is said to enforce the utilitarian management of resources, which is the
economy in the formal sense (*Ibid.*: 320–21).

We see clearly that Pearson has related the issue of surplus
and the development of economic institutions to the larger issues of
the book. Indeed, a substantial part of his paper is devoted to this
relationship. Pearson probes the rationalistic assumptions of the
nineteenth century theorists, from Morgan to Marx and Engels,
who developed what he refers to as the "surplus theorem." The
book as a whole argues the advantages of what Polanyi has termed
the substantive over the formal approach to economies,[2] and Pearson echoes that argument in his critique of the "surplus theorem":

this assumed train of events is based upon a crude confusion of the economy with the state of technology. The economy, to repeat, is a social
process which means that the production, movement and transfer of economic goods may be variously organized. Precisely how these elements of
early economies were organized and integrated is the problem for investigation (*Ibid.*: 327).

Let me not dissemble; I have been much influenced by the
substantive approach advocated by Polanyi and his associates in
this book. Later pages will reveal some of the extent of that influence. For now, however, I would prefer to turn from the more

---

[2]The two approaches and some of the implications of the debate will be
examined in a later chapter.

fundamental issues of human or societal rationality to the specific problem posed in Pearson's paper:

> When employed as the key to evolutionary change, the surplus theorem has two essential parts. There is first the very concept of such a surplus. It is taken to represent that quantity of material resources which exists over and above the subsistence requirements of the society in question. Such surpluses are supposed to appear with advancing technology and productivity, and serve to distinguish one level of social and economic organization from another. The second part of the surplus theorem is the expectation that the surplus has an enabling effect which allows typical social and economic developments of prime importance to take place. Trade and markets, money, cities, differentiation into social classes, indeed civilization itself, are thus said to follow upon the emergence of a surplus (*Ibid.*: 321).

Pearson returns to this issue on a later page:

> The meaning of the concept is clear enough. There is a level of subsistence which once reached provides a measure—so to speak the dam over which the surplus flows. This surplus which is beyond needs however these happen to be defined, is then in some sense available: it may be traded abroad, or used to support the existence of craftsmen, a leisure class, or other nonproductive members of the society. In other words, it becomes the key variable in the emergence of more complex social and economic institutions (*Ibid.*: 322).

In effect, it seems to me, Pearson has raised three questions. *First:* is there, can there be, such a thing as a "surplus"—defined as "that quantity of material resources which exists over and above the subsistence requirements of the society in question"? *Second:* assuming the existence of the phenomenon of "surplus," how exactly does it go about *causing* change in society and economy? And *third:* if you really want to understand socioeconomic change, rather than merely postulate "surplus," why not study the organization and integration of the particular socioeconomic system itself?

Pearson, we have seen, tends to dismiss the very concept of "surplus." Subsistence requirements are clearly relative, he argues, differing from society to society, and therefore what is to be considered "above" subsistence and thus an "oversufficiency" would undoubtedly vary from society to society. He concludes:

There are always and everywhere potential surpluses available. What counts is the institutional means for bringing them to life. And these means for calling forth the special effort, setting aside the extra amount, devising the surplus, are as wide and varied as the organization of the economic process itself (*Ibid.*: 339).

Marvin Harris addresses himself directly to Harry Pearson and the paper cited above, stating in his first paragraph:

The author of this chapter, an economist, set himself the task of destroying the surplus theory of social stratification by showing that the concept of surplus upon which it rests has neither logical nor empirical validity. Since certain aspects of Pearson's criticism of the "surplus above subsistence" notion cannot be refuted, his argument contains much of significance for anthropologists concerned with cultural regularities, but his additional conclusions with respect to the operational framework of economic anthropology inspire vigorous dissent (1959: 185).

Harris is motivated to reply to Pearson, as he makes very clear, because of his conviction that a deterministic approach is vital to any useful effort to penetrate the phenomena of cultural evolution:

To the cultural relativist, Pearson's position will seem to represent the highest canons of scientific procedure and there will be many who will be delighted with the prospect of shuffling off the last remaining coils of the evolutionary serpent. Yet while Pearson pays his respects to determinism, it is only lip service. His denial of the chronological and functional primacy of biological needs and of the techno-environmental adaptations for the fulfillment of these needs is tantamount to a renunciation of the search for order among cross-cultural phenomena. This is not merely because his criticism of the surplus theory cannot be sustained, but because the manner in which he has chosen to refute it inevitably leads to the conclusion that cultural phenomena are essentially the result of whimsical and capricious processes (*Ibid.*: 188).

For Harris, the processes are neither whimsical nor capricious. *Determinism* is the key term in the above quotation: cultural

11

evolution, in his view, reflects the workings of immutable regularities. And not only are there laws and regularities, but for Harris
these regularities are unmistakably expressed in the economically
rational behavior of humans:

I wish to emphasize again . . . that the hypothesis of a cross-cultural tendency to maximize production of food with approximately uniform results
under similar techno-environmental conditions is merely a reasonable hypothesis. . . . Apparent examples of exceptionally irrational uses of the
means of production and the method of the consumption of food will occur
to every ethnologist. Under the present condition of anthropological theory these exceptions have come to be enshrined as sacred bits of anarchy.
No systematic attempt has been made to explain these exceptions in terms
of the rules which they are supposed to violate, and worse, the Boasian
belief that in order to invalidate an empirical law one need merely find an
exception still pervades our discipline. When an effort is made to probe
more deeply into the ecological circumstances surrounding the cherished
examples of the ideological and organizational mismanagement of food
production, it is quite likely that a good many of them will yet be shown
to conform to the hypothesis rather than to invalidate it (*Ibid.*: 194).

Harris, picking up the gauntlet he himself had thrown, made
just such "an effort to probe more deeply into the ecological circumstances" of a classic case of food "mismanagement," that of the
Indian "sacred cow," in his seminal paper, "The Cultural Ecology
of India's Sacred Cattle" (1966). I would be signally ungrateful if I
did not here acknowledge my own debt to Marvin Harris, particularly in respect to this paper; I shall refer to it in some detail in a
later chapter. For now, however, I want to turn from theoretical
underpinnings and ideological motivations, however significant
they may be, to the specific argument Harris offers in rebutting
Pearson.

Harris is most effective in responding to the first issue raised
by Pearson: is there really such a thing as "surplus"? Pearson, it
will be remembered, doubted that there ever was, or could be, a
determinable "absolute surplus," and argued that in all, or most,
societies quantities of food and other goods could often be produced in addition to that perceived as necessary for subsistence.
Since, in such a case, "oversufficiency" was clearly a reflection of

cultural attitudes and perceptions, a "surplus" was inevitably a *social* phenomenon, clearly "relative" and not "absolute."

Harris acknowledges this kind of surplus but calls it an "unnecessary" or "superfluous" variety of surplus, preferring to concentrate on the possibility of an actual "absolute surplus," one that is based on biological factors and is independent of cultural variability. To begin with, Harris notes, humans are biological organisms and as such consume energy in the form of food:

> Actually, the state of nutritional science even now provides us with a basis for roughly calculating the minimum subsistence level of activity for a specific population, if by subsistence level is meant the amount of energy necessary to do nothing except what is biophysically necessary to satisfy the metabolic requirements of the populations concerned. Such a subsistence level is determined by the energy necessary for basal metabolism, specific dynamic action, and the energy gain associated with whatever techniques of food production are employed (1959: 189).

Of course, Harris' concept of "subsistence level" echoes, and presumably derives from, Leslie White's proposal (1973; first printed in 1949) that we view a human society as an "energy-capturing system." This is another reference that will be pursued later in greater depth. For now, let us follow White in observing that a society as a body must, at minimum, replace the energy consumed by that body of people if it is to survive and continue as such a body. In other, if still confusing, words: enough food must be available for enough adults to have the energy to go out and find or produce enough energy to replace the used-up quantity—and so on without end, but always acquiring enough additional energy for enough children to provide for the continuation of the population. This metabolic requirement is clearly what Harris refers to as "subsistence level."

Harris appears to be arguing that simple hunters and gatherers maintain over time a steady subsistence level, producing enough energy to maintain and continue their populations, but no more. He refers, in fact, to the "barbarism of supposing that primitive food-producers have been capable of producing more food than they and their children could eat" (*Ibid.*: 192). In such a "primitive

13

food-producing" society, then, there may well be a fluctuation of available food (energy) from year to year, so that in a given year energy accumulations may exceed, or may fail to reach, subsistence requirements—but viewed over a sufficient time span, productivity in such a society approximates its needs.

One might, following Harris, speculate that if productivity falls too far below the society's requirements the death rate will increase, particularly for the very old and the very young. On the other hand, if accumulations of energy exceed the society's needs for a long enough period, there will be a noticeable population increase. Harris' point, I believe, is that for such a society it all averages out over time. And a temporary abundance in a good year is what Harris refers to as a "superfluous" or "unnecessary" surplus—unnecessary, as I read him, for the understanding or the effecting of evolutionary change.

An "absolute" surplus, on the other hand, exists—if I am still following Harris—when the amount of energy available to a population is *continually* in excess of that which is needed for subsistence. Presumably, the death rate goes down and the rate of live births (or the proportion of surviving children) goes up, and so the population increases, perhaps dramatically. If, nevertheless, the food accumulation (or productivity) *continues* to exceed the subsistence needs of the population, despite the latter's growth, we have a situation of "absolute" or "necessary" surplus:

It is from drafts upon this necessary surplus that both the food-producers and the nonfood-producers are enabled to carry out the nonfood-producing activities which complete the inventory of sociocultural life. The surplus theory proper holds that significant qualitative and quantitative changes in the nature of this surplus will tend to be accompanied by significant changes in social organization, especially those related to an increase in economic, religious, and political specialization, and the development of social stratification based upon unequal access to strategic property (*Ibid.*: 195).

Attention is drawn to the verb in one of the above sentences: "significant qualitative and quantitative changes in the nature of this surplus *will tend* to be accompanied." It seems to me that Harris has answered Pearson's first question—is there such a thing as an "absolute surplus"—quite effectively, but he does not tell us *how* such a surplus actually precipitates change. He says only that the appearance of the surplus "will tend to be accompanied" by socioeconomic changes. But Pearson requested some insight into the mechanisms, given the belief in the necessary connection. Harris appears to admit, at least tacitly, his inability to deal with the second of Pearson's questions:

> The reason why food-producers keep on working is that despite (or perhaps in some cases because of) the presence of a nonfood-producing-class and abundant leisure, there is a shortage of necessary food supplies. The decisive question now becomes: what force or incentive makes the food-producers surrender a portion of their necessary food supply in order to support a class of nonfood-producers?
>
> Undoubtedly, the diversion of food from the food-producing group has not been accomplished in any single uniform manner throughout the world. But wherever we find a nonproducing elite, we may assume that they exist by virtue of their ability to control food supplies. Whatever the initial context of this control, once established, it is probably increased in direct proportion to the size of the surplus above subsistence produced by the food-producers and to the increase in the total population (*Ibid.*: 198).

Harris evades the issue when he writes, "Whatever the initial context of this control, once established," because it is precisely that "initial context" about which Pearson has raised the question!

Let us look more closely. We have Harris' "primitive food-producers" as a baseline—presumably lacking full-time specialists such as artisans, soldiers, officials and other "nonproducers." They enter into a situation of "absolute surplus": more energy is continuously available to the society than it needs for subsistence. Harris has argued, quite reasonably, that such circumstances *make possible* a future in which a complex stratified society has come into existence and in which the food-producers must now support, often at considerable cost to themselves, a pyramid of nonfood-producers who can, with a variety of means, compel the services of the food-producers.

But Pearson asks: how did the transformation take place? Why did those early food-producers allow the body of nonfood-producers to come into existence? Specifically, if I (with my

15

family) can provide enough food to feed ten nonfood-producing families, why *should* I provide the food? This question does not apply to the later situation, when the apparatus of complex societies compels me to so provide, but to the earliest time—before the apparatus has come into existence, or even as it is just beginning to do so.

Visualize a society of "primitive food-producers" of the kind postulated by Harris. They have recently entered into a condition characterized by "absolute surplus." Until now, they have had no full-time specialists, no nonproducing classes. Observing the terms of their socioeconomic rules, they have been, and are, accumulating enough food to satisfy their needs, circulating that food (and other goods) within the society, and consuming it. No doubt, in these present happy circumstances they find they can feed more children and elderly, and can have more elaborate religious ceremonies, than ever before—but that is what happens, as Harris has pointed out, with "superfluous surpluses." The members of our society, however, are now being asked to support not just one shaman but a body of religious specialists, not just one artisan but a whole class of artisans, not just a chief but a hierarchy of rulers with their families and subordinates. What makes them do it? Why go that way?

In our time, of course, we have seen many examples of such change enforced by outside pressures, when subsistence populations must give up shares of their produce through inveiglement into the world economy or because of the imposition of taxes backed by the police or military. The question being asked, however, is how the police, military, and all the rest of the edifice first came into existence! Why change the old way of life without the motivating prior presence of a coercive government or class—particularly when, as Harris himself has pointed out, the burdens inevitably become greater, and the rewards fewer, for the members of the food-producing class?

Harris has convinced me that the concept of "absolute surplus" is a valid and meaningful one and that it constitutes, despite Pearson's arguments, the necessary and enabling factor in the emergence of complex stratified societies. Harris has not convinced me, however, that once given "absolute surplus" the emergence of such societies is inevitable. It may be that his use of the words "will tend" is an indication that he himself is not completely convinced. In any case, as we shall see in a later chapter, there are some contemporary exponents of cultural evolution who also seem unconvinced by Harris' assertion that "absolute surplus" is a sufficient condition, at least in all cultural circumstances, for the development of stratification.

Moving away from this for now, let us note again that Harris has not responded to the second question raised by Pearson: how can the fact of surplus produce the changes—what are the processes, the mechanisms? It seems to me that Pearson has in fact provided the key to the answer when he urges us to seek an explanation of the nature of the transformation from simple to complex—the processes by which stratification emerges—by exploring the ordering of socioeconomic relationships in the actual societies themselves.

In South Asia there had to be a time, somewhere in the past, before the present complex structure that we know as the "caste system" had come into existence. Let us consider it a time of what Harris has called "primitive food-producers." Eventually, and inarguably, the "caste system"—generally accepted as one of the most complex and stratified of all societal systems on earth—emerged into something recognizably like its classic form. The presence of an "absolute surplus" no doubt made that emergence possible, but we have to see whether it had to happen. And also how it happened: what were the "forces" and "incentives" that Harris refers to but does not delineate? What were the mechanisms and processes by which socioeconomic structural transformation was effected?

The goal of this book is to provide answers to these and related questions. The Pearson-Harris debate is of course central, and so had to be reviewed, but it may be remembered that I introduced the debate from a different perspective: that of eclecticism as a valid theoretical position.

Pearson, along with his coeditors Polanyi and Arensberg, challenges the assumption of human rationality, at least insofar as "rationality" may be used to explain economic behavior and development. Pearson is in direct and absolute opposition to the position advocated by Harris. According to Harris, human "rationality" is

17

fundamental, obvious, inarguable and, above all, necessary. Harris' understanding of causality in human affairs and his explanations of social and economic development derive from and require this as their foundation.

How then can I set out to explore and explain a case of socioeconomic change and development—even evolution—while deriving from one approach based upon fundamental and causal "rationality" and simultaneously from another approach that challenges and discards that "rationality" as neither fundamental nor causative?

I can only do it by begging the question. Shameful, but there it is: the typical eclectic waffle. Not to be totally ingenuous, I admit that I have private views on the issue of causative rationality, but I see no reason to make them public, at least at this point. It is sufficient for my purposes to observe that Harris has clarified the problem of "absolute surplus" and Pearson has alerted us to seek the sociocultural processes by which such a surplus leads, when it does, to complexity and transformation. With these, I can move.

It must be borne in mind that the problem, the contending positions, the material drawn upon, and the perspectives employed all derive in large measure from the discipline of anthropology. Students of other disciplines may, for example, find the debate about human rationality naive, or old-fashioned, or even silly. It is not silly to anthropologists, who must wrestle with the implications of an astonishingly wide variety of unexpected and alien cultural responses. Again, anthropologists of all theoretical persuasions are familiar with the need to study and understand the principles of kinship and clanship if we are to penetrate human social behavior; the eyes of nonanthropologists (at least in Western society) tend to glaze over when these topics come up. In this work, I give fair warning, the nature and implications of clan organization are going to be explored in some depth. This is not solely because I am myself an anthropologist, particularly attentive to the issues peculiar to anthropologists; rather, the problem before us, as I see it, is primarily an anthropological one, reflecting anthropological concerns, and capable of solution in terms of anthropological data and theory.

The strategy to be employed in the succeeding pages reflects the peculiar ramifications of the problem under consideration. The problem, as it has been posed, is: How and why did the caste system, a system of stratification, emerge in its classic form in South Asia? Ideally, one might proceed by first defining or delimiting the "caste system" and then move on to a consideration of the factors leading to its emergence.

As I have already noted, however, there is too much disagreement and even confusion on basic issues having to do with both *caste* and *evolution* for me to take this straightforward path. I shall begin, therefore, with a consideration of what has gone before: the traditional Western perception of the South Asian social system and the explanations of origin that have attended that perception. Following that, I shall present my own understanding of the salient features of caste, drawing upon somewhat more modern theories of society and economy. It will then be necessary for me to review some issues that come to the fore when one ponders cultural evolution or transformation.

After all that, I will be ready to take on the problem of how the caste system—as I understand that system, and given my understanding of the processes and conditions of cultural evolution—came into existence.

2

Intimations of Caste

My business is to record what people say, but I am by no means bound to believe it—and that may be taken to apply to this book as a whole.

Herodotus—*The Histories*

Students of South Asia would certainly agree that the caste system reflects complexity and stratification. They would probably further agree that it represents the most complex and stratified society on our planet. But what do we *mean* by "caste"? Alas, here the consensus falls apart.

How, for example, shall we distinguish "caste" from "ethnic group" or even from "tribe"? Almost every observer has a different definition, and different cultures make different distinctions. The literature in English abounds with volumes about "The Tribes and Castes" of every region of British India, while in many Indian languages the word *jati* (or its equivalent) is used indiscriminately for what the English observer separately labels "tribe" and "caste."

In other words, the observer inevitably brings his own perceptions, assumptions, and preconceptions to bear, even in efforts at simple description. The term "tribe," as a case in point, has in recent years been criticized as too general, too all-encompassing, and in the end much too distorting a category (see Fried, 1975). The use of that term by nineteenth century British writers clearly reflected, among other things, the simplistic evolutionary concepts of the time, whereby the original population of Australia, supposedly the most "primitive," was organized in "hordes" while the slightly more "advanced" peoples of Africa, South America, and the hills and jungles of South Asia belonged to "tribes." Only in

Europe and a few other favored spots in the world did we f
highest form of social organization, the "state" or "nation
Fried, *op.cit.*, particularly pp. 88–98).

Involved in all this were notions about the relative super
(or at least the significance) of kin-based versus territory-based
tems, about the presence or absence of central political autho
about the degree of sedentariness of the population, and about
nature of subsistence activities. South Asia, apparently, did
qualify for inclusion in the highest order, and yet the great popu
tion, the degree of specialization to be observed, and numerous oth
factors all militated against calling it a "tribal" society. The catego
"caste" was a convenient in-between one (cf. Senart 1930: 8).

Therefore, before we can move on to our inquiry into origins
we must pause to ask what the term "caste" meant to the people
who first applied it to South Asia. What were outside observers
seeing—or, better, what did they *think* they were seeing—when
they first gazed upon the South Asian social system? For, if Morton Fried has alerted us to the dangers of misusing—even of *using*—
the term "tribe," Julian Pitt-Rivers has demonstrated that use of
the word "caste" can easily distort our ethnographic data, or at
least our understanding or categorization of that data. He warns:

> The problem is not merely to guard against the implications of
> popular usage when employing words as scientific terms. It is a question of
> determining the heuristic status of the words we use. To what extent are
> they able to carry an analytic load? (Pitt-Rivers 1971: 233).

This problem of the observer's bias or preconception is with us
from the beginning. The earliest written account we have—or almost have—is that of Megasthenes, a Greek traveler, possibly even
an ambassador from the court of Seleucus, who visited Pataliputra
(today the city of Patna in the state of Bihar) around 300 B.C. He
wrote up his travels to the courts of the Indian rulers known to us as
Porus and Chandragupta, and his work was accepted as authoritative by all the scholars of classic Greco-Roman times.

Unhappily, today we no longer have Megasthenes' actual account, but only those fragments and references that have survived in
the writings of others. Megasthenes' account was a primary source

21

for the scholar Arrian (Flavius Arrianus), whose work *Indika*, written sometime before 180 A.D., is still available to us. J.W. McCrindle's 1877 translation of the *Indika* was incorporated into R. C. Majumdar's compendium (1960) of all known and surviving references to South Asia by the classic Greek and Roman writers.

According to Arrian, then, Megasthenes noted a distinction in India between what McCrindle has translated as "tribes" and "castes":

The Indian tribes, Megasthenes tells us, number in all 118. And I will so far agree with him as to allow that they must be indeed numerous, but when he gives such a precise estimate I am at a loss to conjecture how he arrives at it, for the greater part of India he did not visit, nor is mutual intercourse maintained between all the tribes. (*Ibid.*: 220).

. . . In India the whole people are divided into about seven castes (*Ibid.*: 224).

And so the "castes" of India are introduced into world discourse. Or are they? Let us remind ourselves that we have just read McCrindle's translation of Arrian's representation of whatever it was that Megasthenes wrote!

An inquiry into the word Arrian/Megasthenes used for "tribe" would take us too far afield, but we must look at the term McCrindle has translated as "caste." Megasthenes, according to Arrian, reported that India was divided into seven μέρη (*merē*), a term that, as Senart has pointed out (1930: 2), is usually translated as "divisions."

In fact, since the word "caste" is, or at any rate is generally accepted to be, of Portuguese derivation, its use by McCrindle is in some measure anachronistic. We are suddenly unsure whether or not Megasthenes was actually referring to what *we* call "castes." Had he in fact observed the *varnas*—or perhaps even something totally different? As a matter of fact, Senart leans in the latter direction, noting that the same term, μέρη,[1] was used by Herodotus to refer to the "divisions" of ancient Egypt—and Herodotus reported that there were seven there, too![2] Senart is clearly imply-

---

[1] *Merē* is the plural of *meros*, meaning part, or division.

[2] As it happens, my favorite translation of Herodotus refers to the Egyptian "classes." Truly, *traddutore, traditore*.

ing that for some reason Greek scholars, from Herodotus to Megas-thenes, assumed that certain kinds of barbarian states, of which Egypt and India were examples, exhibited no more and no less than seven formal divisions.

Let us take warning from this Greek conceit; preconceived notions about the characteristics of a "society" at a given "level of evolution" or "level of sociocultural complexity" or whatever, have been the bane of anthropological research for a century or more, and not just in India.

But we are concerned here with India. Arrian tells us that Megasthenes described the seven μέρη as consisting of:

1) "the Sophists" . . . who are not so numerous as the others, but hold the supreme place of dignity and honour—for they are under no necessity of doing any bodily labour at all, or of contributing from the produce of their labour anything to the common stock, nor indeed is any duty binding on them except to perform the sacrifices offered to the gods on behalf of the state. . . . To this class the knowledge of divination among the Indians is exclusively restricted and none but a sophist is allowed to practice that art. . . . These sages go naked, living during the winter in the open air to enjoy the sunshine. . . . They live upon the fruits which each season produces, and on the barks of trees. . . .

2) "the tillers of the soil" . . . who form the most numerous class of the population. They are neither furnished with arms, nor have any military duties to perform, but they cultivate the soil and pay tribute to the kings and the independent cities.

3) "herdsmen, both shepherds and neatherds" . . . these neither live in cities nor in villages, but they are nomadic and live on the hills. They too are subject to tribute, and this they pay in cattle. They scour the country in pursuit of fowl and wild beasts.

4) "handicraftmen and retail-dealers." They have to perform gratuitously certain public services, and to pay tribute from the products of their labour. . . . In this class are included shipbuilders, and the sailors employed in the navigation of the rivers.

5) "warriors" . . . [who] lead a life of supreme freedom and enjoyment. They have only military duties to perform. . . . As long as they are required to fight they fight, and when peace returns they abandon themselves to enjoyment.

6) "superintendents." They spy out what goes on in country and town, and report everything to the king where the people have a king, and to the magistrate where the people are self-governed. . . .

7) "councillors of state" . . . who advise the king, or the magistrates of self-governed cities, in the management of public affairs. In point of numbers this is a small class, but it is distinguished by superior wisdom and justice, and hence enjoys the prerogative of choosing governors, chiefs of provinces, deputy-governors, superintendents of the treasury, generals of the army, admirals of the navy, controllers, and commissioners who superintend agriculture (Majumdar 1960: 224–26).

Thus Megasthenes' account—or, to be fair, Arrian's account, presumably derived from Megasthenes, but with what errors, additions or deletions we cannot know. What are we to do with it all? We can of course play the game some of my readers have undoubtedly begun, the one traditionally played by those with some knowledge of and much interest in Indian social structure: we can try our hands at reinterpreting these passages. Arrian/Megasthenes have provided us with some tantalizing pieces; can we put the jigsaw puzzle together?

For example, the "sophists" referred to seem to be Brahmans—the description makes them recognizable enough, except for the last set of items. Did the Brahmans of the third century B.C. actually go about naked, dwell in the open and live only upon fruits in season and the "barks of trees"? Or did they only convince Megasthenes that they did? Or did he perhaps confuse Brahmans (presumably a "priestly people") with itinerant holy men and put the two together into one category? It is even possible that Megasthenes was aware of the distinction—supposing that one existed—but that Arrian was not. Might he have derived the final descriptive items from other sources, assuming that Megasthenes and the others were talking about the same kind of "sophists"? And what of the "councillors of state," the seventh "caste"? Might not they have been Brahmans too?[3]

The "warriors" we can easily label *Kshatriya*, the second of the classic varnas, and—somewhat more tentatively—we can spec-

---

[3] Cf. Abbé Dubois (1906: 4–5). I shall return to this later in the chapter.

ulate that "retail-dealers" were *Vaishya*, the third of the classic varnas. But why are they incorporated with artisans, whom *we* know
as *Shudra*, the fourth varna? And what of "tillers of the soil"? Might
they be Vaishya? Above all, of course, what are we to do with the
caste of "superintendents" or *spies*? Perhaps such a caste really existed, or perhaps Chandragupta's Pataliputra was undergoing political turmoil at the time of Megasthenes' visit, or perhaps the
reference to such a "caste" as this reflects perceptions and assumptions of third century B.C. Greeks that bear thinking about.

And that points to the second—and much more meaningful—
thing we can do with such early accounts: we can use them to gain
insight into the *observer* as well as the *observed* and so improve our
understanding of the significance of folk categories and of the applicability of ethnoscience approaches. We must realize that our categories are likely to be as culture-bound as those of Megasthenes, or
those of fifteenth and sixteenth century Portuguese observers who
bequeathed the word "caste" to us.

To begin with, why are we using a Portuguese word? English, after all, contains relatively few words of Portuguese derivation, just as it has few words of Polynesian derivation. It must be
obvious, however, that the ease with which the English language
absorbed the rather obscure term "taboo" and the frequency of its
use in English today, tells us a good deal about the strong need for
the term in *our* ideological system. After all, we have words such as
sacred, forbidden, magical, dangerous, and so on, which individually
convey many—perhaps all—the connotations of "taboo," but we
didn't have "taboo" and apparently we were delighted to acquire it
and ignore the others.

Similarly, we have such terms in English as: *people, race*,[4]
nation, tribe, clan, and even *ethnic group*, any of which could have
been used to translate *jati*. Indeed, some of these have been used in
just this way.[5] We might even have incorporated the Indian term,
"*jati*," into our vocabulary. What we actually did, however, along
with speakers of certain other European languages, was to adopt a

---

[4]Also from the Portuguese? Also of uncertain original meaning?

[5]Contemporary East Indians in Trinidad, descendants of immigrants from
India, tend to translate *jati* as *nation* (Klass 1961: 55–56).

new term, "*caste*," and so we find ourselves endeavoring to determine what exactly we mean by that term—that we don't mean by "*tribe*" or "*nation*," or whatever.

It will not be easy to make that determination; we cannot even be certain of what the term conveyed to the English speakers who first heard it from the Portuguese and adopted it for their own. Indeed, we are not at all certain about what the term meant to the Portuguese, and why they chose this term over all the other possibilities in *their* language.

Julian Pitt-Rivers, for example, doubts the commonly held assumption (see OED 1961: 160) that "*caste*" goes back ultimately to the Latin *castus*, meaning "*chaste*." He prefers the suggestion that "*caste*," or the Portuguese *casta*, entered the Iberian Peninsula originally as the Gothic *kasts*, meaning "a group of animals or a breed of nestlings" (1971: 234).

Still other derivations for "*caste*" have been proposed. *The Columbia Encyclopedia* suggests that it may have been derived from a Portuguese word for "*basket*" (*The Columbia Encyclopedia*, S.V. "Caste" 1963: 357). Presumably, if such were indeed the derivation, it conveyed the sense of "category."

Of course, neither "basket" nor "brood" implies "purity of descent," so such derivations are not as attractive to me—for I have my biases too—as is the derivation from the Latin *castus*, meaning "*chaste*." For my purposes, however, I can leave the problem of derivation to the philologists and content myself with Pitt-Rivers' observation:

> The notion of purity of descent was not essential to the word originally, so that one even finds mention of "the caste of mules", but in view of the preoccupation of the times, especially in Spain, with regard to lineage and purity of blood it is not surprising that *casta* became associated with these ideas, for pure breeding, notwithstanding the mules, was thought to be superior to cross-breeding, particularly in the human species among whom social status was derived from descent (1971: 234).

In other words, whatever the origin of the term, it came to convey the notion of "purity of blood" to the Portuguese (and, as we shall see, to other Europeans after them). Thus, in using the term, the Portuguese were indicating that what struck them most forcibly about the social divisions they observed in India was that the Indians were concerned about maintaining "purity": that is, by forbidding sexual relations and marriage between men and women of different social divisions, the divisions could be maintained as separated and pure "breeds." I agree completely with Pitt-Rivers that this gives us insight into what was striking and meaningful to the Portuguese, at least as they interpreted what they were seeing. And, if the later Englishmen understood the Portuguese language of the period, would it not be reasonable to assume that they adopted the term because they too were struck by the sexual separation of the Indian groups, which they too viewed as an attempt to maintain a kind of "racial purity"?

Well, isn't that what the Indians were in fact doing? So indeed many writers have assumed, and "caste" and "purity of blood" (or, if you prefer, "genetic segregation") have come to be synonymous in the minds of many. But anthropologists today know perfectly well that a "rule of endogamy"—that spouses must be chosen from within a specific circumscribed group—may or may not reflect a desire to preserve the "purity" of the group: Few, for example, would argue that "village endogamy" reflects such a desire. Why, therefore, should *we* conclude, just because the early Portuguese did, that caste endogamy reflected a concern for maintaining "purity of the blood"?

Happily for us, not all foreign observers found it necessary to make such an assumption. Megasthenes, for example, reported only that the social units or divisions of the subcontinent followed a strict rule of group endogamy. According to Arrian's account, he reported objectively and most concisely:

The custom of the country prohibits inter-marriage between the castes:— for instance, the husbandman cannot take a wife from the artizan caste, nor the artizan from the husbandman's caste (Majumdar 1960: 226).

He is telling us that they do not intermarry—and only that. His report does not incorporate any assumption, explicit or implicit, about the origin, significance, or purpose of the practice. It is, therefore, very different from the seemingly similar accounts of later Europeans. Consider, for example, the Abbé Dubois, whose studies derive from the early nineteenth century:

> Another advantage resulting from the caste system is the hereditary continuation of families and that purity of descent which is a peculiarity of the Hindus, and which consists in never mixing the blood of one family or caste with that of another. Marriages are confined to parties belonging to the same family, or at any rate the same caste. In India, at any rate, there can be no room for the reproach, so often deserved in European countries, that families have deteriorated by alliances with persons of low or unknown extraction (1906: 34).

The good Abbé is telling us more than the simple fact that he had observed the Indians to be arranged in endogamous groups; he is also telling us that he believes such a rule to have brought about a condition of what he calls "purity of descent"—because there has been no "mixing [of] the blood"—and, as a result, there has been none of the "deterioration" that Dubois assumes must follow upon such "mixing." We have thus learned a great deal, but mostly about the Abbé's views.

Let us set aside his fanciful assertions, however, and note what we have *not* learned from the Abbé—assuming, and the assumption will have to be challenged eventually, that he has reported the rule of endogamy correctly. Does the existence of the *rule* in itself mean that there is *in fact* no intermarriage? And if there is little or no intermarriage, is there in fact no genetic exchange between the endogamous groups? And, speaking of genetics, given our present understanding of the subject, what are we to do with concepts such as "purity of descent" and "mixing the blood"? Do *we* believe, along with the Abbé, that genetic interchange between members of Indian castes must, or could, lead to "deterioration"?

My point is that "endogamy" and "purity of descent" are unrelated concepts, having to do with totally different categories of phenomena. Where they are fused, as for caste, the fusion reflects culturally biased, or ethnocentric, categorizing. For the very word *caste*, whatever the correct etymology, is usually understood today to imply "purity of descent" and this contributes to the cultural bias that has distorted and continues to distort Western scholarly perception and understanding of South Asian society.

The confusion deriving from the assumption that the Indian rules of endogamy imply "purity of descent" has been compounded by the intermingling of the European notion of "racial purity" with the Hindu concern about "religious purity." Are castes "pure" then, in any terms that make sense to the modern biologist? Can they really be studied, as some are still doing, as genetic isolates—or are they simply social constructs, like the "black" and "white" so-called "races" of the United States, without meaningful genetic boundaries?

Our first concern here, therefore, must be to determine what the caste system *is*, according to analytic and comparative canons accorded reasonably universal acceptance within the discipline of anthropology. Only then do we dare turn to the question of the origins of the system.

South Asian society, we observe, has from the time of the earliest external observation been characterized by some kind of a rule, or set of rules, limiting marriage—which has been required to take place *within* certain categories of relationship, and not between members of certain separated categories. Some European observers, as we have seen, have concluded from this that the endogamous groups were actually biological isolates, the members of which maintained the rules of endogamy in order to preserve that isolation or purity.

In addition, observers—often the same ones—claimed to perceive a second reason for the rules of endogamy. The endogamous castes were said to be not only biologically separate, but *occupationally* distinct as well, and the marriage rules were understood to reflect and maintain this separation too. Thus, to continue a quotation cited earlier, Arrian—presumably quoting, or at least deriving from, Megasthenes—reports:

The custom of the country prohibits inter-marriage between the castes. . . . Custom also prohibits any one from exercising two trades, or from changing from one caste to another. One cannot, for instance, become a husbandsman if he is a herdsman, or become a herdsman, if he is an artizan. It is permitted that the sophist only be from any caste: for the life of a sophist is not an easy one but the hardest of all (Majumdar 1960: 226).

This would certainly appear to be straightforward enough: castes are occupational categories, and one must marry and work in the occupation and caste into which one has been born. A word of caution is again in order, however, because occupation, like marriage, often acquires ethnocentric boundaries or definitions that can make for problems.

Take, for example, the landless agricultural laborers—such as the Paraiyans, Pallans, and Kōnāns—discussed by E. Kathleen Gough in her study of caste in a Tanjore village (1962). She tells us that such people, called *adimai*, were, in the early nineteenth century, permitted to perform only agricultural work, and only for others. They could own no land and were "bound" to their employing households:

A truant Pallan could be returned to his master by force and, except by agreement between two landlord communities, could not change the village of his allegiance and could find no other work (Gough 1962: 23).

On the basis of this, Gough feels justified in translating "*adimai*" as "agricultural serf" and in so referring to them in her text. Now surely these laborers could not be called "free farm workers," nor are they either "farmers" or "peasants." But they hardly resemble the "serfs" of the European feudalism either, except in the one characteristic of not being able to change their place of employment. Apart from that, relationships to the land on which they labor, and to those in authority over them, and even to their fellows, are totally different. In all of these and more, they are closer to the modern "migrant laborer" than they are to the medieval European "serf."

We might also ask why Gough did not translate "*adimai*" as "slave"? Were not the Pallans as bound as any New World plantation slave of the same time period? *Yes*, in terms of labor in the fields, or in terms of any right to change employers, but *no* in terms of social rights. Each *adimai* caste (or effective subdivision of that caste) could determine rules of marriage and social intercourse for itself without interference from the dominant groups. Furthermore, and possibly most important, *adimai* could not be bought or sold in the marketplace; they were not chattels, which for many is the prime characteristic of the slave. This may indeed have been the criterion used by Megasthenes, who, according to Arrian:

tells us further this remarkable fact about India, that all the Indians are free and not one of them is a slave. . . (Majumdar 1960: 224).

Gough's occupational and economic categories are reasonably accessible to us, but can we ever know what Megasthenes meant by "slavery"? Did he really conclude it was absent because there was no slave market? Or was it because there were no house or personal slaves, but only agricultural laborers? Or, for all we know, all of these groups might have been present, but Megasthenes (and I am reaching here) might resolutely have refused to consider people "slaves" as long as their "masters" lacked sexual access to them! We don't know, and therefore we must tread carefully. Were there *adimai* of the sort Gough refers to in the time of Megasthenes, and if so would we—or the *adimai* themselves—agree that "all the Indians are free"?

I am not arguing that we must discard the old accounts, but only that we must use them with caution. Let us proceed with caution, then. From Megasthenes we have learned that in the North India of his time the population was divided into a number of distinct groups exhibiting rules of occupational specialization and marital restriction. Similarly, from the Abbé Dubois we learn that much the same system was in effect—this time in South India—two thousand years later:

Caste assigns to each individual his own profession or calling; and the handing down of this system from father to son, from generation to generation, makes it impossible for any person or his descendants to change the condition of life which the law assigns him for any other (1906: 29).

This information is significant. Just as we have earlier discarded his racial notions, we can put aside as irrelevant Dubois' conclusion that: "Such an institution was probably the only means that the most clear-sighted prudence could devise for maintaining a state of civilization amongst a people endowed with the peculiar characteristics of the Hindu" (*Ibid.*). What is important is that, despite all bias and ethnocentrism, Megasthenes and Dubois, two thousand years apart in time and visitors to different regions of the subcontinent, observed what would appear to be the same socio-economic system.

Even in detail the similarities are remarkable. Megasthenes spoke of a "seventh caste"—the "councillors of state," it may be remembered, "who advise the King." I raised the question of whether they might in fact have been Brahmans, and my question derived in part from Dubois' observation that:

the rule of all the Hindu princes, and often that of the Mahomedans, was properly speaking, Brahminical rule, since all the posts of confidence were held by Brahmins (*Ibid.*: 4–5).

Dubois provides us with much of the detail we wish we had for Megasthenes' visit. He tells us, for example, that the multiplicity of castes can be resolved into "four main castes" known as *varnas:*

Each of the four main castes is subdivided into many others, the number of which is difficult to determine because the subdivisions vary according to locality, and a sub-caste existing in one province is not found in another (*Ibid.*: 14–15).

From Dubois' work we can derive much descriptive data about caste occupations, marital restrictions, and the hierarchical relationships between certain castes. Most helpful of all, we get a sense of the great internal variation of what is nonetheless recognizably one system, but one without centricity or unitary rules.

From the writings of such on-the-scene observers as the Abbé Dubois (and possibly Megasthenes) nineteenth and early twentieth century theorists acquired the information that enabled them to reach their conclusions about the nature and origins of the Indian caste system. This traditional view of the nature of caste is admirably summed up by Nripendra Kumar Dutt in his work on the *Origin and Growth of Caste in India*, in which he acknowledges his debt to European observers and theorists:

Without attempting to make a comprehensive definition it may be stated that the most apparent features of the present day caste system are that the members of the different castes can not have matrimonial connections with any but persons of their own caste; that there are restrictions, though not so rigid as in the matter of marriage, about a member of the caste eating and drinking with that of a different caste; that in many cases there are fixed occupations for different castes; that there is some hierarchical gradation among the castes, the most recognized position being that of the Brahmans at the top; that birth alone decides a man's connection with his caste for life, unless expelled for violation of his caste rules, and that transition from one caste to another, high or low, is not possible. The prestige of the Brahman caste is the corner-stone of the whole organization (1931: 3).

I call the Dutt summation "admirable" because it introduces us, with a terseness I wish I could emulate, to those features most commonly associated with caste, and even to some of the problems scholars have had with those features, or attributes.[6] These, then, are the usually accepted attributes of caste:

a) *Endogamy:* As we have seen, the existence in India of rules restricting marriage to members of one's own group seems to strike observers most forcibly. For some observers, in fact, the rules of endogamy seem to imply a deep concern for the maintenance of purity of descent, and it is possible that the very term "*caste*" originally conveyed that supposed concern. Further, as we see in Dutt, these restrictions are frequently viewed as "rigid," an adjective worth further consideration.[7] We will also want to ask questions about marital exclusivity or restriction. It is clear that rules of endogamy exist, but it is not so clear, as we shall see, just what the boundaries of the endogamous group are.

b) *Occupational Specialization:* There are, Dutt tells us, "fixed occupations for different castes," and Megasthenes made much the same point—but Dutt has qualified the statement, most interest-

---

[6]This should not be taken to mean that I subscribe to Dutt's definition and summation in its entirety, for I do not. It is, however, one of the clearest and sharpest presentations of a particular view of caste.

[7]A very widespread belief, this, asserted by the most influential authorities. Max Weber, for example, refers to "the institution of the castes—a system of particularly rigid and exclusive hereditary estates . . ." (1958: 4).

ingly, with the phrase, "in many cases." When is occupation "fixed" then, and in what cases, or castes, is it not, and with what structural implications?

c) *Hierarchy:* The castes, Dutt has noted, are arranged in some kind of order of precedence "with the Brahmans at the top," and this aspect of the system has indeed been considered of crucial importance by many students of South Asian society. Important questions have in fact been posed by such students: Is there a regular order of precedence? Does it vary from region to region? Are Brahmans always at the top, or can positions in the order be changed? What is the source or basis of the order of precedence? And finally, what exactly do we mean by "hierarchy" and what are the implications of the presence in a society of such a phenomenon?

d) *Commensality:* Caste membership, Dutt reminds us, restricts not only marriage and occupation but eating and drinking activities to members of the caste. Dutt advises us that the restriction on dining with others may not always be as "rigid" as the ones governing marriage and occupation.

e) *Hereditary Membership:* One is born into a particular caste, Dutt tells us (echoing earlier writers from Megasthenes on), and normally remains a member until death, passing membership on to one's children. Further, Dutt notes, expulsion is possible "for violation of caste rules"—so that it is possible to be deprived of one's caste membership. On the other hand, he claims that "transition from one caste to another, high or low, is not possible," and in this I fear he is in error.

There are, needless to say, other ways of viewing or defining caste and the caste system, but Dutt's is surely an adequate introduction for the purposes of this chapter. With it in mind, we can now turn to the explanations people have offered for the origins of such a system.

3

Divine Plan or Racial Antipathy?

If we knew the whole biological, geographical and cultural setting of a society completely, and if we understood in detail the ways of reacting of the members of the society and of society as a whole to these conditions, we should not need historical knowledge of the origin of the society to understand its behavior.

Franz Boas—"Some Problems of Methodology
in the Social Sciences"

In any search for accounts of the origins of Indian society, an obvious first step would be to inquire into the explanations offered by the Indians themselves. The indigenous explanation most commonly referred to in the literature is the one encompassed in a hymn in the *Rg Veda*, a collection of what are usually considered to be the oldest (or earliest) prayers and hymns of Hinduism, perhaps even going back to the time of the arrival of Indo-European speakers in the subcontinent. This hymn, then, is taken to be the earliest Indian reference available on caste and its origins. It appears to describe the origin of the universe—or at least of many of its elements, including humans—through the sacrifice, by divinities, of a "cosmic being" called *Purusha:*

Thousand-headed Purusha, thousand-eyed, thousand-footed—he, having pervaded the earth on all sides, still extends ten fingers beyond it.

Purusha alone is all this—whatever has been and whatever is going to be. Further, he is the lord of immortality and also what grows on account of food.

Such is his greatness; greater, indeed, than this is Purusha. All creatures constitute but one quarter of him, his three quarters are the immortal in heaven. . . .

When the gods performed the sacrifice with Purusha as the oblation, then the spring was its clarified butter, the summer the sacrificial fuel, and the autumn the oblation.

The sacrificial victim, namely, Purusha, born at the very beginning, they sprinkled with sacred water upon the sacrificial grass. With him as the oblation the gods performed the sacrifice, and also the Sādhyas . . . and the rishis. . . .

From it horses were born and also those animals who have double rows . . . of teeth; cows were born from it, from it were born goats and sheep.

When they divided Purusha, in how many portions did they arrange him? What became of his mouth, what of his two arms? What were his two thighs and his two feet called?

His mouth became the brāhman; his two arms were made into the rā-janya; his two thighs the vaishyas; from his two feet the shūdra was born.

The moon was born from the mind, from the eye the sun was born; from the mouth Indra and Agni, from the breath (prāna) the wind (vāyu) was born.

From the navel was the atmosphere created, from the head the heaven issued forth; from the two feet was born the earth and the quarters (the cardinal directions) from the ear. Thus did they fashion the worlds . . . (de Bary 1958: 14–15).

The passage is manifestly a complex one, difficult to understand and full of references not entirely accessible even to the scholar of the language and the ritual. There are contradictions which—granting all measure of poetic, ecstatic license—cause one to wonder whether a number of originally distinct hymns have not been fused. Does Purusha have "a thousand feet" or "two feet," and do those feet give rise to both "shūdras" and the earth itself? Still, there is the hymn as it has come down, and future generations must attempt to do what they can with it.

One of those attracted to the hymn was a codifier of laws who is believed to have lived at some time during the second to first centuries B.C. Presumably a real person, he is known to us as *Manu*, author of the influential *Manu Smrti* (Lawbook of Manu), in which reference is made to the hymn as the explanation or source, as well as the justification, of social difference:

For the sake of the preservation of this entire creation, [Purusha], the exceedingly resplendent one, assigned separate duties to the classes which had sprung from his mouth, arms, thighs, and feet.

Teaching, studying, performing sacrificial rites, so too making others perform sacrificial rites, and giving away and receiving gifts—these he assigned to the brāhmans.

Protection of the people, giving away of wealth, performance of sacrificial rites, study, and nonattachment to sensual pleasures—these are, in short, the duties of a kshatriya.

Tending of cattle, giving away of wealth, performance of sacrificial rites, study, trade and commerce, usury, and agriculture—these are the occupations of a vaishya.

The Lord has prescribed only one occupation [karma] for a shūdra, namely service without malice of even these other three classes (*Ibid.*: 220; brackets in text).

It must be emphasized that, however obscure the original hymn and however tenuous the logic of the derivation of rules of behavior from it, these two passages constitute the orthodox Hindu's explanation and justification of the origin of the caste system and its component elements.

One Indian scholar, N. K. Dutt, argues that the explanation of the origin of caste championed in the Lawbook of Manu (that of the Purusha hymn) was by no means the only one to be found in ancient Hindu writings. There was much early speculation, Dutt claims, and many cryptic passages abound. However, this hymn apparently offered the explanation that Manu liked best, and therefore it was incorporated into the canonical *Manu Smrti* (Dutt 1931: 4–6).

Dutt further advises us that he believes Manu's concern was not primarily with the origin of the castes of India but with the formation of all human diversity, that by the mixture of representatives of the four primary divisions there came about, according to Manu, not just the multiplicity of the present-day Indian castes, but the Chinese, the Greeks, the Scythians, the Dravidians, and so on (*Ibid.*: 6–8).

We must pause to note that once again we have allowed a certain ambiguity in our use of the word "caste" to creep into the text. In the preceding paragraph, the word "caste" is equated with

37

the word "division," as in the "four primary divisions" discussed by Manu. Let us note that the word actually used by Manu is *varna*, one that has given trouble to translators. It can be, and has been, translated as "division" or "caste." On the other hand, de Bary and his coeditors appear to prefer "class," as in the following introduction to a selection from the *Manu Smrti:*

The four classes of those born from the mouth and limbs of Purusha—the brāhman (priest), kshatriya (noble), vaishya (the bourgeois), the shūdra (serf)—formed a well-knit, almost self-sufficient society (de Bary 1958: 219).

This passage seems to imply that the caste system began as a class structure, of the kind we are familiar with in recent European history,[1] which then underwent a strange transformation into the system we view today. If not, how are we to interpret the use of "class" for "*varna*," "bourgeois" for "*vaishya*," and so on?

In short, we have already been presented with two alternative explanations for the appearance of the caste system in India. One is that the varnas—seemingly the precursors of modern "castes"—are of divine origin, basic, immutable, and as much a part of the divine plan as the four cardinal directions. The other explanation, if an implicit one, is that the four original varnas were in some measure comparable to contemporary or historic European "classes."

These varnas, then, must engage our attention, as did the *merē* of Megasthenes/Arrian in the preceding chapter. Dutt, who has given much attention to the issue of what the word "varna" meant to those who first used it, allies himself with the many scholars who have concluded that the term originally meant "*color.*" In other words he believes that at some point in the past the population of South Asia was divided—or believed all humanity to be divided—into four color categories known by the names Brahman, Kshatriya, Vaishya and Shudra (Dutt 1931; 21–23).

And, like so many other writers who translate "varna" as "color," Dutt believes that the "color" referred to is skin color.

---

[1] Indeed, the definitions make the four varnas resemble the four estates of France before the revolution!

Dutt, in fact, prefers "complexion" to "color" as the English trans-lation for "varna" (*Ibid.:* 21), and he concludes that the varnas were thus "racial" categories, reflecting differences in skin color found among the South Asian population at the time the original hymn was composed:

> That the colour question was at the root of the varna system is apparent from the meaning of the word *varna* (complexion) and from the great emphasis with which the Vedic Indians distinguished themselves from the non-Aryans in respect of colour. That class which retained the utmost purity of colour by avoiding inter-mixture naturally gained precedence in the social scale. . . . When the marriage with a Sudra woman was so much abhorred and blamed, we can easily conceive the horror and detestation which a Brahman in his racial pride would feel at the sight of a Brahman woman marrying a Sudra. No words are too strong to condemn such a marriage, and as a deterrent it is enacted that the issues of such a union should occupy the humblest position in society, or rather live outside the society. Thus we see that the development of the intercaste marriage re-strictions was primarily due to the racial differences between the white conquerors and the black natives and the desire of the former to preserve their purity of blood (*Ibid.*).

A number of additional terms and concepts—such as "race," "conquerors," and "Aryan"—begin to clamor for attention as we explore this new explanation of the origin of the caste system. Let us note at the outset that it is surely one of the most commonly held explanations in India as well as in Europe and the United States. In sum, the position is taken that the original varnas were racial categories, set up to maintain "purity of blood" with many, if not all, of the present castes deriving, in their common rule of marital exclusivity as well as in their particular positions in the hierarchy, from attitudes toward "racial" intermarriage in the Vedic period.

I have already indicated that I don't think much of any of the explanations of caste origin (other than my own, of course), but I must confess to a particular bewilderment at the popularity of the "racial antipathy" explanation. I understand, of course, how it fit-ted in with racial views of nineteenth century Europeans, and therefore why it was enticing to them. Enticing as it may have been, however, it lacks internal consistency, since the actual varna colors (Brahman—"white"; Kshatriya—"red"; Vaishya—"yellow"; and Shudra—"black") would appear to be impediments to notions of racial attributes.

Such color designations were of course used in the nineteenth century—and in some places are used even now—to represent supposed "racial" divisions of the human species, but as normally used they are hardly applicable in this case. It is possible to say, for example, that Brahmans, being described as "white," are therefore to be identified with Europeans (as "Caucasians" or "Aryans") and this identification was in fact made. But then, if one is to be consistent, a similar color/race identification is obligatory for each of the others. Are Shudras, assigned to the "black" varna, then to be identified with Africans (or "Negroes")? Perhaps, but such an identification is rarely made with the same assurance accorded to the Brahman/European equation.

And, if consistency is truly our aim, what are we to make of "yellow" Vaishyas? Was this division of ancient Vedic society of East Asian (or "Mongoloid") derivation? Most peculiar of all are the "red" Kshatriyas. Are these noble warriors of Vedic times truly descendants of immigrants from aboriginal North or South America?

Dutt is obviously aware of the inconsistencies, and troubled by them. He states:

The Brahmans were White, the Kshatriyas red, and the Vaishyas because of large absorption of black blood were yellowish like the Mulattoes of America, and the Sudras black, as is described in the Mahabharata (*Ibid.*: 22).

Well, maybe, but certainly a reasonable alternative explanation, solely on the basis of the information given, is that varna "colors" do not refer to "complexion," or supposed skin color, but rather to some kind of spiritual coloration, or aura. Kshatriya were a martial folk, and their spiritual color, like that of the Roman war god Mars, was *red*, a color many people identify with blood and therefore with violence. The Vaishyas, according to Manu, were concerned, among other things, with "trade and commerce, usury" and so is it not unreasonable that yellow, the color of gold, is associated with them? And if not gold, then—since Vaishyas also perform agriculture—the color yellow might reflect ripening wheat. Whatever it was, it was likely to have been an attribute of soul or of occupation, not a description of skin color reflecting "mulatto" ancestry! And, in the same vein, Brahmans would be white *of soul* because of their purity, while Shudras would be characterized, whatever their skin color, by the blackness of impurity.

Of course, I cannot prove any of these assertions, nor do I wish to; I do not advance them with any confidence that they are necessarily correct.[2] I do insist, however, that my explanation, fanciful or not, at least has the merit of consistency, which is more than one can say for the "complexion" explanation of varna so dear, and *so necessary*, to those who assume a racial origin of the caste system.

For varna as "skin color" belongs with the *racial* explanation of caste, not with the classic Hindu *religious* explanation, though through confusion it is sometimes ascribed to the latter. To interpret "varna" as originally meaning some kind of spiritual coloration or quality of soul interferes in no way with the explanation of origin with which we began this chapter. In the divine sacrifice of Purusha, four categories of humans came into existence, each category termed a "varna." "Varna" translates as "color," but why should those who prefer this explanation care whether it originally meant color of skin, color of soul, or even color of traditional garment?

Where it does matter, however—and very much indeed—that varna ascription indicates original skin color, is in the arguments of those who have concluded that the caste system originated out of a situation of racial confrontation and antipathy. In fact, it is fair to say that many of those who have advanced this argument have no interest whatever in Purusha, his reputed sacrifice, or indeed in the Vedas or in the writings of Manu, except insofar as any of these provide indications of "racial" confrontation. They turn to the *Rg*

---

[2]For that matter, I don't even pretend that I am the first to object to the definition of varna as "skin color." Others have made similar objections in the past, and I would particularly recommend the arguments of Oliver C. Cox to the interested reader (1948).

Veda and the *Manu Smrti* because they find in those sources hints—
such as the use of "varna" as "color"—that can be interpreted as
evidence that in Vedic times the population could be divided into
groups exhibiting marked differences of skin color. And, on the
basis of such evidence, they conclude that there were distinct
"races" in Vedic India.

I have argued with the interpretation of "varna" as "skin
color"; whether I am right or not has relevance only for the question of whether the *Rg Veda* and the *Manu Smrti* provide supportive
evidence for the racial explanation. Thus far I have given no attention to the racial explanation itself. Therefore, it now becomes
necessary to turn our attention to the particulars of this explanation
of caste origin, surely the most widely accepted and most influential of all the explanations.

There is hardly ever a "beginning point" in the scholarship
that does not admit, upon investigation, a still earlier point. And
that point, too, had ancestors. Thus, if we seek for the origin of the
"racial explanation" of the caste system, we must begin with the
writings of Herbert Risley, but we must in fairness note that he
was in fact responding to the views of Denzil Ibbetson and J. C.
Nesfield that caste was largely occupational in origin (Ghurye
1950). Let us here, nevertheless, wrench Nesfield and Ibbetson out
of their appropriate position in the order of investigation and consider their views at a later point.

Sir Herbert Risley was a British administrator (Indian Civil
Service), anthropologist, and ethnographer who studied and then
wrote of physiology and society in India in the latter part of the
nineteenth century. His writings, such as *The Tribes and Castes of
Bengal* (1892) and *The People of India* (1908), are recognized as classic
works in the anthropology of India, and have influenced scholars
from the days of Émile Senart and Max Weber to the present. A
brilliant and industrious scholar, he was of course a man of his time
and a subscriber to its intellectual tenets, including the view, mentioned earlier, about sequential or evolutionary relationships between "tribe" and "nation" and "caste":

The primitive tribe . . . wherever we find it, is not usually endogamous,
and, so far from having any distaste for alien marriages, makes a regular

business of capturing wives. . . . In short, when tribes are left to themselves, they exhibit no inborn tendency to crystallize into castes. In Europe, indeed, the movement has been all in the opposite direction. The
tribes consolidated into nations; they did not sink into the political impo-
tence of caste (Risley 1908: 262)

Risley's explanation of the origin of the caste system, therefore, must be understood in terms of some of the commonly held
views of his time, and we will have to examine these views in order
properly to understand him and, where necessary, refute him. But
first, his explanation of the origin of caste:

Whenever in the history of the world one people has subdued another,
whether by active invasion or by gradual occupation of their territory, the
conquerors have taken the women of the country as concubines or wives,
but have given their own daughters in marriage only among themselves.
Where the two peoples are of the same race, or at any rate of the same
colour, this initial stage of what we have called hypergamy soon passes
away, and complete amalgamation takes place. Where, on the other hand,
marked distinctions of race and colour intervene, and especially if the
dominant people are continually recruited by men of their own blood, the
course of evolution runs on different lines. The tendency then is towards
formation of a class of half-breeds, the result of irregular unions between
men of the higher race and women of the lower, who marry only amongst
themselves and are to all intents and purposes a caste. In this literal or
physiological sense caste is not confined to India. It occurs in a pronounced form in the Southern States of the American Commonwealth,
where negroes intermarry with negroes, and the various mixed races, mulattoes, quadroons, and octoroons, each have a sharply restricted *jus conubii*
of their own and are absolutely cut off from legal unions with the white
races. Similar phenomena may be observed among the half-breeds of Can-
ada, Mexico, and South America, and among the Eurasians of India, who
do not intermarry with natives and only occasionally with pure-bred Europeans. In each of these cases the facts are well-known. The men of the
dominant race took to themselves women of the subject race, and the
offspring of these marriages intermarried for the most part only amongst
themselves (*Ibid.*: 263).

I quote at length because of the importance of the passage for
anthropology in South Asia, and also because of the danger that any

43

summary of mine will tend to distortion. This last is a substantial danger, since I am not in sympathy with most of Risley's notions, and consider his supportive assertions as mostly erroneous. I am not aware of any evidence, for example, that his view of marriage in the "Southern States" of the United States ("the various mixed races . . . each have a sharply restricted *jus connubii* of their own. . . .") has any basis in fact—now, or at any time in the past.

Yet, whatever his errors in fact or in interpretation, anthropologists and sociologists, along with writers in other disciplines, have continued to follow Risley's stumbling footsteps to this very day, applying—as he was the first to do—the term "caste" to the social categories of the New World. The sole criterion, for them as it was for him, is whether a society is composed of "races" forbidden (or unwilling) to intermarry with each other. It becomes imperative, therefore, to examine exactly what "race" meant to Risley. We will pursue that question later on in this chapter and also inquire whether that concept of "race" has any utility today.

But now let us return again to India, and to Risley's explanation of the origin of caste. For the moment assuming the existence of "race" and along with it a recurrent tendency for men of different "races" to restrict marriage, how exactly did these lead to the formation of the complex caste system in present-day India? Risley's explanation is on two levels. The first is pseudohistorical, the other pseudopsychological:

it is not difficult to construct the rough outlines of the process which must have taken place when the second wave of Indo-Aryans first made their way into India through Gilgit and Chitral. At starting they formed a homogeneous community, scantily supplied with women, which speedily outgrew its original habitat. A company of the more adventurous spirits set out to conquer for themselves new domains among the neighboring Dravidians. They went forth as fighting men, taking with them few women or none at all. They subdued the inferior race, established themselves as conquerors, and captured women according to their needs. Then they found themselves cut off from their original stock, partly by the distance and partly by the alliances they had contracted. By marrying the captured women they had, to some extent, modified their original type; but a certain pride of blood remained to them, and when they had bred females enough to serve their purposes and to establish a distinct *jus connu-bii*, they closed their ranks to all further intermixture of blood. When they did this, they became a caste like the castes of the present day. As their numbers grew, their cadets again sallied forth in the same way, and became the founders of the Rājput and pseudo-Rājput houses all over India. In each case complete amalgamation with the inferior race was averted by the fact that the invaders only took women and did not give them. They behaved, in fact, towards the Dravidians whom they conquered in exactly the same way as some planters in America behaved to the African slaves whom they imported. This is a rough statement of what may be taken to be the ultimate basis of caste, a basis of fact common to India and to certain stages of society all over the world. The principle upon which the system rests is the sense of distinctions of race indicated by differences of colour: a sense which, while too weak to preclude the men of the dominant race from intercourse with the women they have captured, is still strong enough to make it out of the question that they should admit the men whom they have conquered to equal rights in the matter of marriage (*Ibid.:* 264–65).

To those of my readers who have reacted to the above passage with the feeling that it is this sort of thing that has given pseudohistory a bad name, I can only reiterate my observations that (1) the notion, introduced by Risley, that castes are, *au fond*, maritally restricted *biological* groups is very much still with us; and (2) that a paucity of any recent or adequate criticism of Risley on "race," coupled with a tendency to ignore the question of origin entirely, leaves Risley effectively in possession of the field.

But before we criticize, let us complete the presentation of Risley's argument. Given this principle of racial aversion (apparently only to legal marriages with females of inferior genes, not to copulation with them), how do we get to the full complexity of Indian caste?

Once started in India, the principle was strengthened, perpetuated, and extended to all ranks of society by the fiction that people who speak a different language, dwell in a different district, worship different gods, eat different food, observe different social customs, follow a different profession, or practise the same profession in a slightly different way must be so unmistakeably aliens by blood that intermarriage with them is a thing not to be thought of (*Ibid.:* 265).

If we ask why this "fiction" has taken such hold in India, Risley turns to pseudopsychology for an answer, one that interestingly echoes an opinion of the Abbé Dubois quoted earlier:

it is clear that the growth of the caste instinct must have been greatly promoted and stimulated by certain characteristic peculiarities of the Indian intellect—its lax hold of facts, its indifference to action, its absorption in dreams, its exaggerated reverence for tradition, its passion for endless division and sub-division, its acute sense of minute technical distinctions, its pedantic tendency to press a principle to its furthest logical conclusion, and its remarkable capacity for imitating and adapting social ideas and usages of whatever origin. It is through this imitative faculty that the myth of the four castes—evolved in the first instance by some speculative Brāhman, and reproduced in the popular versions of the epics which the educated Hindu villager studies as diligently as the English rustic used to read his Bible—has attained its wide currency as the model to which Hindu society ought to conform (*Ibid.*).

Despite my explanation, I expect many readers—shocked, disgusted, infuriated, amused, or depressed by the outmoded notions so confidently set forth in these passages—must continue to wonder why I quote at such length. I assure them that my purpose is not to hold Risley up to ridicule. He was an industrious and thoughtful scholar, at the forefront of his discipline, and his ethnographic data are still used.

In the very last passage quoted, for example, we have an indication of a brilliance transcending the limitations of its time. I call it—rightfully, I think—pseudopsychology, but let us note that he had anticipated Gregory Bateson and other students of cognitive processes when he describes the "Indian intellect" with "its passion for endless division and sub-division, its acute sense of minute technical distinctions, its pedantic tendency to press a principle to its furthest logical conclusion." Bateson's use of the term *eidos* (1958: 220) would seem to incorporate very much this kind of cognitive ordering. Risley's suggestion that there is likely to be a relationship between this Indian eidos and the caste system seems a sensible one, and well worth following up.

Risley's tragedy—one that should sober every one of us—is that his brilliance was to no avail because he was constrained to build upon sand. The facts he sets forth so confidently, the assumptions he shared with some of the best minds of his time, have all been exploded and swept away—and therefore so must his conclusions.

Risley believed, along with many other nineteenth century anthropologists and physiologists, that the human species was clearly and demonstrably subdivided into "races": biologically distinct human categories that remained such unless and until "interbreeding" took place, for that resulted in the formation of a "mixed race" now to be distinguished from both "pure" parent "races." Risley cannot be faulted for such a belief, because this was before genetics had arrived on the scene, and because this view was, as we noted, the common opinion of all European scholars.

He might be faulted for his second assumption—that each of these "races" had a characteristic temperament and potential—for while this was indeed widely believed it was nevertheless controversial. This particular notion was asserted first, in the universe of European scholarship, by Arthur de Gobineau, who argued in 1854 for the existence of a "race," variously referred to by him as "white" or "Aryan," that was northern European in appearance and had the greatest—perhaps the sole—capacity among all the human "races" for "civilization." These "Aryans," he argued, brought the blessings of civilization to the known world through conquest, from Europe through Southwest Asia to India. De Gobineau also taught—and many, including Risley believed—that intermarriage by members of this superior Aryan race with members of any of the inferior, darker, non-Aryan races resulted in a loss of the qualities of the superior parent. The degree of loss depended upon the amount of the mixture. The concluding clause of his book starkly asserts that: "when the Aryan blood is exhausted, stagnation supervenes" (de Gobineau 1967: 212). Assumptions derived from de Gobineau are clearly represented in the passages I have cited from Risley, and they are to be found elsewhere in his work.

There is a third assumption of Risley's on which I wish to touch. Obviously related to the first two, this is the notion that at the beginning of Indian history we find the subcontinent occupied by a barbarian (at any rate, uncivilized) indigenous race, the dark "Dravidian." Further, it is assumed that the subcontinent was successively invaded by waves of "Aryans," "white" of skin, who

47

brought civilization and instituted the caste system in a last-ditch effort to maintain their racial purity. Actually, there are two important elements at work here: the belief that the invading "Aryans," whatever their complexions, had a culture manifestly superior to that of the indigenous people; and the belief that caste was not present before the coming the of "Aryans," but was in fact introduced by them to the conquered population.

Now it may well be protested that no reputable scholar *today* believes any of these things. Surely I must know that others besides myself are aware of the findings of modern genetics, and of the essential meaninglessness of concepts such as "racial purity." Am I not kicking a dead horse? Do not, for example, modern Indologists derive more from Max Weber than they do from Herbert Risley?

All this is true, but the problem is that while almost no one today would support the undiluted Risley argument, infusions of Risley abound in the literature—even in the writings of Max Weber! Let me attempt to demonstrate this with a preliminary[3] excursion into the writings of Weber on India before I challenge Risley's assumptions about human variation and Indian history.

In his book, *The Religion of India* (1958), Max Weber appears understandably reluctant to venture too deeply into the morasses of unrecorded history. Still, he admits he cannot completely evade the question "from whence is this caste order, found nowhere or only incipiently elsewhere, and why, of all things, in India?" (*Ibid.*: 123). He wisely cautions us: "The attempt has been made more or less radically to simply equate caste stratification with racial differences" (*Ibid.*). Indeed, he seems to be challenging Risley directly in his discussion, if not actually by name:

one should not assume that the caste order could be explained as a product of "race psychology"—by mysterious tendencies inherent in the "blood" or the "Indian soul." Nor can one assume that caste is the expression of antagonism of different racial types or produced by a "racial repulsion"

---

[3]We shall return to Weber in later pages, for he made important contributions to our understanding of Indian society, if not necessarily to our understanding of its origins.

inherent "in the blood," or of differential "gifts" and fitness for the various caste occupations inherent "in the blood" (*Ibid.*: 124).

Fair enough, but if Weber has discarded the "racial explanation" of the origin of caste, what does he propose in its stead? Now, to be fair, we must note that Weber is not comfortable in the search for origins, and devotes little attention to the question. But he recognizes, as some later scholars have not, that he really ought to say something on the matter, and this is it:

At best we can say that race or, better, the juxtaposition of racial differences and—this is sociologically decisive—of externally strikingly different racial types has been quite important for the development of the caste order in India. But one must see this in proper causal interrelationship (*Ibid.*).

Weber goes on to chart this "proper causal interrelationship":

The name *Arya* remains as a term for the distinguished, the "gentleman." The *Dasyu* was the dark colored enemy of the invading conqueror; his civilization, presumably at least, was on the same plane. The *Dasyu* had castles and a political organization. Like all peoples from China to Ireland the Aryan tribes then lived through their epic period of charioteering, castle-dwelling knights. . . . Ethnic antagonism takes form with respect to contrasts of external bearing and way of life of various social groups. The most striking contrasts in external appearance simply happens to be different skin color. Although the conquerors replenished their insufficient supply of women from among the conquered, color differences still prevented a fusion in the manner of the Normans and Anglo-Saxons.

Distinguished families the world over make it their honor to admit only their peers for courting their daughters while the sons are left to their own devices in satisfying their sexual needs. Here and not in mythical "race instinct" or unknown differences of "racial traits" we reach the point at which color differences matter. Intermarriage with despised subjects never attained full social recognition. The mixture, at least from a sexual union, of upper-class daughters with sons of the lower stratum remained socially scorned. This stable barrier was reenforced by magical dread. It led to the elevation of the importance of birthright, of clan charisma, in all areas of life.

We noted that under the sway of animistic beliefs positions are

49

usually linked to the possession of magical charisma, particularly power positions of a sacredotal [sic[4]] and secular nature. But the artisan's craft in India soon tended to become clan charismatic, finally it became "hereditary." This phenomenon—found elsewhere—nowhere appears so strongly as in India. This was the nucleus of the caste formation for those positions and professions. In conjunction with a number of external circumstances this led to the formation of true castes (*Ibid.*: 124–26).

Weber then goes on to explore some of these "external circumstances" (such as "the weak development of cities and urban markets"), but this is essentially all that he has to say about the formative factors in the development of caste. It is clear, despite his demurral, that he has been much influenced by Risley. For both men, the caste system came into existence in a conquest matrix. Both take it as given that light-skinned "Aryans" had conquered dark-skinned "Dasyus." Both believe that the conquerors had, or soon developed, a strong antipathy to unimpeded intermarriage with the conquered, particularly for the daughters of the conquerors. Both assume that interbreeding (but not *intermarriage*) nevertheless took place between male conquerors and female conquered. For both, the end result of the continuing (and intensifying) antipathy, given the existence of two original "pure" and distinguishable "races" plus a variety of emergent "mixed" groups, was the caste system of India. Finally, for both writers the Indian caste system is seen as just the most extreme example of the widespread human tendency to restrict marriage with those considered alien and—most particularly—inferior.

Where Weber and Risley part company is on the matter of how one accounts for this tendency to restrict marriage. For Risley, as we have seen, it derives from "pride of blood" or what Weber has termed inborn "racial repulsion." But though Weber rejects "blood" or "race" as causal, he fully shares Risley's views on the supposed initial Aryan conquest, on the supposed racial differences between "Aryan" and "Dasyu," and on the supposed differences between the civilizations of the two races at the time of the

---

[4]My guess is that this is a typographical error, and that the word intended here is *sacerdotal*.

conquest. All this, he concludes, is sufficient to generate a *socially* based antipathy to intermarriage, thus obviating any need to invoke an innate "racial repulsion."

Weber's analogy, it will be noted, is with the Norman and Anglo-Saxon in Britain, while Risley's is with the English planter and African slave in the American South. For Weber, Normans prevented their daughters from marrying the conquered Saxons, while they themselves interbred with, but did not marry, Saxon women. The only reason caste did not emerge in Norman England was that physical differences between Norman and Saxon were not as great as between "Aryan" and "Dasyu." Thus, in Weber's view, a socially based antipathy, when compounded by substantial "racial" differences, results in the formation of a caste system.

Therefore, while Weber diverges to some extent from Risley on the causality of caste, the two share certain underlying assumptions and I feel justified in placing their explanations in the same category. After all, both assume that the original speakers of Indo-European languages and of Dravidian languages were, at the time of first contact, physically distinctive to the point of representing different "races." Both assume that the Indo-European speakers established some form of military and political control over the Dravidian speakers, and that as a consequence they occupied as a body a superior sociocultural position. Finally, both assume that the Indo-Europeans, because they refused to countenance intermarriage with the Dravidian speakers, were the ones who laid the groundwork for what was to become the caste system.

Perhaps in the nineteenth century all these propositions could be accepted as given; today they are hypotheses requiring verification. In fact, they are extremely dubious hypotheses, for the weight of accumulated evidence and current interpretation goes heavily against them.

How different in appearance *were* speakers of Indo-European and Dravidian languages four thousand years ago? Did they belong to different "races"? To begin with, contemporary scholars seek explanations of human variation in terms of gene frequency distribution rather than in terms of "fixed" or "pure" categories labeled "races" that are distinguished from one another according to variations in surface features such as "skin color." Second, we have no way of determining what the skin colors of the various populations in South and Southwest Asia (specifically, say, from the Indus to the Caspian) were at the time of the first contact between representatives of those two language families. For one thing, we don't know with any certainty what the distribution of those language families was three to five thousand years ago! One might therefore offer any speculation, however wild, and claim that it was as valid as any other. Perhaps Dravidian speakers were predominantly blond and blue-eyed—who can tell? Perhaps the Indo-European speakers had epicanthic eyefolds like the present population of East Asia. Can we say nothing at all then?

Yes, we can. Even without definite information, it is most reasonable and conservative to assume that populations three to five thousand years ago in the area under discussion exhibited gene frequencies not too far different from those of the present populations. Skin color and hair color lighten as one moves from southeast to northwest in this region, and there are similar gradations in other features, without sharp breaks or discontinuities. As a matter of fact, this kind of continuity and gradation seems to be the rule throughout the world. Contiguous populations exhibit similar gene frequencies, except where there has been massive population movement or displacement, as in present-day Australia and South Africa. There is no evidence that South or Southwest Asia ever experienced such a massive population movement or replacement. In fact, the evidence we have—from skeletal material and from the representations of human beings in pre-Indo-European art—supports the contention that the population five thousand years ago was similar in its range of physical types to the present population. Whether it was or not, however, it is the contention that two very different "races" came into contact that must be *proven*, and not merely *asserted*.

It is equally difficult to determine what the attitudes on intermarriage were during the time in question. Records are nonexistent and comparisons with other societies or situations seem hardly worth the effort without more specific information. If, for example, we were to follow Weber and compare Indo-European speaking invaders with Normans, we would have to ask whether they resembled more the *earlier* Normans—the Scandinavians who occupied the peninsula of Normandy, swiftly adopting the customs and language of the indigenous population, and intermarrying with them—or the *later* Normans who conquered Saxon England barely two centuries later, establishing permanent social distinctions between themselves and the conquered population. Such information is clearly inaccessible. The mere fact of conquest—even if we could be sure of that fact—is no proof in itself that conquerors will hold aloof from intermarriage with the conquered. The histories of the Mongol conquest of China, the Germanic conquest of Rome, the Assyrian conquest of Sumer, the Arabian conquest of Persia—all these and more attest to the fact that the relationship between conquest and intermarriage is by no means simple or obvious.

And that would be the case if in fact we could assume that the Indo-European speakers actually *conquered* the Dravidian speakers of northern India. It is by no means certain that such a thing happened; scholars are in disagreement on the subject. The early assumption, reflected in the works of de Gobineau and Risley, that India was inhabited by savages until the "Aryans" brought civilization, began to give way as archeological research proceeded in northern India. The ruins of the city of Harappa were known by Risley's time, though there was much dispute then (and still is) about who had built and lived in the city, and what relationship, if any, its civilization had to that of later India. But by the middle of the twentieth century, excavations at Harappa, at its sister city, Mohenjo-Daro, and elsewhere in the region, had made it clear that a major civilization, called now the "Indus Civilization," existed in northwestern India along the Indus River and its tributaries and hinterlands long before the languages of the Indo-European family could have reached the area (see Allchin 1968, Fairservis 1971, etc.).

There is, of course, much that we do not know about this civilization. We do not know with any certainty to which family their language, or languages, belonged. Since we have no indication of the presence ever in this area of languages of families other than Dravidian and Indo-European, Dravidian is a reasonable guess, but only that. We have not been able to decipher the Indus script, and we are not certain about the formative stages of this civilization. For example, we do not know the extent to which it may have been influenced by the somewhat earlier civilization of the Tigris-Euphrates valley. Other important questions about the scope and nature of the political and economic structure are still unanswered. We have only fragmentary information about art, religion, and social organization, and much of this is still being analyzed and debated. And, finally, we do not know for certain how the Indus Civilization came to an end.

Still, we can say with certainty that the Indus Civilization unquestionably did exist, and that it flourished sometime during the third millenium before the present calendrical era, coming to an end around, or soon after, 2000 B.C. At its height, its people were gathered in twin cities on the Indus riverine system, plus what were clearly subordinate towns and villages, and what would appear to be trading sites, throughout the region that was to become present-day Pakistan and northern India (Fairservis 1971: 264, *et passim*).

Indus Civilization sites have been found along the Indus and its tributaries, along the Makran coast, southward throughout the Saurashtrian peninsula, down past the Narbada River, and westward almost as far as the present city of Delhi. Standards of measurement and design were controlled over this wide area, which would seem to indicate a substantial measure of central authority. Complex agriculture was practiced, and the broadcast grains (wheat, barley, oats, and rye) of Southwest Asia were known, as were cotton and rice, otherwise associated with East and Southeast Asia. A similarly wide complement of animals was raised by the people of the Indus Civilization: the cattle, sheep, and goats of the west, along with the chicken, water buffalo, and elephant of the east.

Since this industrious, organized, and complex civilization is no longer with us, clearly it must have "come to an end"—but the conditions and circumstances of that "end" are by no means simple or unanimously agreed upon. Oddly enough, one source of uncertainty about the factors leading to the extinction of the civilization is a sharp disagreement about the merits or qualities of the civilization itself. The Indus Civilization has certainly not been accorded unmixed praise and admiration. The archeologist Piggott is most explicit in his expression of distaste, but his views are apparently shared by other British archeologists:

54

The general impression we obtain from the Harappā arts and crafts is indeed one of competent dullness. . . . The pattern of Harappā civilization seems to have precluded great monuments such as temples, palaces, or tombs, wherein an outburst of artistic achievement could redound to the glory of the gods or the pride of a splendid spendthrift monarch. The secrecy of those blank brick walls, the unadorned architecture of even the citadel buildings, the monotonous regularity of the streets, the stifling weight of the dead tradition all combine to make the Harappā civilization one of the least attractive phases of ancient Oriental history. One can grudgingly admire the outcome of its ruthless authoritarian regime rather as one admires the civil engineering of the Roman army in the Provinces, but with as little real enthusiasm. I can only say that there is something in the Harappā civilization that I find repellent (1950: 200–1).

Well, as the Roman engineers might indignantly have responded to Piggott, *de gustibus non disputandum est*. For myself, I have been much moved and impressed by the Indus Civilization art I have seen, from the famous "dancing girl" statuette to the fine animal representations on steatite seals. These latter, along with the specimens of writing on the seals, seem to hint at flourishing schools of art and volumes of written works, which, alas, have not yet been discovered—and may never be, if they were executed on perishable materials, such as palm leaves. One man's "law and order" is of course another man's "ruthless authoritarian regime," and a meticulously laid out city, such as Washington, D.C., might delight some with its order and symmetry, while others see only "the monotonous regularity of the streets."

But there is something here, I feel, besides a simple difference in taste or esthetics. Another archeologist, Walter Fairservis comments on Piggott's remarks:

There is ample evidence that plastering of walls with a mud plaster was common practice. Whether this was decorated in any way we do not know. But certainly a good deal of the monotony of the city's streets was relieved by the wooden superstructures, which may well have reflected in painted, carved, cloth- and mat-covered surfaces the color, exuberance, and humor which is found in the artifacts of the Harappans (1971: 263).

We cannot know, of course, whether Fairservis' speculation is more accurate that Piggott's—but we can note that Fairservis' proposal is not an outlandish one, in view, as he himself notes, of "the color, exuberance, and humor" so clearly manifest in the fragments of Harappan art we do have. What troubles me, to put it bluntly, is not that Piggott finds the artwork unpleasing, but that he finds the entire civilization "repellent." Such repulsion, whatever its source, can lead to a mind-set that favors certain conclusions over others, and not only in the area of artistic criticism.

There is, for example, the puzzling question of whether the Indus Civilization existed for an astonishingly long period—perhaps a millenium or more—without significant change or development in arts, crafts, architecture, and even the arrangement of the streets:

As we look today at the unvarying succession of building phases at Mohenjo-Daro, towering 30 feet above us as we stand on the lowest street-level, we encounter in monumental form the first instance in the story of India of the innate conservatism of thought that is repeated through the centuries; conservatism that may so easily become stagnation, especially when developed in isolation (Piggott 1950: 139).

This passage baffled me when I first read it years ago, and it continues to do so. What exactly does Piggott mean by "innate conservatism of thought"? The only thing that comes to mind is what Max Weber, in a passage cited earlier, calls "race psychology." I might not make an issue of it here, were the notion not present in the writings of other scholars. Thus, Bridget and Raymond Allchin, presumably influenced by Piggott, write:

Summing up we may say that technical uniformity over so great an area is probably unique in the ancient world and that Harappan technology deserves Childe's acclaim as 'technically the peer of the rest' (that is, of Egypt and Babylonia). But its limitations should not be overlooked. The majority of the products are unimaginative and unadventurous, in some ways reminiscent of the products of the Roman provinces but also suggesting that the people of Harappa had their eyes on things not of this world. There are many signs of an innate conservatism, which in many respects demands comparison with Indian conservatism of later times (1968: 136–37).

And A. L. Basham, in his authoritative and influential text, *The Wonder That Was India*, informs his readers:

Probably the most striking feature of the culture was its innate conservatism. At Mohenjo-Daro nine strata of buildings have been revealed. As the level of the earth rose from the periodic flooding of the Indus new houses would be built almost exactly on the sites of the old, with only minor variations in ground plan; for nearly a millenium at least the street plan of the city remained the same. The script of the Indus people was totally unchanged throughout their history. There is no doubt that they had contact with Mesopotamia, but they showed no inclination to adopt the technical advances of the more progressive culture (1954: 15–16).

Basham, of course, is an Indologist, not an archeologist, and his conclusions derive from the writings of Piggott, Childe, Wheeler, and others. Nor, incidentally, is Basham contradicting Childe (1957) on the issue of technical proficiency. Basham agrees that the Harappan people had great technical skill in many respects, but he happens to be particularly interested in the evidence that the Indus people were seemingly deficient in the area of *military* technology—knives, spearheads, and axheads (*Ibid.*: 21). In fact, it is as a result of this technological and military "conservatism" that Basham, along with others, believes that the "end" came:

The Indus cities fell to barbarians who triumphed not only through greater military prowess, but also because they were equipped with better weapons and had learned to make full use of the swift and terror-striking beast of the steppes[5] (*Ibid.*: 27).

D. D. Kosambi, an historian who takes issue with many widely accepted views on the history of Indian economy and society, has been convinced by the archeologists he has consulted that the Indus Civilization was conservative and unchanging, particularly in military technology, and that this conservatism led to destruction by invaders with superior weapons:

This lack of change on the Indus was not due to mere sloth or conservatism but to much deeper causes. It was a deliberate refusal to learn when innovation would have greatly improved matters . . . the simple open-cast

---

[5]This last reference is of course to the horse. Whether chariot riding constitutes "full use" is an interesting question, but not one we can go into here.

bronze celt continued in use as a tool, though the axe and adze with a socket or a hole for the wooden shaft were certainly within the technical capacity of Indus craftsmen. The only specimens of the latter types are found in the top layers and belong unquestionably to invaders from the northwest . . . so also with more efficient weapons such as swords, all foreign to the Indus culture (1969: 64).

The position of archeologists—and of the historians who, perforce, derived from them—on the subject of the extinction of the Indus Civilization, was as follows:

the evidence . . . is reasonably consistent in implying that at some period likely to have been before 1500 B.C. . . . . the long-established cultural traditions of North-Western India were rudely and ruthlessly interrupted by the arrival of new people from the west (Piggott 1950: 238–39).

Let us quickly summarize all the above. It was widely believed that a complex civilization developed along the Indus River and in contiguous regions. This civilization, presumably Dravidian speaking, flourished for at least a millenium (3000 to 2000 B.C.), but was cursed by the first appearance of the unimaginative, unchanging conservatism that was to characterize, according to some people, India in later centuries. For a thousand years, this argument goes, the Indus Civilization stagnated, unwilling or unable to change or to adopt new technology, until it was swept away by a wave of dynamic, aggressive, militarily proficient, horse-riding barbarians from the west, presumably speaking Indo-European languages. These were the ancestors of the Vedic *Aryas*. Now this isn't quite Risley's (or de Gobineau's) view of the Aryan "gentlemen" conquering the Dravidian "dasyus," but I submit that it is certainly a reasonably acceptable substitute.[6]

Thus, a basic issue becomes: was the Indus Civilization really as "conservative" as all that? Personally, I wouldn't have thought

---

[6]The notion of "stagnation," as we have seen, fits in particularly well with de Gobineau's views. I cannot help wondering, incidentally, whether this attachment to a mythical original conquest by "Aryan gentlemen" served as some sort of justification—perhaps unconscious—for the later conquest of South Asia by European "Aryan gentlemen."

that *any* society could be—change, and response to pressures for innovation, seem to be human universals—and I can't help but wonder whether the "repulsion" mentioned earlier played a part in the ready acceptance of the notion of Harappan "stagnation."

But we need not speculate; recent studies have cast doubt on the entire formulation. Raikes (1964), Dales (1965), and Lambrick (1967) have in their writings and research come to question the old interpretations. Their work suggests that the deposition at Mohenjo-Daro—"towering 30 feet in the air"—was laid down not in a millenium but in only two or three centuries. Further, these deposits resulted from changes in the Indus system that were reflected, among other ways, in a series of calamitous floods. Finally, the continual flooding and the accompanying desiccation of the hinterland eventually brought about the desertion of the cities and the breakdown of the political structure. From this perspective, the barbarians—chariot-riding and Indo-European speaking though they may well have been—did not "conquer" the Indus Civilization; they merely moved in upon the collapse of the state and the withdrawal of most of its population. With these new conditions, it is likely that new weapons, new tools, and new subsistence techniques were necessary, though exactly what was introduced by the newcomers and what was developed by the remaining indigenous people is not clear.

The Allchins, writing soon after the work of Raikes, Dales, Lambrick, and others, indicate an awareness of them. They are not prepared, however, to accept fully the implications of the new research, preferring to review it critically, and to conclude that "several causes have been suggested" for the collapse of the Indus Civilization (1968: 143).

On the other hand, Fairservis, writing a few years later, is more critical of the old hypothesis of barbarian destruction. He concludes that such attacks may have played a part in ending the Indus Civilization, but he appears to give much greater weight to the newer hypothesis—that flooding and desiccation led to abandonment. He notes, particularly, that Late Harappan settlements occur in Gujarat, "degenerating, reviving, and finally surviving in new form" (1971: 309; see also 310–11, *et passim*). In fact, he notes that Late Harappan settlements were established in a number of places in west and south India. They appear to merge over time into classical India, and he concludes:

The Harappan civilization can thus be said to have "faded away" rather than to have been extinguished completely (*Ibid.*: 310).

And he also argues:

In this larger sense then the answer to the question as to why the Harappan civilization fell is that it didn't fall! It simply stood at the beginning of the mainstream of Indian culture and faded into that current, having brought to it acts of faith, class morality, aspects of technology, and perhaps a cosmology which heralded the eventual supreme achievement that was medieval India (*Ibid.*: 302).

If we return, therefore, to the subject responsible for this discursion—the "racial explanation" for the origin of caste—we find that none of the three necessary underlying assumptions can stand unshaken in the face of challenge:

1) We do not know what the Indo-European and Dravidian speakers looked like when they first came into contact in northwestern India, but there is at least as much reason—if not more—to assume they resembled each other as to assume that they differed.

2) We do not know the marriage rules of either population, but it is manifestly pointless to derive a set of marriage rules for the newcomers from the "fact" that they were socially and militarily superior to the indigenous people.

3) And, most important, while we cannot yet detail the conditions of intermingling, it is obvious that the old "conquest" theory was much too simple.

Bernard Cohn has put it succinctly for us:

Nineteenth-century scholars sought the origin of the caste system in a racial conflict between the fair-skinned invading Indo-Aryans or Aryans and the darker *Dasas* or *Dasyus*. . . . Today, most scholars agree that the *Dasas* represent the Dravidian peoples, who were probably the descendants of the Indus Valley peoples and clearly had a more highly developed society and economy than the invading Indo-Aryans (1971: 61).

After reviewing and criticizing the "racial explanation," Cohn toys with a few other explanations and then, as has become the custom, simply dismisses the problem:

> The origins of the caste system are undoubtedly very complex, and its direct history will probably never be known. . . . None of the single causal theories has proved satisfactory, and today most anthropologists feel it is fruitless to spend much time in trying to find the origins or trace the history of the caste system to its beginnings (*Ibid.:* 62).

As this work indicates, I cannot accept Cohn's conclusion. The fact that no one has yet been able to come up with a satisfactory solution to a problem is no proof in itself that the problem is insoluble. And while it is perfectly good scientific procedure to demolish proposed hypotheses without having to advance a new one of one's own, it turns out to be bad Indology. After all, we are not engaged in rigorous laboratory research, but are attempting to provide a useful new insight into the complexity of human behavior.

If, therefore, we argue (not "demonstrate," for that is still beyond us) about what caste *is*, and refuse to speculate at all about how it *came to be*, then we have in effect not demolished or discarded the earlier hypotheses at all—we have only discredited them, and indicated our own unwillingness to use them. Our students and readers will have to be forgiven if, lacking alternatives, they return to the discredited hypotheses.

So let us not be of faint heart; that we have failed before does not mean that success this time may not be just around the corner. And by all means let us be eclectic. While I cannot accept Risley's "racial explanation," I am grateful to him for pointing to the entry on the scene of speakers of Indo-European languages. They may not have conquered, or carried all before them by reason of racial superiority, but surely they constitute a factor to be considered.

Indo-European speakers—the so-called "Vedic" peoples or their proximate ancestors—unquestionably contributed much to the development of present-day India. We may not know whether they were warlike or peaceful immigrants, but we do know that they entered the subcontinent from the northwest and moved, over time, eastward through the Indo-Gangetic plain of north India. They contributed to the region—and about this there is no argument—the ancestral forms of the languages presently spoken. No doubt they made genetic contributions as well, although the extent to which present speakers of Indo-European languages in South Asia are descended from the earliest speakers cannot be determined by present techniques. And, of course, no one would dispute that they made significant contributions to the belief system of South Asia—that is, to the religious complexity commonly known as *Hinduism*. The exact nature of this last contribution, however, has been subject to some debate.

A direct continuity is usually claimed or assumed between the religion of the people of the Vedas and the belief system of the contemporary Hindus of India. For some, particularly for many Hindus, it is in fact the *same* religion—modified perhaps, evolved, or even degenerated, but not different. The suggestion, therefore, that Hinduism derives to an important extent not only from the Vedic peoples but also from the earlier, indigenous inhabitants might come as a shock to some—but not, of course, to Indologists. Basham writes:

The earliest civilized inhabitants of India worshipped a Mother Goddess and a horned fertility god; they had sacred trees and animals, and ritual ablutions apparently played an important part in their religious life. Beyond this much has been said and written about the religion of the Harappā people, but in the absence of intelligible texts any efforts at further defining it are very speculative. The salient features of Harappā religion appeared again in a new form at a much later date, and we must assume that it never died, but was quietly practiced by the humbler people, gradually developing from contact with other doctrines and cults, until it gathered enough strength to reappear and largely to overlay the old faith of the Āryan rulers of India (1954: 232).

It might well be argued, then, that much that is crucial to Hinduism derives not from the Vedas and the Indo-Europeans, but from the indigenous "Dasyus." In addition to the items mentioned in the first sentence of the quotation from Basham, one might speculate about the ban on cow slaughter, the concept of transmigration, on asceticism and monasticism, and on much else. And yet, the formal structure of the religion, as well as the assumed source and therefore the authority, is unquestionably Vedic. If a man in India sacrifices a goat to a "mother goddess," is he a Hindu? *Yes*—if he recognizes that she is really a consort of Siva. The point is that the Vedas encompass and incorporate the popular belief system, though the popular system exists distinct from, and probably prior to, the Vedic/Hindu justificatory and explanatory shell.

Might we not apply this conceptual model to *caste*, which after all many perceive as the social dimension of Hinduism? If we do, we might say, following Basham's construction closely, that the indigenous peoples of ancient India participated in a socioeconomic structure that was different from that of the incursive Indo-Europeans. That indigenous structure, furthermore, never died—although we lose sight of it for a while. The available literature describes only the socioeconomic structure of the Vedic peoples, ignoring everything else, but the older system remained in effect—in Basham's words, "quietly practiced by the humbler peoples"— changing and developing over time and in response to new circumstances. Eventually, it reappears to overlay the system described in the Vedas.

However, just as in the case of religion, the Vedic system— which here means the classic varna system—remains the justificatory and explanatory shell. The caste system is clearly not the classic varna system, even though Hindus believe castes have derived (or degenerated) from those varnas. Whatever the justificatory framework for believers, we can say—as in the case of the religious system—that the actuality or content of the socioeconomic system has an ancestry different from that of the framework.

From this perspective, and apart from everything else that has been said in this chapter, we cannot seek the origins of caste in either the Vedic hymns or the racial antipathies of "Aryans," for caste (unlike varna) preceded both Veda and "Aryan" in India.

4

The "Occupation" Hypothesis and Some Other Dubious Proposals

India was a cheerful land, whose people, each finding a niche in a complex and slowly evolving social system, reached a higher level of kindliness and gentleness in their mutual relationships than any other nation of antiquity.

A. L. Basham—*The Wonder That Was India*

Attempts have been made—apparently beginning with Manu, as we have seen—to derive the caste system from the presumed social system of invading "Aryans." For Hindus, that system had a divine origin and sanction. Some scholars, following Risley, have concluded that the system developed in the period just after the "Aryan invasion," as a response to the circumstances of that invasion and the resulting confrontation of "races."

There are other theorists, however, who have sought an explanation for the emergence of caste in a context essentially removed from that of the "Aryan"-"Dasyu" confrontation, and their views—which to some may seem not far removed from the one to be espoused in this work—must now be considered. Are these "economic" explanations? In a sense, but as we examine them closely we will see that they have more to do with "occupation" than with other aspects, or with the whole range, of economic concern.

In general, "occupational explanations" of the origin of the caste system tend to reflect one or the other of only two basic arguments. One is that present (or classic) Indian castes derive originally from occupational associations, or "guilds," which for various reasons became transformed into closed, hereditary, marriage corporations. The second argument is that at some point in Indian history, the priesthood (the proto-Brahmans), presumably hitherto an openly recruited occupational category, closed its ranks to all but the children of priests. Once *they* became a closed marriage-and-descent group, the argument runs, other groups began to imitate them, and the caste system emerged.

The two arguments are clearly not antagonistic to one another and may be supported separately or in tandem, as we shall see when we consider some of the proponents of this category of explanation: Ibbetson, Maine, Nesfield, Senart, Weber, and (quite recently) Harold Gould.

As far as I have been able to determine, the "occupational" approach to the origins of caste begins with—or at least was most clearly enunciated in—the writings of two British scholars and civil servants who labored in India in the 1880s: Denzil Ibbetson and John Nesfield. The honor of priority would seem to go to Ibbetson, since, so far as it can now be determined, he published first.

Sir Denzil Charles Jelf Ibbetson, K.C.S.I., was born in 1847 and entered the Indian Civil Service in 1870, rising through the ranks until he became, in 1907, Lieutenant Governor of the Panjāb. In the fullness of that office, he died in 1908. In 1881, Ibbetson completed a census of the Panjāb District which was published in final form in 1883 under the title, *Report on the Census of the Panjáb*. One chapter of this work, entitled "Races, Castes and Tribes of the Panjáb," apparently excited particular interest among other scholars and civil servants. Risley incorporated a portion of this chapter into an appendix of his book, *The People of India*, in 1908, and the entire chapter was later reproduced as a book in its own right (Ibbetson 1916). It is from this latter volume that all the following quotations have been taken.

Ibbetson begins his chapter on "races, castes and tribes" with laudable directness:

The popular and currently received theory of caste I take to consist of three main articles:—

(1) that caste is an institution of the Hindu religion, and wholly peculiar to that religion alone:

(2) that it consists primarily of a fourfold classification of people in general under the heads of Bráhman, Kshatriya, Vaisya and Súdra:

(3) that caste is perpetual and immutable, and has been transmitted from generation to generation throughout the ages of Hindu history and myth without the possibility of change (1916: 1–2).

He then goes on to argue—quite sensibly, most scholars would agree—that caste is much more than the four "perpetual and immutable" varnas enumerated above; that indeed in many parts of modern India the varnas are not present in their entirety, or at least not easily discernible. And he argues, too:

that caste is a social far more than a religious institution; that it has no necessary connection whatever with the Hindu religion, further that under that religion certain ideas and customs common to all primitive nations have been developed and perpetuated in an unusual degree; and that conversion from Hinduism to Islam has not necessarily the slightest effect upon caste (*Ibid.*: 2).

As far as I am able to determine, Ibbetson thus becomes the first to point out, at least for South Asia, that economic transactions, social relationships, and ideology are not necessarily inextricably intertwined, but can—and on occasion do—assort independently. He may very well have been the first observer of South Asian society to point out that *assertions* of immutability are not of themselves *proof* of it:

the fact that a generation is descended from ancestors of any given caste creates a presumption, and nothing more, that that generation also is of the same caste, a presumption liable to be defeated by an infinite variety of circumstances (*Ibid.*).

Ibbetson sees the complexity that is caste as going back to an unrecorded time when the ancestors of modern Indians found themselves faced with circumstances in the evolution of their society which are common, in Ibbetson's opinion, to all societies. For Ibbetson, we find, bases his explanation of the origin of caste on the assumption of unilineal evolution that derives from the writings of Lewis Henry Morgan and others (including, of course, Spencer and Tylor). This view was widely held by European scholars at the close of the nineteenth century. Thus, he writes:

> Among all primitive peoples we find the race split up into a number of tribal communities held together by the tie of common descent, each tribe being self-contained and self-sufficing, and bound by strict rules of marriage and inheritance, the common object of which is to increase the strength and preserve the unity of the tribe. There is as yet no diversity of occupation. Among more advanced societies, where occupations have become differentiated, the tribes have almost altogether disappeared; and we find in their place corporate communities or guilds held together by the tie of common occupation rather than of common blood (*Ibid.*).

In Ibbetson's view, then, there are two basic principles at work: "community of blood and community of occupation." In some societies, particularly "early" or "primitive" ones, they may be fused, while in more complex societies they are separated. Together, they serve to explain observable social structures:

> In every community which the world has ever seen there have been grades of position and distinctions of rank; and in all societies these grades and distinctions are governed by two considerations, descent and calling. . . . in no society that the world has yet seen has either of these two considerations ever wholly ceased to operate (*Ibid.: 3*).

Given these assumptions about the commonality of human evolutionary experience, and about the principles underlying human society, Ibbetson continues:

> The communities of India in whose midst the Hindu religion has been developed are no exceptions to this rule; but in their case special circumstances have combined to preserve in greater integrity and to perpetuate under a more advanced state of society than elsewhere the hereditary nature of occupation, and thus in higher degree than in other modern nations to render identical the two principles of community by blood and community of occupation. And it is this difference, a difference of degree rather than of kind, a survival to a later age of an institution which has died out elsewhere rather than a new growth peculiar to the Hindu nation, which makes us give a new name to the old thing and call caste in India what we call position or rank in England.

The whole basis of diversity of caste is diversity of occupation . . . (*Ibid.*).

It would appear, then, that in Ibbetson's view Indian society differs only in "degree" from European societies. Caste is simply a form of "position" or "rank," but one in which, because of "special circumstances," the "principle of community of blood" (presumably the basis of English "rank") has become fused with that of "occupation." The sole remaining question therefore becomes: what were the "special circumstances" that started India along its own path?

in India, which . . . was priest-ridden to an extent unknown to the experience of Europe even in the middle ages, the dominance of one special occupation gave abnormal importance to distinctions of occupation. The Bráhman who could at first claim no separate descent by which he should be singled out from among the Aryan community, sought to exalt his office and to propitiate his political rulers . . . by degrading all other occupations and conditions of life. . . . As the Bráhmans increased in number, those numbers necessarily exceeded the possible requirement of the laity so far as the mere performance of priestly functions was concerned. . . . Thus they ceased to be wholly priests, and a large proportion of them became mere Levites. The only means of preserving its overwhelming influence to the body at large was to substitute Levitical descent for priestly functions as the basis of that influence, or rather perhaps to check the natural course of social evolution which would have substituted the latter for the former; and this they did by giving the whole sanction of religion to the principle of the hereditary nature of occupation. Hence sprang that tangled web of caste restrictions and distinctions, of ceremonial obligations, and of artificial purity and impurity, which has rendered the separation of occupation from descent so slow and so difficult in Hindu society, and which collectively constitutes what we know as caste. I do not mean that the Bráhmans invented the principle which they thus turned to their own purpose; on the contrary, I have said that it is found in all primitive societies that have outgrown the most rudimentary stage. Nor do I suppose that they deliberately set to work to produce any craftily designed effect on the growth of social institutions. But circumstances had raised them to a position of extraordinary power; and naturally, and probably unconsciously, their teaching took the form which tended most effectually to preserve the power unimpaired (*Ibid.*: 3–4).

Thus, Ibbetson tells us that an unusually influential priest-hood, in an effort to preserve for all their descendants—however numerous and however superfluous—the perquisites and privileges of their occupation, managed to make that occupation hereditary, and all others eventually copied their example.

The view thus expressed obviously raises many new questions and problems, but before we turn to them it is necessary to emphasize again that Ibbetson's explanation was in accord with widely accepted contemporary theories of the nature and origin of all societies. A decade earlier, Sir Henry Sumner Maine could write: "the primitive Aryan groups, the primitive Aryan institutions, the primitive Aryan ideas, have really been arrested in India at an early stage of development. . ." (1887: 220. First published in 1871). With this perspective, Maine argues, even before Ibbetson does, that:

caste is only the name for a number of practices which are followed by each one of a multitude of groups of men, whether such a group be ancient and natural, or modern and artificial. As a rule, every trade, every profession, every guild, every tribe, every clan is also a caste, and the members of a caste not only have their own special objects of worship . . . but they exclusively eat together and exclusively intermarry (*Ibid.:* 219).

In an earlier passage, Maine argues, even more specifically:

caste is merely a name for trade or occupation, and the sole tangible effect of the Brahminical theory is that it creates a religious sanction for what is really a primitive and natural distribution of classes (*Ibid.:* 57).

A little after Ibbetson, though in the same decade, John C. Nesfield, another British civil servant,[1] argued independently that occupational "classes" existed in India prior to caste formation. He too felt that such a condition was present in all but "savage" societies, though only in India had the "classes" evolved into "castes." Given this, he offers the following definition:

---

[1]Nesfield was an Inspector of Schools in Oudh, and appears to have occupied a social position distinctly lower than that of Ibbetson.

A caste is a marriage union, the constituents of which were drawn from various different tribes (or from various other castes similarly formed), in virtue of some industry, craft or function, either secular or religious, which they possessed in common (1885: 114).

With this, Nesfield formulates a curious equation, a seed unhappily destined to wither in the arid intellectual climate of his time. More than half a century later, as we shall see, Claude Lévi-Strauss arrived at much the same equation. In Nesfield's words:

The differentia of *caste* as a marriage union consists in some community of function; while the differentia of *tribe* as a marriage union consisted in common ancestry, or a common worship, or a common totem, or in fact in any kind of common property except that of a common function (*Ibid.*).

Like Ibbetson, Nesfield believed that occupational "classes" came into existence early in the evolution of Indian society, and like Ibbetson he believed that they might have become "guilds," and thus eventually evolved in the direction of European "classes," had it not been for the presence of Brahmans. Nesfield is even willing to speculate on how the Brahmans were able to effect the transformation:

the only thing that was needed to convert them into castes, such as they now are, was that the Brahman, who possessed the highest of all functions—the priestly—should set the example. This he did by establishing for the first time the rule that no child, either male or female, could inherit the name and status of Brahman, unless he or she was of Brahman parentage on *both* sides. By the establishment of this rule the principle of marriage unionship was superadded to that of functional unionship; and it was only by the combination of these two principles that a caste in the strict sense of the term could be or can be formed. The Brahman, therefore, as the Hindu books inform us, was "the first-born of castes" (*Ibid.:* 115).

We might summarize Ibbetson and Nesfield's approach to the origin of the caste system as follows:

a) Indian society in antiquity was similar to that of any other part of the world. In the earliest stage, India—just like the rest of humanity when in that stage—was characterized by a "tribal" structure in which membership derived from common ancestry, or common totem, or anything but common function.

b) At a later stage of development—again in a pattern believed to be universal for those societies achieving this stage of development—"functional" (or "occupational") groups came into existence, deriving membership more or less at random from the collapsing "tribal" structure. Both Nesfield and Ibbetson seem to imply that this stage was reached after, or about the time of, the invasion by "Aryans," but nothing in their theories makes that invasion a necessary precondition—as it is for Risley's "racial explanation."

c) At this point Indian society began to take its unique path. The priests of the period, who had managed to achieve unusual power and influence, converted their calling into a closed, hereditary marriage corporation: the only man who could call himself a priest, and practice as such, was one who could demonstrate priestly descent on both sides. Given this rule, the priests became Brahmans (a "caste," no longer a "guild") and because of the importance and influence of the Brahmans, the rule was quickly adopted by other "functional" groups at all levels, and India became a "caste" society.

Aspects of the Ibbetson/Nesfield formulation may be found in the works of many writers, even when they reject or ignore the construct as a whole. Thus, Émile Senart, whose criticisms of Nesfield and Ibbetson will soon be reviewed here, joins them in viewing Brahmans as a crucial factor in the emergence of the caste system: "In order to become Brahmans, the aboriginal peoples form themselves into castes and accept the strict caste-rules" (Senart 1930: 175).

For Senart, however, Brahmans were in no way an *occupational* group, at least at first, but rather a segment of the conquering "Aryan" race, living in village-communities and bound into a commonality because of such things as their family structure (very different in Senart's view from that of the indigenous population) and rules of commensality, along with other restrictions on association (*Ibid.:* 175–87). India, in Senart's view, was therefore characterized by an uneasy juxtaposition of superordinate Aryan restricted communities and subordinate indigenous tribal groups, and:

Everything indicates that in the march of Indian civilization the determining influence belongs to the Āryan elements, the aboriginal elements having exerted no more than a modifying, partial, and secondary one (*Ibid.:* 173).

Given this juxtaposition of elements of unequal influence, Senart goes on to argue:

The organization of the tribe, although transformed into a system of castes under the influence of conditions which I am endeavoring to explain, was a natural enough point of contact for conquerers and conquered, given their respective states of civilization.

Nowhere in antiquity have the Indo-Europeans shown any great taste for manual professions. The Greeks and Romans left them to slaves or intermediate classes, freedmen and members of the household. The Āryans, settled in villages and at first completely pastoral in occupation, had even less need to follow them in India than elsewhere. Manual labour was destined in general to remain the lot of either the aborigines or of the peoples whose hybrid or doubtful origin related them to the same level.

Both these groups, in becoming artisans, brought with them their tradition and the desire to be assimilated to the analogous organization of the superior race (*Ibid.:* 202).

Senart has thus rejected (for reasons yet to be reviewed) the arguments of Nesfield and Ibbetson that "tribe" evolved into "guild" and the latter into "caste" solely because of the particular power and influence of the Brahmanic guild or protocaste. Instead, he joins Risley in assuming that an "Aryan" population invaded South Asia at a particular time (or times), conquered the indigenous population and maintained themselves as distinct from the conquered. He departs from Risley's position, however, by denying any "racial" factor in this population distinction—although he apparently shares Risley's assumptions about the primitive nature of the indigenous institutions when compared with those of their conquerors.

Senart is therefore unwilling to join Risley in ascribing all influence in the formation of caste to the conquerors and none to the indigenes. Similarly, as I have noted, he refuses to join Nesfield and Ibbetson when they seem to trace the evolution of caste from the indigenous "tribal" structure. He opts for a kind of sane middle course, proposing that it is the juxtaposition of "Aryan" and "tribal" systems that is the source of caste, with the "Aryan" as the most influential of the two elements.

But if "racial antipathy" and "occupation" were not the sources of caste, why then the exclusive nature of caste? Senart concludes that Aryan social institutions, such as family structure, are the source of caste exclusiveness. But then why are there occupational distinctions? Having denied the likelihood of prior occupational grouping, he finds himself forced to predicate a kind of "occupational antipathy" as characterizing the early Aryan. Thus we see a progression: invading Aryans maintain themselves as separate from both tribal indigenes and half-breeds through the strength of their family and other social ties. Given their own inborn antipathy to manual labor, the Aryans restrict their own occupational options, relegating manual labor of all kinds to non-Aryans. Within the Aryan category, Brahmans emerge as a dominant social and occupational group—they are now a "caste." At this point the Nesfield/Ibbetson suggestions become operant, as the non-Aryans, now menials and artisans, follow the example set by their betters and convert into castes.

Max Weber objected to this view that Brahmans began as a nonoccupational, social, subdivision of the Aryans:

The Brahmans have never been a tribe. . . . Originally, the Brahmans were magicians who developed into a hieratic caste of cultured men. . . .

The general stages in the development of the Brahmans into a caste is clear, but not its causes. Obviously, the priesthood of the Vedic period was not a closed hereditary status group even though the clan charisma of certain priestly sibs was established in the eyes of the people alongside the personal charisma of the ancient magician. . . . The magicians had invaded the circles of ancient priestly nobles and, finally, had taken over their legacy.

The ascent of the Brahmans from magical "family chaplaincy" explains why the development of priestly "office" remained quite alien to the Hindu priesthood. Their position represents a specialized development from the universally diffused guild organization as of magicians and their development into a hereditary caste with ever-rising status claims. . . .

Since the knowledge of the Brahmans was secret, the monopoly of education by their own progeny resulted automatically. Thus, alongside

73

educational qualification for the priesthood there appeared qualification by birth (1964: 58–59).

It must of course again be noted that Weber was really concerned with the analysis of what caste *is*, and very little with how caste *came to be*. Nevertheless, certain assumptions about origin are clearly implicit in his writings, whether or not they were always apparent to him as such. Thus, he writes:

> "Caste" is, and remains essentially social rank, and the central position of the Brahmans in Hinduism rests primarily upon the fact that social rank is determined with reference to Brahmans (*Ibid.:* 30).

So if caste equates with social rank, which is determined with reference to Brahmans, and if Brahmans began, as Weber believes they did, as a magician's guild that became hereditary by acquiring the "legacy" of "ancient priestly nobles," we are not, in the end, much removed from the arguments of Ibbetson and Nesfield.

Now I am in no way attempting to argue here that all of these writers—Ibbetson, Maine, Nesfield, Senart, and Weber—share the same view on the origin of the caste system. The differences between and among them should be apparent even from the brief passages quoted. What I do argue is that underlying all their differences—in concern, in presentation, and in explanation—is one common assumption: the desire for occupational separation is at the root of the caste system. Whether one argues that the system began when protoguilds incorporated, or when Aryans turned away from manual labor, or when early priest-magicians made their occupation hereditary and were copied by others—that same assumption is operative.

This means we must turn our attention directly to that assumption, ignoring peripheral questions such as whether Indo-Europeans have an inborn antipathy to manual labor, or whether contemporary Brahmans are in fact descended from prehistoric "magicians" instead of from "priestly nobles." The issue for us becomes: does the caste system reflect—now or in the past—an organizing principle of occupational exclusiveness, involving the protection and maintenance of the occupational corporation?

74

I have classified Émile Senart with Ibbetson and Nesfield, if with some misgivings. Like them, he attributes the development of the caste system to the proto-Brahmans. Still, he puts primary causal emphasis upon social factors, such as differences in family structure. This part of his argument, of course, makes him vulnerable to the lines of attack used against Risley, such as whether there ever was an Aryan conquest. On the other hand, Senart, perceiving the difference between his views and those of Ibbetson and Nesfield, attacked *them* most effectively:

The real weakness . . . is shown by the inordinate importance attributed by Ibbetson—who agrees with Nesfield on this point—to community of occupation. If this really constituted the primitive bond of caste, the latter would have shown less tendency to split up and disintegrate; the medium which originally united it would have maintained its cohesion.

Experience shows, on the contrary, how caste-prejudices hold apart people who should be united by the same occupation carried on in the same place. We have seen what a variety of occupations may separate members of the same caste, and this not only in the lower classes but even in the highest. Nowhere is the abandonment of the dominant profession sufficient in itself to cause exclusion. Occupations are graded according to the degree of respect which they inspire, but the degrees are fixed by conceptions of religious purity. All trades not involving pollution, or at least enhancement of impurity, are open to every caste. Nesfield himself states that Brahmans may be found carrying on all trades 'except those which would entail ceremonial pollution and consequent loss of caste'. . . .

Many castes take their name from their dominant occupation but this only refers to a generic denomination, the application of which does not at all necessarily correspond to the limits of the caste. Baniā (merchant) is, like Brahman or Kshatriya, a designation in which it would be very incorrect to see the name of a caste; to do so would be to unite in a single province a number of groups which, having neither the right to intermarry nor to eat together, themselves form distinct castes. Agricultural castes are numbered by dozens in a single district, and the Kāyasths, or scribes, of Bengal, in spite of a common professional name, are really divided into as many castes, distinguished by geographical or patronymic names, as there exist among them endogamous groups with particular usages and special jurisdictions. It is the same everywhere.

It may be that in certain cases a local professional title embraces a group wholly united in a single caste. This will be the exception. The bond of occupation is extremely frail, and its unity is broken by the slightest accident. It certainly does not constitute the pivot of caste. . . . There is nothing more simple and natural than that castes and guilds should meet at certain points, for both are corporations. . . .

To grant to community of trade a place among the motive-forces active in shaping the destiny of the caste is a very different matter from claiming it to be the all-sufficient origin of the system. The first proposition is obviously as reasonable as the second is inadmissible (1930: 163–66).

I suppose I quote Senart at such length partly because I want to atone for the somewhat disparaging report I gave earlier of his views on the origin of caste. However unsound we may find his proposals, there can be no doubt of his brilliance in disposing of the essential premises of the "occupational" theory of caste origin. Risley took enthusiastic note of them, and indeed since their appearance few have raised their voices in support of the arguments of Nesfield and Ibbetson.

Senart's points are particularly interesting because they reflect crucial aspects of the complexity of caste, and force us to turn away from simple explanations or even descriptions. It is not true, he reminds us, that all castes have hereditary, characteristic, or caste-specific occupations. The fact that *some* castes may be characterized in these ways does not mean necessarily that *all* castes may be so characterized. Indeed, some obviously never have been. And Senart notes that throughout India we find many situations in which (a) members of a caste subdivision engage in a number of quite different occupations without in any way affecting the cohesion of the body as a closed marriage group, and (b) substantial numbers of people from different castes follow the same occupation—without any movement whatever to fuse, because of identity of occupation, into one new marriage group.

The anthropologist D. N. Majumdar, in his book *Races and Cultures of India* (1961), takes a rather indulgent view of the many theories on the origin of caste; at least, he presents summaries of a number of these theories with minimal comment or criticism. He is moved, however, to reject the "occupational" (or "functional," as he calls it) explanation each time he encounters it, arguing:

Endogamy does develop when a section of a caste takes to a new technique or adopts a new occupation, but people of different castes following the same occupation do not form a caste. . . . the few occupations followed in India do not account for the innumerable castes that one finds in any particular region. Agriculture claims more than 67 percent of the population and thus a constellation of castes and tribes can be identified with agriculture as their main economic pursuit. That makes the functional interpretation of the Hindu social system extremely dubious. . . (Majumdar 1961: 291, 296).

Majumdar's views should not be interpreted as a contradiction of Senart's observation that members of a caste can engage in different occupations without becoming separate marriage groups. True, as Majumdar notes, the pursuit of different occupations *can* lead to fission within the caste, and indeed does, particularly when the differences in occupation precipitate a significant difference in income and social position. But the point Senart was making is that differences in occupation do not inevitably and invariably lead to fission, for there is hardly a caste in India today—from those ranked highest to those ranked lowest—where members are restricted, *by the caste itself*, to only one occupation.

Limitation of opportunity, in other words, or the pressures of the community, may now, as in the past, have so constricted the situation that all members of the caste (or better, all males) follow one single occupation. Nevertheless, the entry of the members into new occupations is rarely the occasion for expulsion from the marriage group. Some men might be expelled because the occupation being followed was repulsive to the rest of the group, and others might separate themselves, as Majumdar has noted, perhaps because they believed their new occupation placed them above their fellows. All of this, however, is very different from saying that a caste is an *occupational group* and the mere fact of taking up a new occupation is in itself sufficient grounds for expulsion or fission.

The significant issue is, of course: in the beginning, did those who pursued the same occupation—whether it was that of "magician" or "barber" or "farmer"—thereby band together and form an hereditary marriage group? Majumdar joins Senart in asserting that

77

this never happens in India today, and there is no evidence that it ever happened in the past, at least to an extent significant enough to account for the origin of the system.

More than that, Majumdar—like Senart before him—points out that the exact obverse situation apparently occurred throughout Indian history. In all parts of India today, and clearly in the past as well, we find instances of two or more endogamous groups engaged in the same occupation living side by side, without any indication whatever of a propensity toward amalgamation because of their common occupation.

Therefore, it can surely be argued that if such amalgamation was in fact the way the system came into existence we should be able to note some indication of it, either in terms of an event in the past or of a residual tendency, however obscure, in the present. Risley (1908: 259ff.) uses this argument forcefully in his dismissal of the occupational explanation, and the argument still seems logically unassailable.

In any case, proponents of the occupational explanation of the origin of castes have never replied to the objections raised by Risley, Senart, and Majumdar. In fact, this explanation of origin has pretty much disappeared from the literature as a serious proposal—at least until comparatively recently. In 1971, Harold Gould proposed what is essentially a version of the occupational explanation, though he does not cite either Ibbetson or Nesfield.

Gould is aware, however, of recent archeological findings and their implications. He is convinced that the caste system had its origins in the Indus Civilization, which, he believes, was at first "not basically different in technology and social structure" from the preindustrial states of the Fertile Crescent. He is convinced, in fact, that the Indus Civilization derived in no small measure from the developments in Mesopotamia and Egypt (Gould 1971: 9–10). Thus, like the Mesopotamian states, the early Indus Civilization was characterized, as Gould sees it, by the presence of ranked occupational specialists. In neither case, of course, was this caste, but:

The transition to the caste system occurred when Hinduism matured into an institutionalized religion and began transforming the social

78

organization of Indian state systems to accord with its metaphysical, philosophical, theological and ritual presuppositions. This was the achievement of the Brahman priesthood. By sociological processes that are still far from understood, because they are so inadequately documented, this priesthood evolved into a stratum of religious specialists situated at the apex of Indian society and empowered to set the standards of religious belief, moral conduct, and occupational rank for virtually the entire subcontinent (*Ibid.*: 10).

Gould appears to imply that the Brahman priesthood was present in India before the coming of Indo-Europeans. This is an interesting and, as far as I know, an original speculation. For the rest, however, the arguments and objections posed by Senart, Risley, and Majumdar apply as much to Gould as to other proponents of the occupational explanation. Gould in no way refutes them—he simply ignores them. Nor does he give any reason for his assertion that Brahman priests, when they established the caste system in ancient South Asia, behaved in a way so remarkably different from those of their ecclesiastic brothers in other societies. He can refer only to "sociological processes that are still far from understood." But this is another way of saying that he doesn't have any idea why it happened, and—while candid—such a statement can hardly be termed an explanation.

* * *

If the reader has followed me, without too much discomfort or disagreement, through these past two chapters, he must—like me and like many before me—have arrived at the conclusion that the major traditional explanations offered for the emergence of the caste system simply do not stand up under the weight of scholarly criticism.

Caste did not originate in the moment of divine creation of the human species, or at least the evidence for this is lacking. Caste could not have originated in the revulsion of conquerors at any association with the conquered, nor can it be attributed to any other dimension of supposed "Aryan" superiority over "Dravidian" inferiority, since the latter equation is a figment of nineteenth century perception and not in accord with whatever we know of the historical record. And finally, there is no evidence, past or present, to support the assertion that caste originated when those of like

79

occupation (particularly priests) banded together and made their occupation hereditary. There is, in fact, evidence to refute it.

Where then does that leave us? What other explanations have been set forth? Not many, and none with much success. Senart, in his review of the subject (1930), isolates only four lines of explanation, which he labels: "Traditionalist" (those who would derive caste from the varnas, in terms of Hindu religious literature), "Occupationalist" (Nesfield and Ibbetson, and the position explored in the preceding pages of this chapter), "Racialist" (the arguments of those who, like Risley, see caste as deriving from instituted laws of endogamy), and finally his own, which he calls "Brahmanist" and which I have argued is close enough to the "Occupationalist" explanation to be subject to the same kind of criticisms.

In J. H. Hutton's comprehensive review and discussion of the question of the origins of the caste system (*Caste in India*, 1969; first printed in 1946), we find an excellent analysis of the positions held by various distinguished writers. It is so complete, in fact, that I urge any readers interested in pursuing the matter further to consult Hutton's Chapter IX, "Other Theories: Factors in the Emergence of Caste." For example, he disposes swiftly of the view that caste is "the ingenious device of Brahmans" by noting: "So deeply rooted and pervasive a social institution as the caste system could hardly have been imposed by an administrative measure" (*Ibid.*: 170). In the succeeding pages, he examines the suggestions of some twenty or more scholars and demonstrates, quite effectively, that almost all are essentially variations, permutations, or combinations of the racial and the occupational explanations we have been examining.

Thus, he views the approach of Gilbert Slater, in his book, *The Dravidian Element in Indian Culture* (1924), as a special amalgam of "both functional and racial" theories of origin. Slater argued (as Gould would, years later) that caste had its origins among the "Dravidians" before the "Aryan" invasion. First, occupations became hereditary, then—as a result of the racial antipathies of the conquering "Aryans"—caste took on its final characteristics (Hutton 1969: 177). Let us note in passing that Slater's book is indeed a significant part of the body of scholarly literature on South Asia. Among other things, he offers a powerful additional argument against the "Aryan" explanation of the origins of caste:

notoriously the caste system is much stronger, much more elaborate, and plays a much larger part in social life in South India than in North India; and it reaches its highest development in that part of India which is most effectively cut off from land invasions from the north . . . (Slater 1924: 52–53).

How, then, can one possibly assert a northern, or "Aryan," origin for the system? Slater's attention to "Dravidian" elements is an important corrective, therefore, for earlier overemphasis on supposed "Aryan" contributions to South Asian civilization. However, his explanation of the origin of the caste system is, as Hutton suggests, only a combination of earlier, already discarded explanations, breaking no new ground.

In fact, Hutton is able to find only one approach that could be classified as novel, that of the British social anthropologist Arthur M. Hocart, as set forth in his book, *Caste: A Comparative Study* (1950). Hocart, who was deeply interested in the interplay between religion (particularly ritual) and social organization, suggested that the caste system came into existence, and has maintained itself, as a social arrangement for ordering ritual observance:

> The conclusion we have arrived at on modern evidence is that the caste system is a sacrificial organization, that the aristocracy are feudal lords constantly involved in rites for which they require vassals or serfs, because some of these services involve pollution from which the lord must remain free. . . .
>
> The sacrificial basis of caste appears still more clearly when we ascend further back to the old ritual literature. There the worthy or excellent castes are those which alone are admitted to share in the sacrifice, with whom alone the gods hold converse. . . .
>
> If one section may not concern itself with the inauspicious ritual of death for fear of contaminating the auspicious ritual of life, then some other section must handle death and decay, for these are inexorable facts which must be dealt with. A hereditary group is therefore necessary to deal with them. These men are the serfs, the *śūdras* of later writings, the *dasyu* or *dāsa* of the Rig-veda. . . . In conclusion, castes are merely families to whom various offices in the ritual are assigned by heredity (1950: 17–20).

Again, in accord with my eclectic propensities, I am not inclined to dismiss Hocart out of hand. For example, I think he performs a service in reminding us that the caste system has an ideological dimension which it is perilous to ignore. His explanation of the origin of the caste system, however, has never been adopted, and for good reason. Despite Hutton's contention that it is unique, there are certainly echoes in it of racial and occupational modes of explanation—and perhaps even of the "Aryan" hypothesis. More important, Hutton contends that Hocart:

offers no explanation of the taboos on commensality and intermarriage which are essential to the caste system. . . . In any case, it is perhaps less unconvincing to suppose that the performance of the ritual was first associated with particular groups because that was their customary work than that association with the ritual led to the formation of the caste (1969: 177).

There are many other objections that one could raise: if ritual observance leads to the formation of hereditary, exclusive groups, where else in the world do we find similar phenomena? Why *does* exclusive right or obligation to perform a particular ritual lead to the formation of hereditary groups? Indeed, many of the objections Senart has raised to the occupational explanation are pertinent again: why, for example, do we find such a profusion of castes, some sharing ritual practices with other groups but each remaining, nevertheless, resolutely endogamous?

In the end, Hutton confesses himself dissatisfied with all of the approaches and assays an effort of his own:

Probably enough emphasis has not been laid in previous theories of the origin of caste on the geographical aspects of the situation. The fact is, many roads of migration have led to India—and have ended there. This has resulted in the accumulation of a large number of societies of very different levels of culture and very varying customs in an area in which they have neither been mutually inaccessible nor without some measure of individual isolation. The mere inescapable necessity of finding a *modus vivendi* on the part of a number of different cultures has probably played a not unimportant part among the various factors that have combined to cause the caste system to develop (*Ibid.*: 191).

Hutton also draws attention to a "complex of beliefs in *mana*, taboo and magic" which he feels is characteristic of much of South

82

and Southeast Asia, and which he feels provides the ideological underpinning for the caste system. However, the passage I have just quoted appears to represent what he obviously considers to be fundamental to the emergence of the caste system (since he makes no claim for it elsewhere in the region he considers characterized by "mana" and "taboo"). For him, geographical isolation combined with a continuing series of invasions by peoples "of very different levels of culture and very varying customs" to produce the caste system.

In spite of Hutton's disclaimers, this does have some ear-marks of an updated version of Risley's original argument. Instead of one invasion, we are invited to note that there have been many invasions. Instead of "racial antipathy" it is suggested that "varying customs" and different levels of culture brought about the need for exclusive hereditary groups. Many of the objections we have heard before (and Hutton has used in the same chapter!) are again applicable. If "invaders" are responsible for the caste system, then why, as Slater has pointed out, is the system stronger in the south than in the north—and strongest of all in the regions that have seen the fewest invasions? And, again, is not the subcontinent of Europe also both geographically isolated and yet subject, over the past three or four millenia, to continued invasion by many peoples exhibiting a similar range of cultural level and variation? Why did the caste develop in India and not in Europe? Hutton's explanation is, in the end, like the approaches he criticizes, no explanation at all. Nevertheless, adequate or not, Hutton's proposed explanation brings us to the end of the line, for—apart from Gould's—there are no more after his.

It is obvious that the discussion came to an end not because there was any sense that the problem had been solved, but rather because fifty years of controversy and suggestion had produced very little in the way of a generally acceptable solution. *All* the explanations offered for the origin of the South Asian caste system had effectively been eliminated; *nothing* remained standing amid the debris. Understandably, there was a desire to turn to more profitable lines of inquiry.

And there was a second reason for dropping the matter. During the first half of the twentieth century, sociological and anthropological theory had been moving from a search for origins toward a concern for an understanding of *present* phenomena. Increasingly, it was argued that without records or other hard evidence any assertion about derivations or prior forms of social systems constituted unscholarly excursions into "pseudohistory"—or what Pocock has somewhat forcefully labeled "speculative paleontology" (Bouglé 1971: ix). It was far more profitable, and far more meaningful and interesting, to explore the nature of societies, to perceive the elements present and to explicate their interrelationships. This was, of course, true for the entire spectrum of sociological and anthropological interest and not just for South Asia, but it was equally true for the latter as well.

Indeed, one of the first to move in the direction pioneered by Émile Durkheim, Marcel Mauss, and others—one who was in turn to influence later writers such as Louis Dumont—was Célestin Bouglé, the eminent French sociologist. His classic work on the caste system, *Essais sur le Régime des Castes*, was first published in 1908 in the *Travaux de l'Année Sociologique*, a series founded and edited by Durkheim. The work was translated into English by D. F. Pocock and was published in 1971 under the title, *Essays on the Caste System*.

Bouglé is primarily concerned with the *system* that is caste, rather than with its origins. But he wrote at a time when the lines were not yet so carefully drawn, and one could, permissibly, ask *both* questions. Thus, after reviewing the writings of Risley, Nesfield, Senart, and others referred to in this chapter, he permits himself to conclude, before turning to questions of structure and function:

> We refuse, and rightly, to attribute the creation of the caste system to the interested calculations, artifices and conspiracies of the Brahmans: it was born and grew, rather from the concurrence of collective and spontaneous tendencies. It is a mistaken fear to think that we can exaggerate the control that religion exercises over the Hindu soul. These tendencies are subject, for the most part, to the influence of ancient religious practices. . . . It is the habit of the closed cult of the first familial groups that prevented castes from mingling: it is the respect for the mysterious effects of sacrifice which finally subordinated them to the caste of priests. . . . a sort of arrested sociological development characterizes Hindu civilization. India has prolonged, indefi-

nitely, a phase that other civilizations have only passed through—or rather, she, like the others has developed the primitive principles but in an adverse direction to the general one. Where other civilizations have unified, mobilized and leveled she has divided, specialized and hierarchized (Bouglé 1971: 60–61).

Bouglé's explanation is not satisfying; we perceive within it echoes of Weber and hints of Hocart. The reference to "collective" tendencies apprises us, if we needed to be, that Bouglé is a student of Durkheim. And Bouglé's other adjective—*spontaneous*—should give us pause: is he implying a cause that is unknowable, undefinable, and unpredictable? Somehow, perhaps only in my imagination, Bouglé seems weary of the problem, and eager to push on. Still, he was willing to consider the matter, and that is more than we can say for his translator, a half century later, who chides the master gently for discussing what has become, in the interim, the undiscussible:

The argument is conducted in synchronic or, better, achronic terms and the sudden movement into the diachronic comes as a jar to the mind. This . . . can only be called a breakdown, a regression to an earlier mode of thought. . . (*Ibid.*: xii).

Pocock seems to be implying that the discussion of caste must eschew the historical sequence of events; it must be constrained to the "achronic" or timeless dimension of the "ethnographic present."

Which is not to say that this was a bad thing. My own feeling, as the previous pages should indicate, is that the investigation into the origins of the caste system had, given the extent of our knowledge, come up against a dead end. Furthermore, the ensuing concentration upon the "achronic" unraveling of the nature of the caste system has produced major contributions to the understanding of South Asian society and culture, and indeed to the understanding of human society and culture in the most fundamental terms. In fact, it is necessary to consider briefly some of these findings and interpretations before we dare move on to still one more effort at an explanation of the origin of the system. Thus, we shall at least have the advantage over predecessors such as Risley

85

and Nesfield. We will have a much more finely tuned comprehension of the system to speed us on our way.

In addition, we shall have the advantage of being able to draw upon much more acceptable approaches to the evolution of society, for research and analysis has continued in this area just as it has in the area of structural and functional analysis. Our difficulty is that contemporary interest in cultural evolution has largely ignored the problems and implications of caste and concentrated on other issues, using examples from other parts of the world. Therefore, in a succeeding chapter we shall have to review contributions to the understanding of cultural evolution that were not available to Maine, Risley, Senart, and the others.

The final task, of course, will be to bring together contemporary approaches to social structure and contemporary approaches to cultural evolution into a meaningful, if eclectic, fusion that will enable us to perceive a new solution to our old question: how and why did the caste system come into existence in South Asia?

5

The Units of the Caste System

It is much easier to say what caste is not than what caste is.

Taya Zinkin—*Caste Today*

What can we say about caste at this point? So far, we have observed that most of the population of South Asia is reportedly divided into a number of demarcated groups. In our citations, these groups have been variously labeled "varnas," "jatis," and—most commonly, in English and other European languages—"castes." We have been informed again and again that "endogamy" is a primary distinguishing characteristic or attribute of "castes" and that commonality of occupation is the next most important.

Still, there have been disturbing hints that common occupation is characteristic of many who are not in the same caste, and that sometimes men of the same caste follow different occupations. On the other hand, some of those called by the same label ("Brahman," "Bania," etc.) in fact belong to different marriage groups. We find caste continually referred to as "corporation" without having this term defined for us. We have been told that castes may, in addition, sometimes be characterized by "rules of commensality" and by ritual exclusivity. Finally, it would appear that these castes are arranged in some kind of order, some system of ranking or stratification—but exactly what this signifies has not been made clear. In this chapter, I propose to explore these and related issues. My concern here is with structure: caste in South Asia viewed as a socioeconomic system.

Some of our problems, as I think has been clearly enough demonstrated in the preceding pages, derive from differences in perception, assumption, and interpretation on the part of those attempting to convey a description of the system. The meanings and applicability of terms are not universally agreed upon in anthropology, let alone in the social sciences in general. We are constrained to wander in a universe without common measurements, accepted boundaries, and familiar features. We are all like the blind scholars in the parable dubiously attributed to India, running our hands over whatever part of the elephant we can reach, and, in our individual darknesses, desperately but inadequately attempting to comprehend the whole.

But, to be fair, some of the difficulty in this case may be attributed to the complexity and seeming intransigence of the matter at hand. The caste system is not a simple proposition, nor is it easily described and encompassed. Brilliant writers have pondered it, and if they have come up with different and even mutually exclusive perceptions, they have probably not been all wrong; my own suspicion is that many of them were more than a little right.

Let us seek our baseline. Obviously, the term "caste system" can not be applied to any *homogeneous* society, made up of persons who are, essentially, undifferentiated equals—persons who have equal access to occupations, spouses, and various forms of activity and association. Following this line of reasoning, Max Weber saw "caste" as "social rank" (1958: 30). In other words, it reflects the occurrence of a "class system"[1] exhibiting "closed status groups."[2]

Most scholars of South Asian society would agree, I think, with the main thrust of Weber's delineation: the caste system reflects a class-structured society, in which the units are accorded sharply distinct degrees of "social honor" and in which membership in the units is by birth. Bouglé, it seems to me, has said much the same thing, but he has sharpened our focus so that we may distinguish the Indian caste system from other, seemingly similar, class structures:

---

[1]"Ownership or nonownership of material goods, or possession of definite skills constitutes a class situation (1958: 39)."

[2]"Status" reflects a concern for the presence or absence of "social honor" and a "closed status group" is one in which membership is only by descent (*Ibid.*).

The spirit of caste unites . . . three tendencies, repulsion, hierarchy and hereditary specialization, and all three must be borne in mind if one wishes to give a complete definition of the caste system. We shall say that a society is subject to this system if it is divided into a large number of mutually opposed groups which are hereditarily specialized and hierarchically arranged—if, on principle, it tolerates neither the parvenu, nor miscegenation, nor a change of profession (1971: 9).

These perceptions of Weber and Bouglé give us our starting point: we can agree that the South Asian system is a complex, stratified one that is different from other complex, stratified societies because of the nature of the component units. And this brings us swiftly to the many questions we must address if we are to gain a better understanding of what caste is, and how it came about. Let us begin with two issues about which, unfortunately, there has always been disagreement: (a) What exactly are the "units" or "groups" which, taken together, comprise the system? (b) What is the "system" and how does it function over time?

In this chapter I will deal only with the issue of the nature of the "units," those human aggregations which we want to call "castes."

We have already noted that Indian society has traditionally been divided—by orthodox Hinduism—into four groups, the varnas: Brahman, Kshatriya, Vaishya, and Shudra. And we have also noted that most observers of the contemporary South Asian scene agree that, whatever the origin and ancient roles of these varnas, in recent (or historical) times the varnas have not really been "castes." That is, they themselves are not endogamous bodies, nor are they occupationally distinct in any way; they lack organization, coherence, and even mutually acceptable definition. Hutton puts it this way:

As a matter of fact none of the four terms for *varna* now represents anything but groups of castes. All Brahmans do not intermarry, but there are many endogamous Brahman castes. . . . the whole of the Kshatriya *varna* is claimed by Brahmans to have been extirpated by Parasurama, but if so it has been replaced by manufactured Kshatriyas, and in any case Kshatriya rank is claimed by many whose title is one of function or of

89

creation rather than of inheritance. Numbers of Sudra castes have taken to wearing the insignia of the twice-born, and some of them gain acceptance, after a time, as doing so legitimately (1969: 66–67).

There are, in short, many jatis in South Asia claiming to be of a particular varna, and the claim may be denied or accepted by other jatis in turn claiming membership in the varna. Since, however, there is never intermarriage between members of two different jatis (whether of the same varna or not) there is no way to effectively oppose the claim of another jati to membership in one's varna. Thus, as Hutton points out, some in India may argue that there are no "true" Kshatriya jatis any more, or no "true" Vaishya, but such assertions in no way prevent jatis from claiming membership in either varna. The caste system seems to function perfectly well in spite of all this. Indeed, it appears to function despite the fact that there are regions in India without Kshatriyas, or without Vaishyas—while in almost any part of the subcontinent there are jatis to be found which have never been assigned to *any* of the four varnas!

"Varna," Hutton suggests, is a term best translated as "group of castes," and we can leave it at that. It may be of some ritual, social, and occasionally even economic, significance if one's jati is accepted as belonging to a particular varna, or to none of them. The varna itself, however, has no unity, no formal organization, no leadership, and—most important—no control over its members. The claim in India to varna membership might be likened to the claim in England to be of "Norman blood." Such a claim might generate support from the genealogist, doubt from the historian, and amusement from the geneticist; it might affect one's socioeconomic standing in certain circumstances, but it is of little real use to the analyst of the present social system.

Increasingly, therefore, the attention of those who would understand the caste system has been directed to the social category called "jat" or "jati" over most of South Asia—and this is the category usually referred to nowadays as "caste." Is the jati, then, the unit we are seeking: endogamous, organized in some fashion, with control over its members?

The answer, unhappily, is no. Adrian Mayer has dealt with

the matter most clearly and succinctly. Discussing the "caste" as a category, he observes:

> In some ways this is nothing but a category composed of subcastes, rather than a group in its own right. For, though the caste is endogamous, the smallest endogamous units are the subcastes. Again, the caste as a whole has no mechanism for settling disputes, for adjusting the status of members, and so forth. Only in relations with other castes is the caste a significant unit. For people of other castes do not, as a rule, regard the caste as the sum of the constituent subcastes, but see it as an undifferentiated group (Mayer 1970: 5).

Where does this leave us, then, in our search for the effective unit of the system? We learn that the caste (or jati) is endogamous, and is viewed by outsiders—those of other castes, as well as foreign observers—as an "undifferentiated" and perhaps indivisible body. The same thing, however, might have been said of varna; it, too, is endogamous in the sense that marriages may be observed to take place within it,[3] and its internal divisions, too, may not always be apparent to outsiders. We have now learned that the jati, like the varna, is without unity, organization, or leadership. Most of all, as Mayer points out, it too has "no mechanism for settling disputes, for adjusting the status of members, and so forth." Thus we observe that the caste, like the varna, has no control over its membership.

This issue of "control over membership" is a vital one, for—as we have been told by practically everyone—endogamy is the prime distinguishing characteristic of the caste system, and those who violate the rule are punished by expulsion, usually referred to as "out-casteing." But who enforces this rule of endogamy, who has the power of expulsion? Clearly not the varna—and, as we now see equally clearly, not the caste (the jati).

Mayer draws our attention to the social unit he calls the "subcaste," defined in the passage quoted above as "the smallest endogamous unit" within a caste. In other words, we are finally talking about that body of people in the South Asian countryside which exercises control over the conditions of membership by de-

---

[3]But not in the sense of a *rule* of endogamy, enforceable and enforced!

termining the boundaries of permissible marriage and of other behavior, and by punishing (by expulsion or whatever) those who are
found in violation of the rules. Such a body may consider itself a
local representative of a more widespread "caste," and even of a
still more widespread "varna," but such allegiances carry no political constraints. That is, there is no submission to any caste or
varna authority—because there is no such authority!

Mayer was not the first to use the term "subcaste"; he notes
that he derives it from G. S. Ghurye. Indeed, he even quotes
Ghurye's view that:

There is ample reason why, to get a sociologically correct idea of the
institution, we should recognize subcastes as real castes (Mayer 1970; quoting from Ghurye 1950: 20).

That Mayer does not entirely subscribe to Ghurye's conclusion is interesting. Apparently he considers "caste" just as *real* as
"subcaste," though he acknowledges the "penetration" of Ghurye's
observation. My own view is that, given the importance from a
structural perspective of what Mayer, Ghurye, and others refer to
as "subcaste" (whatever the "reality" of *other* units), I could only
wish they had chosen a stronger, more discrete term for the category. Manifestly, this unit is not *sub-* anything—it is *the* unit of
endogamy, organization, and political control within the system,
for there is none other!

Unhappily, however, no one term is in use for this social
category in South Asia (or even in the literature on South Asian
society). For the region of Madhya Pradesh in which he conducted
research, Mayer reports the use of the term *biradari* to represent
"subcaste" (1970: 152). In the part of the West Bengal with which I
am most familiar, the term *sômaj* is most often used, though the
term *mojliś* is also known, and in other parts of the Bengali-speak-
ing area it is indeed preferred. Still other terms for this social
category—the endogamous unit within the jati—are in use in other
parts of South Asia. One can therefore understand why Mayer—
and before him Ghurye, and beside them many others—chose the
English term, "subcaste," over any of the localized Indian names.

But, I repeat, we are concerned here with the determination

92

of the basic sociopolitical unit of the South Asian social system. I have opted, therefore, to part company with Mayer, Ghurye, et al., and shall henceforth designate the category with the much more accurate and meaningful term, *marriage-circle*.

We lack sufficient information about the variety of ways marriage-circles may be organized in different parts of the subcontinent. Just as the name differs from region to region (and perhaps, in some cases, from caste to caste), so too do the conditions of marriage-circle organization. Mayer, for example, refers to what he calls "kindred of recognition":

This is the population within which marriages are made and/or kin links can be traced through mutual kin. These two features tend to go together, for people will not make marriages with families about which they know nothing, and the information runs along kinship channels. The kindred of recognition forms a large and rather amorphous body, being much the same for the members of a single village's subcaste group (for they are usually inter-related). . . . The kindred of recognition is, in the instances I have recorded, a *de facto* endogamous body, for it contains enough people to satisfy the search for partners. . .(1970: 4).

Mayer then goes on to contrast this "*de facto* endogamous body" with one described by E. Kathleen Gough for Kumbapettai in Tanjore:

where the definite number of eighteen villages forms an apparently *de jure* endogamous unit, and this may be a fundamental difference between types of local structure (*Ibid.*).

Thus we observe two structurally different types of marriage-circles. One, Mayer's *de facto* type, constitutes a network radiating outward from any given component family. The second, Mayer's *de jure* type, is composed of a specified number of families residing in a specified set of villages. Many interesting questions could and should be pursued: What is the distribution of these types in geographic, social, and economic terms? What other types, if any, remain as yet unreported?

Such questions must resolutely be ignored here; what is important for us is that marriage-circles are found throughout South

Asian society; in principle, every family on the subcontinent belongs to one. Further, the marriage-circle—whether of the *de facto*, the *de jure*, or whatever, variety—is everywhere in principle the endogamous body with the power to control the behavior of the membership.

Now this is a very big statement. How can we be certain that marriage-circles of every region and station have this power when, as we have just seen, jatis and varnas lack it? For one thing, we can infer it: the system is characterized by a rule of endogamy and so somewhere within the system there must be a unit capable of enforcing such a rule—and these are the "smallest endogamous units." Further, the field anthropologist observes the unit in action as soon as he or she reaches the South Asian countryside.

My own experience has been primarily with what Mayer has labeled the *de jure* variety (Klass 1966, 1978), where the endogamous body is a set of families claiming and accepting common membership in one jati, and residing in a specified set of villages. Elsewhere (Klass 1978: 59–76), I have described in some detail the marriage-circles I observed, and I gave some examples of the "marriage-circle assembly" in action. This latter was, for my area of research, the specific legislative, judicial, and executive body responsible for administering the affairs of the marriage-circle and for controlling the behavior of the members. Let us look, then, at the South Asian marriage-circle from the perspective of the field anthropologist.

To begin with, an Indian marriage-circle reflects both territoriality and kinship, and to ignore one of these organizational principles is to distort one's understanding of the structure. A marriage-circle is, on the one hand, a kin group: Mayer's "kindred of recognition" or even, in Nur Yalman's words, an "endogamous kindred" (1962). It contains *all* those families with which a given villager considers himself related (by blood, marriage, or whatever), and it contains, in principle, *all* the families with which marital arrangements may be made by members of that villager's family. Following Yalmen, we may say that this body includes all those too closely related to be acceptable as marriage partners, all those to whom one is already related by marriage, and all those sufficiently distantly related to be eligible for marriage.

Beyond this body, it should be noted, are not only (and obviously) total strangers who are therefore not acceptable as marriage partners, but also some who are in fact perceived as kinsmen. These are the members of distant marriage-circles *of the same caste*, who are assumed to derive from the same origin, but who are too distant in space and too different in behavior to be acceptable in marriage.

And, on the other hand, the *de jure* marriage-circle is a territorially circumscribed body. It is composed of all the families in a given geographic area who belong to a specific jati: all the Brahmans, say, or all the Barbers, or all the Sweepers, in a demarcated area. Such an area has specified boundaries—north, south, east, and west—and it contains a particular number of villages. Let us suppose, for example, that we refer to the total geographic area enclosed between River A and River B from east to west, and from a railroad track in the north to an escarpment in the south. Let us imagine that there are, in all, some seventy-five villages within this area, but that Brahmans of a particular jati are found in only twenty of these, and that the Brahmans average some ten families in each of the villages in which they are found. The marriage-circle of the Brahman jati in this area would therefore consist of some two hundred families residing in some twenty villages scattered over the area. Note that in this area there are also villages with *no* Brahmans, and perhaps even some villages containing Brahmans of *another* jati, who have their own marriage-circle and who do not associate—at least in terms of marriage exchange—with the alien Brahmans whose marriage-circle intersects with their own.[4]

As we have seen, Mayer derived his example of *de jure* subcaste from a paper written by E. Kathleen Gough. In that work (1956), Gough refers to a marriage-circle of Smārtha Brahmans of Tanjore living in some eighteen villages (see also Gough 1962). In my own research, I noted a marriage-circle of Kanauj Brahmans

---

[4]The *de facto* marriage-circle described by Mayer appears to constitute a network, but a territorially-based one, for it is made up of all the families of one's jati, in a circle around one's own, within a manageable distance, in terms of travel and of monitoring (see, for example, Srinivas 1954).

who lived in twelve villages in the area northwest of the town of Asansol in West Bengal. Carpenters, in the area I studied, belonged to a marriage-circle within the same approximate area that was composed almost entirely of villages other than those to which the Brahmans belonged. Bauris—the ritually polluted ploughman caste of the region—were found in almost every village in which the Brahmans were to be found, but their marriage-circle also stretched much further to the east (Klass 1978).

The point is, the geographical distribution of a marriage-circle of any particular caste represented in a given village need not coincide with that of any other caste of that village. We find that every marriage-circle is in principle independent of all others, both those of the same jati and those of different jatis. Each marriage-circle has its own independent leadership; each sets up, and *enforces*, its own rules and regulations.

Max Weber has provided us with the term *verband*, usually translated as "corporate group" and defined, according to Weber, as: "A social relationship which is either closed or limits the admission of outsiders by rules" and in which the "order is enforced by the action of specific individuals" (1964: 145).[5] From what we have seen, it is clear that neither varna nor jati can be termed a verband. It is equally clear that the Indian marriage-circle is just such a verband. As a matter of fact it is a special *kind* of verband. To use Weber's terminology again, it is an *autocephalous* verband—one with its own leadership and internal control, admitting of no other, or higher, level of authority (*Ibid.*: 148).

---

[5]"Corporation" (or "corporate group") has of course been defined differently by other writers. Morton Fried, for example (1967: 207–12), approaches "corporate group" in terms of ownership of common property, and as he seeks to unravel the evolution of complex political systems he explores the development of the division of functions (such as *ownership, management, interest*, etc.) in a corporate group. I have been influenced by Fried's work, as will be demonstrated in a later chapter. My problem here, as one might suspect, is that I see the validity of both Weber's and Fried's approach to "corporate group." I can use one in analyzing the structure of caste and the other in exploring the emergence of the system. Unhappily for me, neither approach to "corporate group" makes any provision for the other. What, then, do *I* mean by "corporate group"? Depending on the problem, and for the purposes of *this* essay, I mean either Weber's or Fried's definition—and in the end I mean *both*, properly synthesized.

Thus we have come to the end of our search: if the caste system is characterized by a rule of endogamy, active and enforceable, then it is the verband—the *de jure* or *de facto* marriage-circle—that is the body, and the only body, with the power to enforce the rule.

It is, of course, necessary to bear in mind that there is much regional variation in the internal regulations of marriage-circles. Certain marriage-circles, for example, are composed of exogamous subunits, or patrisibs, usually referred to as *gotras*. In such cases, the rules require not only that all marriages be contracted within the marriage-circle, but, in addition, that *no* marriages be contracted between families of the same gotra. The variations are many. Marriage-circles found in the same village, but representing different jatis, may have different rules about internal exogamy: some may exhibit gotras, some may have other types of exogamous subunits, some may forbid only the marriage of close kin. Some marriage-circles extend the boundary of endogamy to include one or two contiguous and closely related marriage-circles of the jati; some permit hypergamous unions with women of other jatis in special cases, and so on. The variations, interesting and important though they are, must not obscure the larger fact: the marriage-circle is ubiquitous in the South Asian countryside, and it is everywhere and at every level an autocephalous verband, enforcing its own rules and controlling the behavior of its members.

In the South Asian countryside, *marriage* and *death* are invariably viewed as life crises. The appropriate observation of these events requires the participation of substantial numbers of the affected family's marriage-circle. In other words, the head of the household in which the marriage of a girl, or the death of an adult person, is to be solemnized, must invite to that event the representatives of as many households of his marriage-circle as he possibly can.[6]

---

[6]Again, let us not ignore or forget variation: some marriage-circles place greater emphasis on marriage than on death as the event to be marked, some invite guests to solemnize other life crises (such as birth), and so on. In some cases, entire households are invited, and in some cases only household heads. Wealthy families can invite and feed many more guests than can poor ones (whatever the group's range of wealth), and there are innumerable other permutations and variations.

Thus, everywhere, in every marriage-circle, there is a characteristic event bringing together a substantial number of household heads. These events occur with a sufficient frequency within the marriage-circle to permit the body to function as a verband, capable of controlling the behavior of its members. Should it become impossible to have such gatherings with sufficient frequency, attendance, and/or representation, then the marriage-circle will divide into smaller units which have the necessary capacity.

In every village, then, of every region of traditional sedentary, agricultural South Asia, every household is normally a constitutent member of such a marriage-circle. All households are in principle equal to each other; at least, each household is entitled to one vote, through its head or representative, at those occasions when a vote is taken. Such occasions occur (a) when a substantial number of household representatives are gathered together for the observance of some member's life crisis, and (b) when the leadership of the marriage-circle converts the gathering at the event into an official assembly of the marriage-circle for the purpose of deliberating some matter of concern to the body. Further, in an emergency, the leadership may call a special gathering of household heads.

The marriage-circle assembly may deliberate a variety of matters, but the most serious and ubiquitous problem—one that seems to receive the attentions of almost every marriage-circle at one time or another—is that of the marriage of a member to an outsider. Almost everywhere, the rule is that spouses for children must be chosen from households belonging to the marriage-circle. In those cases where there can be an exception to the rule (i.e., cases of permitted hypergamy, or where certain outsiders are invited to join the jati, etc.) it is understood to be just that, a special exception to what everyone knows to be the rule.

But every marriage-circle has many rules—and not just about marriage—and all are enforced by the marriage-circle assembly. A miscreant may be ordered to pay a fine, or he may be beaten, or punished in other ways. The most serious punishment, and the one most likely to be held out as a threat to the household that has contracted an unacceptable marriage, is that of "out-casteing" or expulsion from the jati. We have already noted that the jati has no power to expel anyone. Technically, therefore, the marriage-circle has the power to expel the miscreant person or household only from the verband itself, but the members of the latter see themselves as representing the jati, and they may term their action an expulsion from the jati—or even from the entire varna.

Whatever else such an expulsion may mean—for there is great variation from region to region and from caste to caste in terms of whether expulsion carries with it deprivation of livelihood, loss of living quarters, etc.—it always means, specifically and intrinsically, that the expelled household is henceforth out of the pool of prospective spouses. Their children are not eligible mates for members of their former marriage-circle, and they are forever barred from seeking mates within the marriage-circle.

It is this eventuality, and not military power or divine sanction or economic deprivation, that underlies the authority of the marriage-circle and enables it to function as a verband. Further, the strength of the verband in this regard is a reflection not so much of the internal organization of any verband as it is of the fact that the entire society is composed of such bodies, each with a rule restricting its members from marrying outsiders!

In a society in which substantial numbers of persons are free to contract marriages with whomever they please, such an expulsion would be an inconvenience, but hardly a catastrophe. If, for example, you are a citizen of the United States, or of any other Western nation, and you are excluded from marriage with other members of what has been your ethnic or religious, or whatever, body of association, you are of course perfectly free to join another such body—or to move freely among the many people without such primary allegiances. You may reasonably assume, therefore, that neither you nor any of your children will experience particular difficulty in finding a spouse—at least, not for the sole reason that there are *no* potential spouses available. What we are discussing in these pages, however, is a society in which *every* household belongs to an endogamous marriage-circle. If, in such a society, a household is expelled from its marriage-circle, where shall the members seek mates? The answer, in principle and often enough in fact, is *nowhere*.[7]

This ubiquitous rule of endogamy, along with its dramatic enforcement through expulsion, has unquestionably captured the imagination and attention of students of South Asian society. It is necessary for us to note again, therefore, that a marriage-circle, and most particularly its assembly, is concerned with many matters other than misalliance and its prevention. In broad terms, the marriage-circle assembly (as all such bodies are continuously aware) is concerned with the maintenance of the marriage-circle over time, and the continual protection and enhancement of its membership. One might legitimately inquire, at this point, why it is so desirable that the marriage-circle be preserved, maintained, and enhanced. The question is indeed legitimate, but the answer must be saved for later.

In any event, the marriage-circle seeks, as a body, to preserve and enhance itself, and it does this, to begin with, by seeing to it that all members observe all the rules of the body. These include: *marital rules* (such as endogamy—but also, and variably, patrisib exogamy, prevention of widow remarriage, certain kin avoidances within households, and so on), *dietary rules* (such as those on eating with persons of other castes, accepting food from persons of other castes, acceptable or nonacceptable foods, and so on), *occupational rules* (activities and occupations permitted and not permitted for members of the marriage-circle), and many others.[8]

We must note again that details of the rules vary greatly from

---

[7]There are, needless to say, some loopholes, some special exceptions and occasional possibilities. Very low-ranked castes, for example, in some cases permit expelled individuals of much higher-ranked castes to join their marriage-circles (*pace* Dutt). There is no happy solution, however, anywhere in South Asia, and so expulsion from the marriage-circle has always been, and still remains, a formidable threat and therefore the most effective source of control by a marriage-circle over its membership.

[8]Note that these rules function to maintain the marriage-circle, not to maintain "purity of blood." Thus, hypergamy, hypogamy, caste adoption, and other such "violations" of "purity of blood" may be perfectly acceptable in cases where they pose no threat to the maintenance of the body—however much they may astonish the foreign observer preoccupied with questions of "purity," or even of "descent."

region to region and from caste to caste. Nevertheless, the rules for each marriage-circle are stated, specific, and known to all the members of that body. One marriage-circle, for example, will not permit its members to eat meat of any kind, while another permits the eating of mutton and fish, though not of beef and pork. One marriage-circle permits its members to engage in any occupation or activity that does not involve the taking of plant or animal life, while a different group permits any activity to its members, barring only that of removing the bodies of dead dogs from the streets. In one marriage-circle a widow may never remarry or even live with another man, in a different one a marital union of sorts is permitted for widows, but only with men who have themselves been married before. We may find a marriage-circle in which a man is punished severely for sexual association with a woman of any other caste, and still another one in which a man may have sexual relations with (though not marry) women of certain specified other castes. Here, a man is punished if he touches—or even speaks to—his younger brother's wife, there he is punished if he shaves himself or cuts his own toenails. And so on and on.

One might say that the point is not *what* the rules are, but the fact that there are *always* rules—meticulously defined and rigorously enforced—to distinguish the marriage-circles from all others, even of the same jati.[9]

In addition, a marriage-circle can modify, drop, or add any rule—for who is to forbid it? Changes in the rules, therefore, are or can be an agenda item for any marriage-circle assembly. The abandonment of dowry, the acceptance of a new occupation or practice, a change in dietary or marital restriction—all of these, and many more, are referred to in the ethnographic literature. Sometimes the modifications in the rules constitute responses to internal stresses—as in the case of abandonment of dowry, say—and sometimes they reflect changing economic circumstances or new dimensions of interaction with the world beyond the marriage-circle. The experiences of the Jadavs of Agra (Lynch 1969) and the Chamars of Senapur (Cohn 1955) are but two classic examples of marriage-

---

[9]See Freed (1957) for a discussion of the role of boundary setting rules in the maintenance of group identity and control.

circles enforcing, rather than preventing, change, but they are more than enough by themselves to bury forever the charge, or assumption, that the caste system is "rigid."

Finally, a marriage-circle—when circumstances demand, and to the extent that it can—strives to protect and support its members in their daily relations with other people. It is this particular aspect of a marriage-circle's behavior that has caused some people to liken caste to "guild."

The marriage-circle must come to the aid of a persecuted member, as in the case of the Senapur Chamars who were beaten by fellow villagers for observing the new Chamar rule to eschew scavenging. If men of the dominant caste of a village refuse to pay the village barber what he feels he is entitled to, he may complain to the leaders of his own marriage-circle. If they feel his complaint is justified, they may decide to help him relocate to another village—and then refuse to permit any other members of the marriage-circle to replace him in his former village despite the entreaties of the lords of that village, who are now faced with the awful prospect of cutting their own hair and nails!

It is obvious that we are now moving from *unit* to *system;* the two are in any case inextricable. The units, the marriage-circles, control the behavior of their members by threatening expulsion. This threat has teeth because everybody in the society belongs to a marriage-circle—this is a society composed of autocephalous verbands—and so the expelled person is not only cut off from his traditional source of spouses, but he will not be able to find another source! Similarly, the members of the dominant caste in a village cannot exceed certain bounds in their treatment of subordinate villagers because each of these belongs to a marriage-circle of his or her own. If the subordinate villager's marriage-circle can exercise control over a necessary occupation, the group can protect the fellow member. In a society in which people may be forbidden by their own marriage-circle even to cut their toenails, there are going to be a lot of "necessary occupations." Thus, for a marriage-circle to be a meaningful and effective body, it must be part of a system of autocephalous bodies—and the system, we begin to see, has social, economic, and ideological ramifications, some of which will have to be explored further.

We began this discussion with the observation that caste society is a stratified society. Having examined the units of the system, we are in a position to say that it is a particular type of stratified society—one in which the individual articulates with the total society as a member of an autocephalous verband (specifically, in this case, a marriage-circle), rather than solely as an individual, or even as a member of a "social class."

E. R. Leach makes a similar point, though he does not appear to be aware of the structural implications of marriage-circle, or subcaste, as opposed to caste:

a caste does not exist by itself. A caste can only be recognized in contrast to other castes with which its members are closely involved in a network of economic, political and ritual relationships. Furthermore, it is precisely with these intercaste relationships that we are concerned when we discuss caste as a social phenomenon. The caste society as a whole is, in Durkheim's sense, an organic system with each particular caste and subcaste filling a distinctive functional role. It is a system of labour division from which the element of competition among the workers has been largely excluded. The more conventional sociological analysis which finds an analogy between castes, status groups, and economic classes puts all the stress upon hierarchy and upon the exclusiveness of caste separation. Far more fundamental is the economic interdependence which stems from the patterning of the division of labour which is of quite a special type (1962: 5).

My debt to Leach is obvious. He draws our attention to the *system*, and to the need to examine economic interdependence—an issue, as he notes, all too frequently ignored in much of the literature on caste. It is not clear to me, however, why Leach urges us to explore the economic dimensions of caste solely in Durkheim's terms. To describe the caste system as an "organic system" is somewhat tautological, at least to a functionalist, and it provides little insight into how the caste system differs from other social systems (all of which, presumably, are "organic systems"). The only difference that Leach can point to is that in the caste system "the element of competition among the workers has been largely excluded." There is evidence, as we shall soon see, that this supposition does not always hold up. Thus, Leach offers important insights—for example, he advises us to view caste "as a system of labour division" rather than only as a system of ritual and social hierarchy and separation—but his vision is limited, perhaps because he does not have at hand the kind of analysis of the units of the system that we have just gone through.

In the light of that analysis, we are able to inquire: what kind of economy do we find when autocephalous verbands, arranged in a complex stratified society, engage in economic exchanges?

6

The Economy of Caste

Technology is the hero of our piece. This is a world of rocks and rivers, sticks and steel, of sun, air and starlight, of galaxies, atoms and molecules. Man is but a particular kind of material body who must do certain things to maintain his status in a cosmic material system.

Leslie A. White—*The Science of Culture*

In this chapter I want to examine, in some depth, the caste system in one of its dimensions, that of an economic system. My approach derives from what has come to be termed *economic anthropology*, rather than from the discipline of *economics* itself; after all, I lay claim to being an anthropologist, not an economist.

There are many complexities and problems in our path, through which we will have to wend our way with care. Only a few anthropologists have provided us with the kind of data we need, and the economists have not been much more helpful. In addition, the very field of economic anthropology is in an exciting but confusing state of flux as contending scholars debate both the meaning of the data and the applicability of classic economic theory to the world beyond "Western Civilization." I must pause, therefore, before attempting an analysis of the system to clarify the system of analysis I will be using.

In recent years, two approaches have been championed (and of course attacked) by anthropologists interested in economy and society. One of these approaches is customarily referred to as *ecological anthropology* and derives from the writings of Leslie White, Julian Steward, and others. The second has come to be called the *substantivist* approach to economic analysis, and derives from the work of Karl Polanyi and his associates. I have found it advisable to make use of both of these approaches, however uneasy the fit, in my efforts to understand the economy of caste.

First, therefore, we shall consider the South Asian ecosystem—the interaction between humans and the physical environment of the subcontinent—leaning heavily upon the insights of Marvin Harris, the anthropologist who has made the most significant contribution to our understanding of this topic. Then we must turn to the workings of the South Asian economy, and it will be necessary to examine the arguments of Karl Polanyi, because the best analysis of South Asian economic processes available to us is that of Walter C. Neale, a student of Polanyi's and a "substantivist" economist.

But Neale wrote as an economist, not as an anthropologist, and so to complete the work of this chapter we will have to turn to the ethnographic record. Specifically, we will use E. Kathleen Gough's account of economic transactions in the early days of the village of Kumbapettai to see how caste functions as a *socio*economic system. Throughout this chapter, our concern is with both economy and society, with human institutions and with the exchange of goods and services, with the material universe and with the ideological one. The task is to fit data and theory together, so that the two levels of concern become integrated.

A quick flourish of the flag of eclecticism is in order as we begin. It is certainly instructive to note that while the second half of the nineteenth century witnessed an increasing polarization in the social sciences between materialists (such as Marx and his students) and functionalists (such as Durkheim and his students), the second half of *this* century has witnessed a curious rapprochement between the two polar theories. The students of Durkheim urged us, as does Leach in the passage quoted at the end of the last chapter, to view society as an organism, analogous to a living creature. Leslie White has reminded us, however, that any living organism is invariably imbedded in the material universe of matter, motion, and energy:

Plants are, of course, forms and magnitudes of energy. Energy from the sun is captured by the process of photosynthesis and stored up in the form of plant tissue. All animal life is dependent, in the last analysis, upon this solar energy stored up in plants. All life, therefore is dependent upon photosynthesis (1973: 370–71. First printed in 1949).

With this biological dictum to guide him, White could turn to society-as-organism with a materialist perspective. For, if every biological organism is basically an energy-capturing system, then so too is every social or cultural organism. White concludes that "culture is a mechanism for harnessing energy" (*Ibid.*: 369)—and suddenly the seemingly unbridgeable chasm between the two theoretical positions has ceased to exist! At least, once we agree that a social organism is an "energy-capturing system" then it must follow that the social organism is bound by the laws of the material universe, and most particularly by the laws of thermodynamics, and is therefore amenable to materialist analysis. White arrives swiftly at the following:

We can now formulate the basic law of cultural evolution: Other factors remaining constant, culture evolves as the amount of energy harnessed per capita per year is increased, or as the efficiency of the instrumental means of putting this energy to work is increased (*Ibid.*: 368–69).

Some scholars, such as Harry Pearson perhaps, might consider this statement more of an inference, or an hypothesis—or even a pious hope—than a "law," but we need not trouble ourselves about that now. White's perceptions, we can note, led directly to much rewarding research and theoretical clarification. Anthropologists have returned to the long-evaded questions of cultural evolution because of White's work. This is important because culture *has* evolved, and continues to do so. We ignore that at peril to our discipline. And so, because of White, we understand more about the sequences and processes of cultural evolution than ever before.

At the same time, anthropologists—as a direct result of the work of cultural ecologists—are becoming more and more convinced of the validity of Durkheim's perception, referred to by Leach in the passage cited earlier, that the institutions and elements of an "organic system" do indeed all fulfill "functional roles." If this means, as it is usually taken to mean, that no social organism

107

can survive over time if any of its institutions are massively dysfunctional, then surely it must follow that the society's economic/
ecological relationship with its material environment *also* cannot be
dysfunctional. In other words, there cannot ever be an "irrational
economy" continuing over a significant stretch of time.

And this perception brings us back to South Asia, the economy of which has long been characterized as "irrational." Marvin
Harris, in his penetrating paper,[1] "The Cultural Ecology of India's
Sacred Cattle" (1966), reviews a wide-ranging body of literature, all
of which reflects a view that the economy of South Asia is now,
and by implication has always been, wasteful, impractical, irrational, and—in short—uneconomic.

This view of the economy focusses on what is perceived as
Indian misuse of cattle. To summarize points made in the works
cited by Harris, the traditional argument is that in India there is,
apart from an enormous and hungry human population, an additional population of some two hundred million cattle. These animals, it is believed, are "worshipped" by Hindus and are therefore
bred and kept alive for reasons having nothing to do with their
propensities for producing milk or meat. They compete with humans for scarce food resources; they stray freely and graze with
abandon and without hindrance in country rice field and urban
fruitstand. And finally, so the litany runs, they constitute a total
waste of meat—and this in a protein-poor land—since beef is forbidden to Hindus.

In challenging this traditional view of South Asian economy,
Harris is, as always, explicit about his theoretical interests and
concerns:

I have written this paper because I believe the irrational, non-eco-
nomic, and exotic aspects of the Indian cattle complex are greatly over-em-
phasized at the expense of rational, economic and mundane interpretations.

My intent is not to substitute one dogma for another, but to urge
that explanation of taboos, customs, and rituals associated with the management of Indian cattle be sought in "positive-functioned" and probably
"adaptive" processes of the ecological system of which they are a part. . . .

---

[1]See also Harris (1974) and "Gross Energetic Efficiency of Indian Cattle in
their Environment," by Stewart Odend'hal (1972).

In spite of the sometimes final and unqualified fashion in which "surplus," "useless," "uneconomic," and "superfluous" are applied to part or all of India's cattle, contrary conclusions seem admissible when the cattle complex is viewed as part of an *eco-system* rather than as a sector of a national price market. Ecologically, it is doubtful that any component of the cattle complex is "useless," i.e., the number, type, and condition of Indian bovines do not per se impair the ability of the human population to survive and reproduce. Much more likely the relationship between bovines and humans is symbiotic instead of competitive. It probably represents the outcome of intense Darwinian pressures acting upon human and bovine population, cultigens, wild flora and fauna, and social structure and ideology (*Ibid.:* 51–52).

Harris then proceeds to analyze the ecosystem, particularly in terms of the human/bovine interrelationship. I shall attempt to summarize some of his findings.

When we refer to "the ecosystem of South Asia" we are talking about the ways in which the enormous human population of the subcontinent (India, Pakistan, Bangladesh, etc.) provides, and has provided over the millennia, for its needs. Some 80 percent of the human food energy requirements of the area (Harris calls these "calorie rations") derives from grain crops, primarily from rice and wheat, and the proportion of each sown reflecting local environmental conditions. Unlike horticulture, or kitchen gardening, in which humans can provide all the necessary labor, grain production almost everywhere *requires* the labor of animals in addition to that of humans.[2] In South Asia, this has meant the participation of bullocks (cattle or water buffalo) in the various stages of crop production: preparation of the fields, plowing, irrigation, harvesting, and transporting.

Viewed therefore from the perspective of the ecosystem, Harris points out, the primary function of cattle in South Asia is to provide the crucial traction without which no crop of significance

---

[2]Only very recently, and in only a few areas of the world, has it been possible to replace much of the animal, and some of the human, labor with that of machines such as tractors. Dr. Creighton Peet has pointed out to me, however, that the Newar farmers of the Kathmandu Valley raise rice and other crops for market without the use of any animal labor whatever (see Bista 1976: 20). This apparent exception to the rule calls out for thorough investigation.

could be produced in the area. Citing the appropriate literature, Harris, demonstrates that *working* cattle and buffalo (that is, castrated males) are in minimal if not indeed short supply. Since oxen cannot replace themselves, a substantial herd of cows (and a lesser number of bulls) must always be present to replenish the herd of working animals. The primary function of *cows*, it follows, is to provide replacements for working animals, not to provide milk or meat!

According to Harris, the next most important function of South Asian cattle population, from an ecological perspective, is to provide the fuel with which the grain crop is converted into food—that is, into something humans can eat:

In India cattle dung is the main source of domestic cooking fuel. Since grain crops cannot be digested unless boiled or baked, cooking is indispensible (*Ibid.*: 53).

Harris notes, of course, that the cattle population also provides a substantial portion of the protein requirements of South Asian humans in the form of milk, milk products, and meat.[3] He argues, however, that if the quality or quantity of milk or meat production from Indian cattle is not up to that of the West, that fact must be equated with the traction and fuel producing qualifications of the animals, which would be much less important in modern Europe.[4]

Finally, Harris points out, cattle in South Asia make all their contributions to the ecosystem without drawing significantly upon energy resources needed by humans. After all, cattle feed in South Asia primarily upon fodder (straw and other crop residues) and wasteland grass and shrubs, none of which can be used for food by humans.

It will be noted, of course, that Harris is concerned only with

---

[3] I would add that milk and milk products provide protein needs primarily for the elite (upper class, or higher caste) who otherwise consume little animal protein. Beef—that is, the meat of dead cattle and buffalo, which is frequently termed "carrion" in the literature because the animals from which it came were not formally slaughtered for food—provides protein for those at the bottom of the social continuum.

[4] In addition, as Harris notes, other parts of the animal are utilized, particularly the hides, which constitute the base for "India's huge leather industry—the world's largest" (*Ibid.*: 54).

the physical needs of the human population in South Asia. We do not see them, as he discusses ecosystem, as socially or culturally distinctive; there is, for example, no mention of caste. No matter. Harris' ecological analysis is most revealing and illuminating. Further, it cannot be negated merely because a few of his arguments are open to challenge or modification.

Some economists,[5] for example, have questioned whether the system is necessarily ideal: is a *more* effective use of the elements possible? Could fodder, say, be replaced in the cattle diet by something else or could cow dung be replaced by another fuel so that fodder and dung could be available for use as fertilizer? Might not the cattle be bred into better milk and meat producers without necessarily lessening their traction contributions?

Functional analysis, which includes ecosystem analysis, always risks the too easy conclusion that "all is for the best, in the best of all possible worlds." But Harris' work rises triumphantly above all these cavils, for what he has shown us is how the system works and *has worked*, and for that I am grateful.

But there are questions. What is the role of caste in all this? Why have so many students of South Asian society and economy insisted that the economy is "irrational"? Why have they not perceived the functioning ecosystem that Harris describes?

One reply might be that while the ecosystem clearly functions in the way that Harris has outlined, the system and its functioning may not be all that clear to the people who participate in it; in functionalist terms, one might say that the South Asian ecosystem is *latent*, not *manifest*. Elsewhere (Klass 1966: 60; 1978: 100), I have discussed the Bengal villager who was unable to see that the bull calf he sold with much regret in the cattle market eventually returned to him, in principle if not in fact, as the ox he purchased in the same market to pull his plow. The farmer had an ideological aversion to hurting a calf in any way—and castration would unquestionably hurt the animal—but he did require an ox for plowing. Put another way, the farmer participated fully within his ecosystem, but had difficulty—for reasons growing out

---

[5] See Heston (1971), Dandekar (1969), Raj (1971), etc.

of his belief and value system—perceiving the process and its consequences.[6]

Such ideological barriers to contemplation of consequences can lead to difficulty, especially when persons in such a system are asked to explain the system to outsiders, or to respond to externally derived proposals for change. High-caste villagers, for example, do not permit their minds to dwell on the fact that all the dead cattle of the village are consumed by the lower-caste people of the village. Such upper-caste people cannot be expected to appreciate the importance of the contribution made by such meat to the diet of poorer villagers, and consequently offer few objections to proposals by outsiders for the disposal of carrion in ways that will prevent others from eating it.

We may wonder: How can people participate in an ecosystem and maintain it over time when they are ideologically unable to perceive or accept the system as it is? It sounds difficult, and it may well be for other societies, but it is apparently possible in the caste system because of the structural relations between the elements. If this is so, we cannot deal adequately with "ecosystem" without understanding "caste."

One might ask, of course, why the expert—and most particularly the economist—could not perceive the inherent "rationality" of the ecosystem, especially when he has Harris to guide him. After all, he is not blinkered by the villager's ideology. True, but scholars too have their ideological perspectives, and in a not too different way theoretical concerns and disciplinary interests can interfere with their perceptions. A glance now at some of the consequences of such differences in the particular case of the South Asian ecosystem may help us to understand why some anthropologists have found it necessary to part company with classic economic theory.

Economists tend to focus on "market"—on the interplay of

---

[6]He brings to mind the grieving American, described by Jessica Mitford in her book *The American Way of Death* (1963), who has squandered large quantities of money on "embalming" and on silk-lined coffins for his deceased relatives, but who cannot, or will not, permit his mind to dwell on what happens to coffin and corpse after the moment of interment.

"supply" and "demand"—and surely this is understandable and commendable, given the nature and demands of their discipline. Anthropologists, on the other hand, given the nature of *their* discipline, tend to focus on the small community and its inhabitants—on the actual agriculturalist, for example, and his fellow villagers—with all the needs and problems of such a community. From the perspective of the field anthropologist, the "national price market" can seem very remote.

It should not surprise us, therefore, to find this divergence of perception underlying the debate over the "rationality" of cattle utilization in South Asia. Thus, the economist Alan Heston, in his paper, "An Approach to the Sacred Cow of India" (1971)—written, he tells us, to "support the traditional view," that is, of the economist—takes sharp issue with the ecological interpretation advanced by Harris. Heston argues that a good program of culling—in other words, cow slaughter—would probably result in a far more efficient system of cattle utilization for South Asia than the one described by Harris.

Heston presents evidence that 24 million cows out of the total Indian herd of 54 million would, if properly provided for—as they would be if the weak and useless ones were not around to compete for food and care—likely produce as much milk as the total South Asian herd does now! And, he goes on, a similar culling of weak and sick oxen would result in fewer but stronger oxen providing the same amount of traction power as at present. Since, according to Heston, larger, healthier animals produce more dung than scrawnier, sicklier ones, even dung production would not be much affected by the introduction of an effective culling procedure. The end result of such a procedure would be: maintenance of milk, traction, and dung production at present levels; a concurrent saving in fodder; and a significant increase in farmland, for with fewer cattle to graze more land would be available for cultivation.

Heston's proposal for culling the total cattle herd undoubtedly makes sense from the economist's perspective—that of the "national price market"—but from the anthropologist's perspective there are suddenly many problems. Joan Mencher, in her "Comment" on Heston's paper, begins by noting that she finds it "amazing for several reasons," particularly because:

Heston considers an isolated aspect of the economic system without reference to the rest of the system; he attempts to deal with the economics of
cattle without considering patterns of cattle ownership, patterns of land
ownership and tenancy, and the facts of agriculture as it is actually prac-
tised in India's villages (1971: 202).

Mencher, an anthropologist, is inviting us to consider the
impact of a culling program of these dimensions—in which almost
half the national herd is destroyed or otherwise removed—upon
the prototypical village household. In such a household, she reminds us, traction for the fields derives from the efforts of one
team of two oxen, however "sickly," and milk in the diet derives
from "one scrawny cow," who may yet surprise us with just one
more calf.

Other anthropologists commenting on Heston's paper make
similar points (see Nag 1971, Harris 1971, and Horowitz 1971).
Heston's proposal may be excellent from the perspective of the
national economy, but it is obvious to any anthropologist, on the
basis of his field observations, that what may be economically
sound on a national level can spell total economic disaster to the
very villager the program was designed to help![7]

It should no longer surprise anyone, therefore, that anthropologists—since the days of Bronislaw Malinowski—have chafed
at the approach to economic analysis provided them by the formal
discipline of economics. One can understand why many anthropologists (if by no means all) turned eagerly to the analytic approach to economics suggested by Karl Polanyi (1957).

Any attempt here to explore in depth the differences between
(and among) anthropologists and economists on the knotty issues of
"economic anthropology" would take us too far from the concerns

---

[7]The retort, of course, is that the village household need not be left with but
half a cow and one ox; cooperatives and other forms of mutual aid can come into
play. But now we are introducing still more change into the traditional system in
order to make it "rationally" economic, and—apart from the fact that each novelty is
likely to raise as many new problems as the culling proposal—the original question
had to do with the nature of the ecosystem and its functioning, and not with
advantages or disadvantages of any revised system.

of this book.[8] For our purposes, I think it useful, and sufficient, to cite one anthropologist on the subject. Conrad M. Arensberg—one of the coeditors, along with Polanyi and Pearson, of *Trade and Market in the Early Empires*—devotes considerable attention to the differing perspectives of the two disciplines, noting:

> Not free human nature, nor free individuals, nor even any hard and fast psychological attributes of man, within his biological and physiological limits as an animal, give the anthropologist his starting point. In treating any culture patterns, even those of economic institutions, the anthropologist selects . . . "patterns of interaction". . . . anthropology is deeply committed to this priority of social patterns in any scheme for the understanding of the substantive economies of the human record. Our discipline is preconditioned to derive specific motivations, whether "economic" or otherwise, from such arrangements, rather than from abstract human nature or needs (1957: 100).

Clearly, Arensberg is pointing us in the direction of structural analysis. He is implying that the approach to economic analysis of Marcel Mauss is more useful to anthropologists than that of Adam Smith—and he is reminding us that our primary concern is with patterned interaction and exchange.

To Karl Polanyi's specific proposals, then. This economist urges us to distinguish sharply between—and then consider the consequences of—two divergent meanings of the term *economic:*

> The substantive meaning of economic derives from man's dependence for his living upon nature and his fellows. It refers to the interchange with his natural and social environment, in so far as this results in supplying him with the means of material want satisfaction.
>
> The formal meaning of economic derives from the logical character of the means-ends relationship, as apparent in such words as "economical" or "economizing." It refers to a definite situation of choice, namely, that between the different uses of means induced by an insufficiency of those means. If we call the rules governing choice of means the logic of rational

---

[8]See LeClair and Schneider, *Economic Anthropology* (1968), for a presentation of many arguments—their own as well as those of others—against the approach advocated by Polanyi.

action, then we may denote this variant of logic, with an improvised term, as formal economics.

The two root meanings of "economic," the substantive and the formal, have nothing in common. The latter derives from logic, the former from fact. The formal meaning implies a set of rules referring to choice between the alternative uses of insufficient means. The substantive meaning implies neither choice nor insufficiency of means: man's livelihood may or may not involve the necessity of choice and, if choice there be, it need not be induced by the limiting effect of a "scarcity" of the means . . . (Polanyi 1957: 243–44).

There is so much here to ponder. For example, the suggestion that "the necessity of choice" is implicit in the "formal" meaning of economics must certainly disconcert some anthropologists who champion the "formal" over the "substantive" meaning. After all, anthropologists have long been aware that choice is only *sometimes* present in marital exchanges: how dare we assume that is *invariably* present in economic exchanges?[9]

Polanyi is clearly responding to anthropological concerns about the nature of economic transactions. He does not deny the applicability or the validity of "formal" economic analysis, but he does challenge the somewhat ethnocentric assumption that it *must* apply to *all* human societies:

This view of the economy as the locus of units allocating, saving up, marketing surpluses, forming prices, grew out of the Western milieu of the eighteenth century and it is admittedly relevant under the institutional arrangements of a market system, since actual conditions here roughly satisfy the requirements set by the economic postulate. But does this postulate allow us to infer the generality of a market system in the realm of empirical fact? The claim of formal economics to an historically universal applicability answers in the affirmative. In effect this argues the virtual presence of a market system in every society, whether such a system is empirically present or not. All human economy might then be regarded as a potential supply-demand-price mechanism, and the actual processes, whatever they are, explained in terms of this hypostatization (*Ibid.*: 240).

---

[9]For discussions of the implications of the presence—or the absence—of *choice* in marriage arrangements, see Lévi-Strauss (1969), Homans and Schneider (1955), Needham (1960), Klass (1966), Rosman and Rubel (1971), etc.

If economists insisted that the market system was universal, what could anthropologists do, even when they seriously doubted its presence in a society under study?[10] Polanyi offers an alternative: he directs our attention to the "substantive" meaning of the term. Following Polanyi, anthropologists interested in economic exchanges can turn their attention to the patterned "interchange with . . . natural and social environment, in so far as this results in supplying . . . the means of material want satisfaction."

Well, is this not in fact, without significant addition, the "ecological" approach of Leslie White and others that we have just been considering? Indeed, there does seem to be an apparent ease of fit between "ecosystem" analysis and "substantive" economic analysis, and one might have expected there to be much fruitful interchange between the two. Apparently, however, ecologists and culture-materialists (such as Marvin Harris) were troubled because Polanyi and those who followed him questioned the automatic assumption of inherent "rationality" in human economic behavior. This, as we have seen, leads to the questioning of the implacability of "surplus" as an agent of evolutionary change. Since I, as an eclectic, can simply ignore the issue of inherent "rationality" I feel quite comfortable with both approaches.

In fairness, however, it should be noted that there is an important area of difference between the two approaches. While both ecological analysis and substantive economics are concerned with the same thing—the interaction between humans and their environment—they call for different perspectives. Ecological analysis, as we have seen, tends to view the interaction from the environmental end, focussing on such matters as caloric return and energy utilization. But Polanyi asks us, in essence, to view the same interaction from the human .end and focus upon the implications and consequences of "instituted process."

For "process," Polanyi argues (*Ibid.*: 248), "suggests analysis in terms of motion . . . changes in location, or in appropriation, or both," while the word "instituted" leads us to a consideration of "internal organization," or structure.

And so, having enjoined us to seek our understanding of

---

[10]See Herskovits (1952) for a lengthy treatment of this issue.

economic behavior not only in the physical environment but also in the interplay of process and structure that manifests itself in human social institutions, Polanyi turns to an issue that could not be raised as long as the formal approach was the only one available: How many different systems are there of patterned economic interchange and integration?

Empirically, we find the main patterns to be reciprocity, redistribution and exchange. Reciprocity denotes movements between correlative points of symmetrical groupings; redistribution designates appropriational movements toward a center and out of it again; exchange refers here to vice-versa movements taking place as between "hands" under a market system. Reciprocity, then, assumes for a background symmetrically arranged groupings; redistribution is dependent upon the presence of some measure of centricity in the group; exchange in order to produce integration requires a system of price-making markets. It is apparent that the different patterns of integration assume definite institutional supports (*Ibid.*: 250–51).

I view this passage as a kind of prospectus for research. Are there really only *three* integrative patterns—or are these merely the first ones we have, the ones that Polanyi was able to isolate? Is the relationship between integrative pattern and institutional support— say, between "redistribution" and "centricity"—always what Polanyi has hypothesized? What variations, permutations, and even exceptions will we find in empirical reality? Such a prospectus, such a generation of new hypotheses where before we had only sterile assumption, is of inestimable value for field research. Even the fact that Polanyi's concerns and terminology are occasionally at variance with those of anthropology[11] should not blind us to the importance of his contributions to the discipline.

---

[11]I refer particularly to the fact that "reciprocity" and "exchange" are sometimes difficult to distinguish from each other when one is analyzing *social* relations. I prefer, myself, to refer to Polanyi's three types of economic integration as: *reciprocal exchange, redistributive exchange,* and *market exchange.* There are other issues one might raise from an anthropologist's vantage point; for example, Polanyi claims to be concerned with all aspects of economic activity, but the three integrative patterns he sets forth are really patterns of *distribution* and are of only minimal utility for investigations of *production* and *consumption.*

Polanyi has taken us a major step forward—if for no other reason than that he has released anthropology forever from having to approach all economic behavior everywhere as if it were market-exchange behavior. The test of a new approach is of course in the new insights and applications it generates; the utility and importance of Polanyi's suggestions are attested to by the papers in the volume *Trade and Market in the Early Empires*—such as the one by Harry Pearson—which derive from Polanyi's formulations.

One of these papers, entitled "Reciprocity and Redistribution in the Indian Village," was written by Walter C. Neale (1957). Since my own views about caste as an economic system derive in large measure from this paper, I will turn to it now. Neale, as we shall see, not only follows Polanyi's substantive approach but obeys his dictum that one must look at the human end of the social/environmental interaction, at structure and process. Along with Harris' ecological analysis, Neale's work may help us to see that interaction in its entirety.

Neale has subtitled his paper "Sequel to some Notable Discussions," and he begins by reviewing the various conflicting positions taken since early in the nineteenth century on the Indian village structure and on its economic processes. He notes, for example, the contribution of Sir Henry Maine, in *Village Communities in the East and West* (1887) and in other works:

The importance of his discoveries lay in their emphasis upon the corporate unity of the village economy, upon its system of collective responsibility, and above all on status as a rationale of motivation, and as the principle on which the village economy was organized and integrated (Neale 1957: 222).

Neale is of course aware of the controversy precipitated by Maine's analysis.[12] Nevertheless, Neale finds Maine's perceptions extremely useful. Using Polanyi's substantive approach and Maine's insights, Neale is able to move to a level of analysis of Indian village economy clearly superior to the ones attained "by the

---

[12]He refers approvingly, for example, to Baden-Powell's trenchant criticisms of Maine, and particularly to Baden-Powell's observation, in his work *The Origin and Growth of Village Communities in India* (1908), that there is much geographical variation in village structure in India, and therefore no likely original or "pure" type.

more usual terms of economic theory or by the vaguer terms of pre-capitalistic, barter, or subsistence economy" (*Ibid.*).

Then, with data on village economic activity deriving from the Indian province of Oudh during the eighteenth century, Neale argues that a grain crop was produced in a village through the varied activities of the villagers, who shared among themselves a substantial portion of the results of their labors. He concludes, however, that the sharing, or parceling out, of the results of the combined labor of the villagers reflected neither market-exchange rules nor any kind of "primitive communism":

The village did not hold its lands in common but it did have common officials and servants: watchman, headman, clerk, blacksmith, carpenter, herdsman, washerman, barber, priest and potter. These officials and servants received their remuneration in a share of the cultivators' grain heaps. . . . Throughout the year there was no exchange or payment for services rendered. The herdsman watched the cows and the blacksmith made the implements and repaired any ploughs that broke. . . .

Distribution . . . took place in three stages: From the standing crop; from the undivided grain heap of each cultivator; and from the heaps after the cultivator had contributed to the Raja's heap. . . .

There was scant regard for economic rationality in the distribution. . . .

Each villager participated in the division of the grain heap. There was no bargaining, and no payment for specific services rendered. There was no accounting, yet each contributor to the life of the village had a claim on its produce, and the whole produce was easily and successfully divided among the villagers. It was a redistributive system (*Ibid.:* 224–26).

Harris, we remember, pointed out that the production of a grain crop was the most important activity of the South Asian countryside; the primary contribution of cattle was that of labor for grain production. Neale now gives us some insight into the *human* contribution to the production of the crop, and even more insight into how—once the crop is produced—it is distributed to all concerned. Neale tells us there was no buying and selling between villagers, no interaction of supply and demand. There was, in short, no "marketplace" within the village. Rather, in Neale's (and Polanyi's) words, there was a "redistributive system." Conceptu-

ally, there was a flowing together of the crop to a central point—
the "grain heap"—from which it would flow outward again as it
was redistributed to all those who were understood to have a right
to share in it.

Thus we see the ecosystem of South Asia in action: a crop of
grain is produced through the combined labor of cattle and humans, and the particular (redistributive) economic rules govern the
movement and allocation of the produce.

Still, we need to know more. How does *production* take place?
Are the rules for this dimension of the economy the same as for
distribution? And who sets up the rules, interprets them, and super-
vises the allocative processes? Most of all, what has this to do with
"caste"? Could not such a system occur in a *non*caste society?

The economist Neale has relatively little to say about caste
and the caste system, for he perceives these as phenomena essentially separate from the redistributive economic system. In fact, he
sees caste as having an economic dimension of its own, one having
to do with the exchange of *services:*

> Intertwined with the redistributive system of family-village-
> kingdom was the caste system through which crafts and their services were
> organized. No contract, no bargaining will account for its structure. It was
> founded on reciprocity. Every member of each caste contributed his ser-
> vices and skills to the support of every member of the other castes. Its
> sanction was religious, while its function was largely economic. Rather
> than a simple dual symmetry, a multiple symmetry underlay the caste
> system: a large number of groups were sharing out their services among
> each other although they acted independently. Each caste was economi-
> cally entirely dependent upon the performance of their duties by the other
> groups. . . .
> Briefly, it can be said that relationships were reciprocative in regard
> to services, and redistributive in regard to agricultural produce (*Ibid.:* 227).

Alas, *too* "briefly," I suspect. For one thing, there seems to be
an implication in this passage that *castes* are concerned only with
services; it is almost as if Neale forgets that those engaged in crop
production are equally members of castes of their own. Let us
remind ourselves of D. N. Majumdar's observation, cited in an
earlier chapter:

121

Agriculture claims more than 67 percent of the population and thus a constellation of castes and tribes can be identified with agriculture as their main economic pursuit (1961: 296).

Given this fact, it is obvious to any student of the ecosystem that the caste system—in any economic analysis—must be approached in terms of agricultural production. Exchange of services is clearly a secondary function—much as milk production is a secondary function of the cattle herd—and, however important, must be considered only after (and in terms of) agricultural production.

Neale is also a bit too "brief" when he says: "Every member of each caste contributed his services and skills to the support of every member of the other castes." No doubt such a thoroughgoing and all-encompassing exchange is called for if we are to apply terms such as "symmetry" and "reciprocal exchange." Nevertheless, it is simply not true—and I doubt that it ever has been—that every caste contributes services and skills to every other caste. After all, what need have landless laborers of carpenters and blacksmiths? Do we not know that certain castes, such as those of priests and barbers, everywhere limit their services by their own internal rules so as to exclude from the exchange system certain low-ranked castes of their region? If such exclusion is structural, rather than exceptional, what happens to the notion of "reciprocity"?

Anthropologists and economists, we have seen, look for different things when they examine village economy. Let us therefore turn to the ethnographic record to see how the caste system in actual manifestation relates to Neale's system of redistributive exchange.

There are of course many fine sources to draw upon; I propose here to use only one, E. Kathleen Gough's account of caste and agricultural production in Kumbapettai, a village in Tanjore (1955a; 1955b; and 1962). For one thing, we were introduced to this study in the preceding chapter. For another, Gough was able to penetrate into the past of her village, and can tell us about the founding of Kumbapettai in the last quarter of the eighteenth century, as well as about the changes that were introduced in later centuries. We are thus able to examine the way the system functioned in Kumbapettai in the early days without having our attention distracted by later changes and events.

Gough's account is particularly useful for our purposes because it provides us with data roughly comparable in time to that used by Neale, but for a distant and seemingly different part of South Asia. Neale's data was from Oudh, in the north central Hindi-speaking region long under Muslim control. Gough's derives from the far south, from a Tamil-speaking region long part of the Hindu Vijayanagar empire and, at the time under discussion, part of an equally Hindu Maratha kingdom. Surely, if we can detect similarities and congruences we have a right to conclude that there are pan-Indian structural regularities, despite all regional and other variations.

According to Gough, the Maratha Raja established a multicaste village on the lands of what was to become Kumbapettai. If there had been any previous settlement, it had been destroyed during a period of warfare, and the land was uninhabited at the time our narrative begins. However, the Raja did not simply throw the village open to settlement. Instead, he turned the land of the village over to four family clusters of one caste—in fact, of one marriage-circle:

four exogamous patrilineal lineages of Smārtha Brahmans of the Maranad Brahacharnam subcaste, an endogamous group today distributed in eighteen villages in the north-west of the district. The system of land management is not entirely clear, but my informants thought that the lands were permanently divided into a number of shares (*pangu*) of approximately equal value. Each of the four lineages controlled a fixed number of shares by hereditary right, but lands corresponding to the shares were rotated between the lineages in triennial periods. Every three years, the eldest competent man of each lineage similarly allotted a portion of the lineage's shares for usufruct to the head of each patrilineal extended family household within his lineage (1962: 21–22).

Though the Brahmans had the right to apportion and reapportion the land assigned to them, they apparently had no right to sell it or otherwise dispose of it to outsiders. Gough terms the land "impartible"; she implies, however, that the Raja had given the Brahmans and their descendants usufruct rights for as long as he was satisfied with their management and productivity. In return for this gift, the Raja received a substantial share of the harvest, which occurred twice annually. The amount of the Raja's share

123

varied over the years, from forty to as much as sixty percent of the total harvest.

The rest of the harvest, we are informed, belonged to the Brahmans. A substantial part of their portion provided for the subsistence needs of the entire village, and the remainder, if any, "was sold for cash, apparently by separate Brahman households, to merchants of the town" (*Ibid.*).

What we have here, so far, is clearly the "family-village-kingdom" system that Neale has described for Oudh in the same period.

But now let us look more closely into the system of agricultural production, as Gough describes it for us. Are we, for example, observing farmers, each producing a rice crop on his own lands, by his own labor and that of others? Apparently not, since Brahmans, at least these Brahmans, *cannot engage in the activities of farmwork!*

Religious rules prohibited them from ploughing the earth, ostensibly because this required taking the life of small insects and so was ritually polluting (*Ibid.*)

Whatever the reasons, we find that these Brahmans, like so many others in South Asia *seemingly* engaged in agricultural pursuits, are forbidden by the rules of their own caste (as manifested in their marriage-circle) to stand behind a plough or to cut a blade of grass. One is almost tempted to wonder whether they might have obtained their grant of land from the Raja under false pretenses in the first place.

What in fact happened, of course, was that, upon acquiring the right to grow crops on the land of what was to become Kumbapettai, the Brahmans soon acquired sufficient families of agricultural laborers to perform the actual work of planting, growing, and harvesting the crop—activities the Brahmans were forbidden to perform themselves, but which they might without difficulty direct and supervise. And so, in Kumbapettai, this agricultural work came to be performed exclusively by families deriving from two specific castes: Kōnān and Pallan. The details of the roles they played in village economic life are extremely illuminating:

In the uplands of south-east Tanjore, Pudukottai, Ramnād and Madura, where grazing grounds are extensive, Kōnāns were in some areas independent sheep- and cattle-herders, owing only a tenuous allegiance to higher castes. In the delta, where grazing ground tends to be confined within village establishments, some entered serf-like relationships with landlords of higher caste. It is possible that the Kōnāns were independent pastoralists in Kumbapettai before the village was fully irrigated and granted to the Brahmans. . . .

Whatever their origins, about a dozen Kōnān families were settled at an early date in Adichēri [the "serf-quarter," a district of the village] as *adimai* (serfs) of the Brahmans. Each of the four Brahman lineages is said to have controlled two or more Kōnān households and distributed their services between the several households of the lineages. The right of service of a Brahman lineage was normally inherited patrilineally; many Kōnāns still know to which lineage their ancestors were attached. A serf might, however, be transferred from one lineage to another if rearrangement of numbers became desirable. Kōnān men did garden work and tended the Brahmans' cattle; women cleaned the houses of their husbands' masters, but were forbidden to enter the kitchen. Each family received materials for house-building, the use of a garden in Adichēri, the right to fish in the village bathing-pools, and gifts, including clothing, at marriages, deaths and festivals. Men were paid by their masters a fixed quantity of paddy each month; women and boys received separate smaller amounts. Like other non-Brahmans, Kōnāns further eked out their livelihood by keeping goats, chickens and cows.

The Dēvendra Pallans, whose ancestors had served the Brahmans in their previous village, were *adimai* in a stricter sense. The Kōnāns appear to have accepted serfdom from choice as an assurance of livelihood. Some communities of their caste in other areas were independent pastoralists, and if a suitable opportunity presented itself they were free to leave Kumbapettai for agricultural work elsewhere. But Pallans were by law everywhere the serfs of landlords. A truant Pallan could be returned to his master by force and, except by agreement between two landlord communities, could not change the village of his allegiance and could find no other work. Pallans were attached to Brahman households in the same manner as the Kōnāns. They received daily payments in grain and similar gifts on special occasions, but their total remuneration was less than that of Kōnāns. Their work was also more arduous, for between them men and women performed practically the whole work of grain cultivation of the village (*Ibid.*: 22–23; parentheses hers, brackets mine).

Gough has illuminated many issues well worth further consideration. In an earlier chapter I questioned whether "adimai" should really be translated as "serfs." On the basis of the preceding quotation, even if we were to agree that Pallans were indeed serfs, what are we to say of Kōnāns—who were free to change their place of labor and residence? Again, in a later chapter I shall consider some of the implications of Gough's account of how the Kōnāns became adimai. For now, however, I want to focus exclusively on the relationships of agricultural production.

According to Gough, the men and women of the Pallan caste of Kumbapettai performed "the whole work of grain cultivation of the village"; could not one indeed conclude, on the basis of this account, that Pallan *and Kōnān* men and women—together—performed *all* Kumbapettai agricultural, horticultural, animal husbandry, and fishing activity? And, if that was the case, we might inquire what the *rest* of the inhabitants of the village did! Well, as I have already observed, the Brahmans directed and supervised agricultural activity, without engaging in any of it directly themselves. The Brahmans also administered the affairs of the village; they were, in fact, the *allocative center* referred to by Polanyi and Neale. The other castes provided a variety of services, but before we turn to them let us complete our examination of the adimai/Brahman relationship.

We have seen that, while both Kōnān and Pallan were called adimai, they actually performed different tasks—and this was neither by virtue of individual ability or interest, nor because of position in the socioeconomic system (since both were adimai), but solely because of membership in the respective castes. Pallans performed agricultural labor, Kōnāns did garden work, housework, tended cattle, and so forth. Furthermore, it is clear from the passage quoted above as well as from the rest of Gough's paper, that whatever the personal relationship between a Brahman and a "serf," such a relationship was constrained by, and dependent upon, the more primary *intercaste* relationship:

although each Pallan household is attached to a particular land-owning family, the Brahmans in many contexts deal with the Pallans as a collectivity. In particular, individual offenses against the privileges of the upper castes are apt to provoke heavy fines imposed on the street as a whole, or corporal punishment administered to random individuals (*Ibid.:* 44).

To go just one slight step further than Gough, we find the Brahmans as a "collectivity" dealing with the Pallans as a "collectivity," and this of course means *caste* with *caste*—or, as we now know, *marriage-circle* with *marriage-circle*. By what authority, then, may Brahmans visit punishment upon adimai? Gough informs us:

> In the late Marātha period the heads of the four Brahman lineages formed a group (*panchāyat*) responsible to the government for the village's administration and the collection of revenue. Their duties included the periodic allocation of lands and servants to separate households, the common control of the village specialist castes, and the organization of Pallans for such joint tasks as the digging out of the irrigation channels before the sowing season and occasional forced labour on government projects such as irrigation works and road-building. The *panchāyat* was also concerned with the administration of justice among the Brahmans and within the village as a whole (*Ibid.:* 36).

We have already seen that the members of the Brahman marriage-circle in Kumbapettai were supervisors of agricultural and related activities. Now we learn that they were also authorized by the government to supervise irrigation, roadbuilding, and other supravillage activities, and to administer justice to those who performed these tasks. Neale's "kingdom-village-family" system is clearly before us.

And, finally, we see that the Brahmans—our "allocative center"—have also been given "common control of the village specialist castes." With this information, we can turn from "crop production" to "services."

In the time period under consideration there were in Kumbapettai—apart from Brahmans and adimai—four types of village servants, each apparently represented by one household of a specific caste: "namely, Barbers, Carpenters, Potters and Village Temple Priests" (*Ibid.:* 23). Gough uses capital letters for each of these categories—they are, after all, occupations normally not capitalized in English—because each term is actually a translation of a caste name. Let us look, then, at the activities and relationships of these marriage-circle representatives in Kumbapettai:

Barbers were required to shave the body hair and a portion of the head hair and to manicure finger-nails of Brahman and non-Brahman men,[13] twice a month, and to shave the heads of Brahman widows at similar intervals. They were also herbalists, leeches and dentists. Women of the caste were midwives for all castes above Ādi Drāvidas. Carpenters made wooden ploughs, bullock-carts, paddy-storage chests and other wooden utensils, and doors, window-frames and pillars for houses. Though they did odd jobs for all the castes, their work was overwhelmingly for Brahmans. For in this period few families other than Brahmans owned ploughs or bullock-carts, and only Brahman houses had doors and window-frames. Even today, most non-Brahman and Pallan families live in windowless, thatched mud shacks and hang a grass mat before the doorway.

Kumbapettai Pūsālis[14] were similarly employed primarily by Brahmans, who built and managed the village temple. Twice daily they made ritual offerings of cooked food, incense, water and flowers before the deity, sacrificed goats at festivals, provided flower garlands for marriages, and received offerings for the goddess from Brahman and non-Brahman families after the successful birth of a child or a calf or the satisfactory conclusion of an illness.

Each of these servant groups received, as their main source of livelihood, shares from the total grain harvest of the village in February and September. Individual Barbers in addition received six measures of paddy after harvest from each man and widow in the village whom they regularly served; Priests and Carpenters received six measures from each Brahman and non-Brahman house. . . .

Potters (unlike Barbers, Carpenters and Pūsālis) often undertook work for Pallans as well as non-Brahmans. For their work was both ritually neutral and also essential to the lower castes. Perhaps partly because their work was as much oriented to the lower castes as to the Brahmans, Potters, unlike other village servants, derived their maintenance in separate grain-payments from the households of all the castes (*Ibid.*: 23–25).

---

[13]Gough uses the term *non-Brahman* to encompass all castes other than Brahman and Pallan. The latter are referred to in the text as Ādi Drāvida, or "ancient Dravidians."

[14]"Village Temple Priests."

Thus the potters constitute something of an exception to the rule that services are provided primarily for the dominant castes of the village and secondarily for other service castes, but not for the laboring castes; the Potters provided services for all the other castes of the village and received payments in grain from all of them. The other non-Brahmans in Kumbapettai worked primarily for Brahmans and received grain payments primarily, if not indeed exclusively, from them.[15]

According to Gough, even in the early days of Kumbapettai other specialist services were available to the Brahmans—and, to a varying extent, to other castes. However, except for the services of four families of Pallan watchmen (who received biennial grain shares at harvest time), these were not provided by actual residents of Kumbapettai:

> Kumbapettai drew the specialist services of Washermen, Blacksmiths and Goldsmiths from families of Mānāngorai, the village to the south, who held hereditary rights in both villages. These families were remunerated in the same way as the Barbers, Pusālis, Carpenters and Pallan watchmen. Washermen washed clothing for occasions such as marriages and also washed polluted cloths used during menstruation, childbirth and delivery. In addition, they provided lamps for temple festivals, decorated marriage booths and strewed cloths before funeral processions. Goldsmiths made gold and silver necklaces, ear-rings and bangles from metal provided by their patrons, and Blacksmiths made ploughshares and metal vessels. *The work of all these castes was performed primarily on behalf, and under the authority, of the landlords whose villages they served* (*Ibid.*: 25; italics mine).

There were still other castes providing still other services—to the village as a whole or to individual families within it—but surely the point has been made in sufficient detail. The rules governing

---

[15]I suspect the exception is of little moment, even for the income of the Potters themselves. We have seen that Pallans acquired their grain in the form of "daily payments" from the Brahmans for whom they worked. My own field observations were that such "daily payments" even today are rarely more than enough for the laborer's family meal. If this were the case in Kumbapettai, Potters could hardly have considered Pallans as among their more important customers. Still, even Pallans needed an occasional pot.

duty and remuneration vary, as do the rules concerning which other castes may or may not be served. Some service castes live within the village, and some without; some are ranked high in ritual terms, and some are ranked low. Indeed, were we to consult the ethnographic literature for India's villages we would find the range of variation—for conditions of residence, ritual purity, nature of duties, permissible clients, and terms of remuneration—to be startlingly great.

My point, however, is that the structural principles appear to be essentially the same, whatever the variations in detail. Throughout India, as in Kumbapettai, we find that the families in a given village who control agricultural production constitute the dominant caste or castes (see for example, Srinivas 1955, 1959). Further, they supervise the distribution of services as well as the production and distribution of the crops.

Reciprocity—or reciprocal exchange—may be present, but it does not appear to be the meaningful diagnostic characteristic of the socioeconomic system. What Gough noted in Kumbapettai is simply one example of what Neale predicated for all India as the instituted economic system: a redistributive exchange system, in which the dominant caste in a village, under the authority of the government, controls the production of the crop, the distribution of it, and—as we have determined from Gough's account—even the allocation of services.

We have learned something more from Gough, too. Participation in this complex redistributive exchange system is not by individuals (or families) acting as discrete social units. Rather, the units participate as—because they *are*—village representatives of regional castes, manifested in specific marriage-circles. Each of these marriage-circles articulates with the total economic system by providing, or controlling access to, a specifiable set of commodities or services, with the dominant caste of the village serving as allocative center for the redistributive exchange.

Each caste group was virtually homogeneous in occupation and wealth, Brahmans being considerably wealthier than their non-Brahman servants, and non-Brahmans slightly wealthier than Ādi Drāvidas. The overwhelming majority of economic relationships were hereditary and caste-determined. In spite of the proliferation of castes, specialization was simple from an economic point of view. In most cases, different specialist groups did not co-operate in the production of a single object. . . . A single household, and in some cases a single worker, could control each of such skills as cultivation, cattle-tending, pottery-making, laundry work and barbering. . . . Economic relationships were overwhelmingly between separate households of different castes and were dyadic: Cowherds, Agricultural Serfs, Barbers and Washermen were not involved in each other's relationships with landlords. Within the village, apparently, all economic relationships consisted of the provision of goods and services in direct exchange for paddy, the chief source of livelihood (*Ibid.*: 26–27).

And, to go outside the village, we might argue that the Brahmans were in effect providing a service for the ultimate owner of the land, the Raja, by supervising the production of the crop, managing the distribution, and administering the affairs of the village. In return, they received *their* share of the harvest. Does this not help us to understand why the Raja chose Brahmans, who could not by their caste rules themselves engage in the activities of farming, as the "landed gentry," as the people competent to see to it that the village was prosperous, peaceful, and productive?

"Farming" as we know it in the West is of course one way of producing a crop in a complex, mixed agriculture society, just as the production of milk and meat are the two functions of cattle with which we are most familiar. Undoubtedly, classical South Asia knew "farming," just as South Asians knew that cattle produced milk and meat, but the dominant mode of production was something other than farming.

If we attempt to combine the perspectives of ecosystem analysis and substantive economics, we find that the contours of the South Asian system are quite distinct. It is a mixed agriculture system and a complex society, but we observe that the integration of cattle into the system is more thorough than in the West, and that the socioeconomic complexity is likewise very profound and very specific.

We find that the massive grain heap needed to support the subcontinent's population derived from innumerable villages in which the production of a crop reflected the complex interaction of what Gough calls "simple" specialists. Each of these represented a

131

marriage-circle with the right, or obligation, to contribute a particular specialty, and each participated in the web of activities leading to the production of the crop, to the full utilization of both land and animals, and to the maintenance of equipment and human personnel.

Further, this participation was through the mechanism of what Gough calls "dyadic" relationships.[16] Such a system worked despite the absence of magistrate or mayor, or other political authorities, because the economic system itself provided the sociopolitical center: the Brahmans, or any of the other dominant land-controlling castes. These castes were not composed of "farmers," but of *supervisors* of production and distribution.

Given all this, I am satisfied that one may view the South Asian caste system as a crucial integral feature of a particular redistributive economic system. South Asia, we have seen, is characterized by a complex agricultural system in which land and animals and human specializations interact to produce a crop large enough to maintain an enormous population. The village was (and is) the locus of this production, and it is the place where most of the subcontinent's population live. Not all the population, as represented in a given village, is necessary for the activities of grain production: some people care for animals and some provide maintenance services. Through these various activities and services, all claim shares in the crop.

But this is a stratified society: not everyone has equal or even equivalent access to the basic resource—land on which to grow a crop.[17] And in this particular stratified society, we have observed that control and access is neither by individuals nor by households—nor, for that matter, by tribes, clans, nations, or whatever. Rather, as we have seen, the South Asian socioeconomic system is structurally inseparable from "the caste system." Whatever else *caste* may be on sociological or ideological levels, it is clearly the crucial element of the economy.

---

[16]Others refer to these as *jajmani* relationships. See, for example: Wiser (1936), Beidelman (1959), Kolenda (1963), etc.

[17]This statement reflects the approach to stratification advocated by Morton Fried. More on this in a later chapter.

In classic South Asia, then, redistributive exchange is the economic integrative system in a stratified society in which the differential access to basic resources is *solely* by the representatives of corporate groups. The "corporate group"—Weber's verband—is of course the *marriage-circle* we became acquainted with in the previous chapter: autocephalous, and able to maintain control over its members because the body is in principle occupationally homogeneous and invariably endogamous.

On the basis of the material considered in this chapter, however, we have achieved new insights into occupational homogeneity and the rule of endogamy among South Asian castes. Apparently, the system is most effective when the component castes are *both* occupationally homogeneous and endogamous, as in the case of Gough's Kumbapettai, but there is no reason why the system cannot continue to function adequately even when members of a caste engage in different occupations and vary in degree of individual prosperity. Thus, this attribute of caste has undergone modification, but the system remains.

Endogamy *is* crucial, however—but not for the reason most frequently asserted. Most writers, from the Abbé Dubois on, argue that the rule of endogamy is crucial for the maintenance of the *castes*. Of course it is, but much more important is that the rule of endogamy is necessary for the maintenance of the total *caste system*. In other words, the issue is not "purity of descent" but maintenance of distinct boundaries over time between the units. Without these boundaries, this particular structure lacks any mechanism for enforcing *all the rules of the system*. Everything rests on this keystone of distinct and bounded units, and therefore upon endogamy. Were it ever to become possible for individual households—in large numbers and with ease—to continue over time outside the bounds of the marriage-circle, the system would undergo massive structural revision.

None of the many changes and stresses South Asia has experienced in the last century, however, has significantly affected the rule of endogamy. Occupations change, rules of diet and association have been drastically revised, even the ideological underpinnings of the system have been challenged and in some cases swept away. But, still, an expelled household—of any marriage-circle, of

133

any region—finds it almost impossible to obtain spouses for children. And the system continues, remarkably unimpaired.

I am speaking, of course, not of the cities but of the South Asian countryside, for that is where we find the caste system with which I am concerned in this work—a system of agricultural production and economic distribution in a stratified society—and it is the origins of *this* system which I seek.

7

From Clan to Caste

The English have very peculiar opinions on the subject of perfection.
They insist that . . . mankind have arisen, by degrees, from the state
of savages to the exalted dignity of the great philosopher Newton. . . .

Mirza Abū Tāleb Khān—*The Travels*
of Mirza Abū Tāleb Khān (1814)

It should be apparent that this book is not intended as any
kind of comprehensive disquisition on the nature and functioning
of castes, or of the caste system of South Asia. Many dimensions of
caste—many problems of great moment to those interested in the
subcontinent—have here been barely touched upon, and some
have been ignored entirely.[1]

Why, for example, do I give so little attention to ideology, to
the findings of symbolic analysts on such issues as pollution, hierarchy, values, and so on? As I have tried to make clear, my concern in writing this book is with the emergence of the system, and
I have endeavored to restrict my account of the system to those

---

[1] It will have been noted that jajmani relationships have been mentioned only
once, and that in a footnote. Again, nothing has been said here about the rules of
food and water prestation (giving and accepting), and little about the rules of commensality (eating together). Unquestionably, commensality and prestation are important for any understanding of the *consumption* dimension of economic behavior
(see Marriott 1959, 1960; Freed 1963), but as far as I can determine neither consumption nor prestation nor commensality nor jajmani require further explication
for the purposes of this work.

features which, in my opinion, must be reviewed if we are to approach the questions of origin and transformation.[2]

On the other hand, I am fully aware that in the end *all* aspects of the system are significant for any understanding of the entire system and its origins. The dilemma is a painful one. I am not one of those who think that only economic, ecological, and technological dimensions of culture are always and everywhere crucial and must take priority in any analysis.[3]

The concern at the moment, however, is with a problem in cultural evolution—the emergence of a particular system of stratification—and no one has argued convincingly that for this kind of problem any dimension of culture plays a role equal to, let alone greater than, that of economy, ecology, and technology. Instead, the arguments for focussing on these three, as I have been doing, are many and cogent, and have been advanced persuasively by an increasing number of scholars, including White, Steward, Sahlins, Service, Fried, Harris, and many more. To follow their lead, therefore, requires no justification; to ignore it, or to move contrary to it, might.

And yet, having delivered myself of all that, I propose to turn first to an exercise in symbolic analysis in my effort to penetrate the unrecorded past and to speculate about the conditions that might have led to the emergence of the caste system. I will take all the help I can get, in this most difficult of all anthropological enterprises, the search for origins.

The question before us now is: What kind of socioeconomic system preceded the caste system in South Asia? In the next chapter, the question will be: How do we get from "*pre*caste" to "caste"? For my first question, I have found two studies particu-

---

[2] I urge all readers who wish to learn more about the South Asian social system to consult the appropriate literature. I would particularly recommend Mandelbaum (1970) for a description of the system and Dumont (1970) for an analysis of it.

[3] I do not see, for example, why one must assume that economy, ecology, and technology must invariably constitute the "core" of the culture, while social structure and ideology are always to be relegated to "superstructure." As Rosman and Rubel demonstrated, to take just one case, the rules of marriage and of status inheritance are clearly the "core" issues for any meaningful analysis of potlatch variations on the Northwest Coast of North America (1971).

larly illuminating. One of these studies, Paul Kirchhoff's "The Principles of Clanship in Human Society" (1968), deals with broad issues of evolutionary potential for social forms. On the other hand, Claude Lévi-Strauss, in "The Bear and the Barber" (1963), specifically uses *caste* in his analysis of structural difference, and so I have given his work priority of attention as I seek to identify the unit from which caste—and the system from which the caste system—ultimately derives.

Claude Lévi-Strauss has long been interested in the role of reciprocity, in the form of social exchange, in creating and maintaining bonds of affiliation in human societies (see, of course, Lévi-Strauss 1969). In "The Bear and the Barber" he compares and contrasts two structural types usually assumed to be profoundly different from each other. The structural type denoted by the word "bear" in the title of the paper is labelled "totemic": he considers it characteristic of classic Australian aboriginal groups, among others. By "barber" he is referring to the caste system of India.

Lévi-Strauss' primary concern in this paper is, as I have indicated, with a problem in symbolic analysis. He argues, for example, that "totemic ideas appear to provide a code enabling man to express isomorphic properties between nature and culture" (1963: 2). For instance, he reports that there is a widespread practice in India of naming not only castes, but clans within castes, with terms denoting occupations or manufactured goods. Lévi-Strauss compares this with the practice of "totemic" societies, such as those of Australia, where the tendency is to name clans after plants and animals, and he concludes:

in India, where products or symbols of occupational activities are clearly differentiated as such and can be put to use in order to express differences between social groups, vestiges or remnants of totemic groups have come to make use of a symbolism that is technological and occupational in origin (*Ibid.*: 7–8).

His reference to "vestiges or remnants" must not be allowed to go without comment. Lévi-Strauss is most emphatic in stating that he is not interested in the issue of evolution or even of sequence:

I never refer to a past or present institution but to a classificatory device whereby discrete elements of the external world are associated with the discrete elements of the social world (*Ibid.*: 7).

While we must respect his intentions, surely we are entitled to note, for our purposes, the implication of sequence in his work—whether Lévi-Strauss is concerned with it or not. Thus he has noted that "vestiges or remnants of totemic groups" are to be detected among contemporary castes, but nowhere does he suggest that similar "vestiges" of caste are to be noted among totemic groups. There is an unavoidable implication that he assumes that caste evolved (or otherwise derived) from some prior structural form in which "totemism" was much more pronounced, for only "vestiges" remain. His final paragraph in this paper is therefore relevant:

societies are not made up of the flotsam and jetsam of history, but of variables; thus widely different institutions can be reduced to transformations of the same basic figure, and the whole of human history may be looked upon merely as a set of attempts to organize differently the same means, but always to answer the same questions (*Ibid.*: 10).

If by *transformation* Lévi-Strauss means, as I am sure he does, *change from one form to another*, then his concern and mine (for this book) are not so far apart. I speak of *emergence* in preference to *evolution* only because I want to avoid fruitless debates about whether a change is from "simple" to "complex," or involves a shift to a different "level of integration." But the concern in a work such as this cannot be merely with "change" alone. I am also concerned with "sequence" and I therefore react with interest to the implication that caste may reflect an earlier "totemic" condition.

Let us turn, then, to the similarities and differences that Lévi-Strauss has detected between a "totemic" and a "caste" society. To begin with, he points out that "totemic" groups are characterized by a rule of *exogamy*—as opposed to the "caste" rule of *endogamy*. That is to say, in a "totemic" society we observe a number of discrete social divisions or segments (variously labeled "clans," "sections," "subsections," or whatever), each of which is named after or otherwise identified with a particular animal, plant,

138

or insect. Men of such a group—that is, an exogamous unit of the society—equate themselves (and are equated by others) with the totemic life form. They claim to be descended or otherwise derived from it, and are customarily forbidden to eat the totemic object, although they are free to eat the totemic objects of sister groups of their own society.

All the groups ("totemic clans") of the society engage in the same subsistence activities (presumably, hunting and gathering) and provide for the needs of the members with—it would seem, for Lévi-Strauss—a minimum of economic exchange. There are few specialists, and no specialist "clans." Each "clan," however, obeys the rule of exogamy: a male and a female of the same "clan" may not marry each other, and so the spouse for each member of the society must be sought in a "clan" or "section" other than his or her own.

In effect, therefore, what Lévi-Strauss perceives among "totemic" societies is a relative absence of economic exchange between component social units, coupled with a required spouse exchange between the units. In contrast, he observes, "castes" are rarely economically independent. Instead, they engage in a complex system of exchange of goods and services with each other, while each strictly observes a rule of endogamy, marrying offspring only *within* the group and never making marital exchanges with any other group. We may conclude, therefore, that when Lévi-Strauss discusses "caste" societies his concern is with the endogamous unit, or what I have referred to as the "marriage-circle"—though he, of course, uses only the somewhat ambiguous term "caste."

In Lévi-Strauss' own words:

An Australian section or sub-section actually produces its women for the benefit of the other sections, much as an occupational caste produces goods and services which the other castes cannot produce and must seek from this caste alone. Thus it would be inaccurate to define totemic groups and caste systems as being one exogamous and the other endogamous. These are not real properties existing as such, but superficial and indirect consequences of a similarity which should be realized at a deeper level. In the first place, both castes and totemic groups are 'exo-practical': castes in relation to goods and services, totemic goods in relation to marriage. In the second place, both remain to some extent 'endo-practical': castes by virtue of the rule of endogamy and Australian groups as regards their preferred type of matrimonial exchange, which being mostly of the 'restricted' type, keeps each tribe closely self-contained and, as it were, wrapped up in itself. It would seem that allowing for the above restrictive considerations, we have now reached a satisfactory formulation, in a common language, of the relationship between totemic groups and castes. Thus we might say that in the first case—totemic groups—women, that is, biological individuals or natural products, are begotten naturally by other biological individuals, while in the second case—castes—manufactured objects or services rendered through the medium of manufactured objects are fabricated culturally through technical agents. The principle of differentiation stems in one case from nature and in the other from culture. . . .

In totemic systems, men exchange culturally the women who procreate them naturally, and they claim to procreate culturally the animal and vegetable species which they exchange naturally: in the form of food-stuffs which are interchangeable, since any biological individual is able to dispense with one and to subsist on the others. A true parallelism can therefore be said to exist between the two formulas, and it is possible to code one into the terms of the other. Indeed, this parallelism is more complex than we believed it to be at the beginning. It can be expressed in the following tortuous way: castes naturalize fallaciously a true culture while totemic groups culturalize truly a false nature (*Ibid.*: 8–9).

It must be apparent that while Lévi-Strauss starts with the ethnographic datum he moves swiftly to the realm of metaphor. His primary interest is clearly with fundamental, or underlying, structural principles. Though he begins by talking of *Australian* totemic groups and *Indian* castes, it is necessary for us to perceive that he is really concerned with the *essential* "totemic group" and the *essential* "caste" and not with any actual group of people in either Australia or India.

But if his approach enables him to reveal for us underlying structural principles, relationships, and congruences, it also requires him to limit the attention he can give to ethnographic details. For example, it seems to me that he has oversimplified (at least for the needs of this book) the matter of economic specialization and exchange among even the simplest of hunting and gathering societies. Thousands of years ago, perhaps hundreds of thousands of years ago, substances common in one locality and rare in others were exchanged over enormous distances. Flint, obsidian, amber, and salt are examples of such items, but by no means exhaust the list. Such exchange was of course reciprocal—between equals—just as exchange between units of the caste system, as we have seen, is redistributive. Since such matters are irrelevant for his purposes, Lévi-Strauss simply ignores them. Similarly, while Lévi-Strauss refers to economic exchange between "castes" he is not concerned with the details of that exchange, as we have been in the previous chapter.

If there is oversimplification in his presentation of economic exchange within the two societal types, we must expect a similar absence of attention to detail on the issue of exchange of marriage partners. He focusses, for example, on *endogamy* as the integrative principle of "caste" but has nothing to say about *exogamy* in such a society. But the phenomenon of exogamous subdivisions of castes—such as gotras—is much too prevalent in India to be ignored.[4] Clearly, we are dealing with a structural principle relating to the integration of the *marriage-circle*, just as endogamy relates to the integration of the total system.

In no way, of course, does this weaken Lévi-Strauss' essential argument. His "caste" (my "marriage-circle") is a body without significant internal economic exchange, without specialization of household against household. It is likely, however, to contain a large number of people scattered over a very wide area. Such a body (reminiscent of a total "totemic" society) may therefore require an integrative principle if it is to maintain itself over time, and it should come as no surprise, given the illumination provided by Lévi-Strauss, to find *exogamy* as the principle.

And, finally, what of *endogamy* in the "totemic" situation? Lévi-Strauss introduces but does not pursue this issue, but we may note that it is almost unavoidably present as a feature of the total system. Lévi-Strauss concentrates on the exogamous unit— the "totemic" clan—but *unit* implies *system of units*, and we may be certain that the units are exchanging marriage-partners within a

---

[4]The *gotra*, or exogamous patrisib, is found among castes throughout India, but exogamy within the caste takes other forms as well (see Kolenda 1978: 14–18). Internal exogamy is not the invariable rule, but it is certainly extremely common among the castes of India.

definable boundary. If, as is almost invariably the case everywhere, the human universe contains aliens or outsiders, then endogamy must be present, too: members of "totemic" clans cannot marry with people who do not belong to exogamous "totemic" clans, or even with those who belong to unfamiliar clans. Lévi-Strauss slights *endogamy* of "totemic" clans because he is concerned with internal structure; for his purposes, a "totemic" clan society might almost be said to exist in a vacuum. For my purposes, concern for internal structure must be matched with concern for relations between groups.

Having made these points, let me put them to one side for the moment. It is more important here to be clear about what we have learned from Lévi-Strauss; later, and with the aid of the insights he has given us, we can turn to other questions.

We may remember the passage by John Nesfield, the nineteenth century theorist on the origins of caste, that was cited earlier:

The differentia of *caste* as a marriage union consists in some community of function; while the differentia of *tribe* as a marriage union consisted in a common ancestry, or a common worship, or a common totem, or in fact in any kind of common property except that of a common function (1885: 114).

Nesfield, like Lévi-Strauss, contrasted "tribe" and "caste" in terms of economic behavior, and also noted the relationship between economic behavior and the fact that a caste constituted a "marriage union"—but there the similarity between the two scholars ends. It is not merely that Nesfield was unaware of the phenomenon of exogamy/endogamy; Nesfield's problem was that, given his time, he could deal only with surface attributes.

Lévi-Strauss bids us see structural contrast between "totemic" society and "caste" society and then bids us peer further and note, *at a deeper structural level*, an inherent similarity or congruence between the two. In both cases, we see that we are dealing with nonhomogeneous societies, for each is made up of discrete, definable units (in one case "clan" and in the other "caste"). In each case, the units must have a regularized, or structured, interrelationship if the society is to continue as a system. In the totemic, or tribal, case, the structured exchange is of marital partners,[5] since the economy, to Lévi-Strauss, is too generalized to permit the kind of specialization of production or service that might require structured economic exchange. In the case of "caste," such a structured economic exchange is in existence and is the integrative feature of the socioeconomic system—and marriage exchange between "castes" does not occur. There are, we see, significant structural similarities.

All of this is very much in accord with our previous findings. If, as I have argued, marriage-circle endogamy is necessary to preserve and maintain the total caste system (the integrative feature of which, Lévi-Strauss tells us, is structured economic exchange), then *gotra* exogamy—within the marriage-circle—may also be an integrative feature, but at a subordinate structural level. I have suggested that while exogamy is the integrative feature of the *total* society in the "totemic" condition, and endogamy the integrative feature of the *total* society in the "caste" condition, exogamy may serve to integrate the *component unit*—the marriage-circle—in the case of the caste system. We are dealing with levels of structural complexity that bear an organic relationship to one another.

Is the structural congruence we have been shown by Lévi-Strauss solely a result of some set of universal sociological or psychological principles at work, or does it, perhaps in addition, also reflect genetic relationship? Lévi-Strauss may not care, but some of us wish to know whether we are dealing with homology or analogy.

Once we raise the issue of genetic relationship, we are faced with a curious problem. Since, by Lévi-Strauss' definition, a "totemic group" society has the simplest kind of subsistence economy known to us, we are unable to ask what came before it. Not so with "caste," again according to Lévi-Strauss, for there we see specialization and complex interchange of goods and services. A society such as the one Lévi-Strauss has subsumed under the heading of "caste" cannot be traced too far back in time, and so if the structural similarities with "totemic groups" are significant, would it not be reasonable to assume that something on the order of "totemic groups" preceded "caste" in actual evolutionary sequence?

---

[5]Actually, Lévi-Strauss speaks of exchange of "women," but I find this unnecessarily limiting.

Unhappily, Lévi-Strauss—understandably, of course, given his interests—has not provided us with the kind of detail we need to approach such questions. For example, while we may at this point know something about the nature of caste, we definitely need to know much more about "totemic groups." What does "clan" really mean, at least for the purposes of this work? How many varieties of clans are there, and which varieties must we distinguish among here? Finally, what happens to a "clan-type" society when economic stratification is in the process of coming into existence? In other words, can we trace the development of a "totemic group" society into a "caste" society, assuming that such a thing has ever taken place?

For answers to these questions—or at least for a prologue to the answers—we must turn to the work of another theorist, Paul Kirchhoff. True, Kirchhoff's writings have received much less attention than those of Lévi-Strauss, for his most important paper, "The Principles of Clanship in Human Society," was written originally in 1935 and did not see publication until 1955—and then only in a rather obscure journal. It has since been reprinted, however, and brought to the attention of a wider audience. I shall quote from the version of Kirchhoff's paper that appeared in the second edition of *Readings in Anthropology, Volume II: Cultural Anthropology*, edited by Morton H. Fried (1968).

Kirchhoff was concerned—in 1935, we must bear in mind—with the need to reopen and reconsider the issue of cultural evolution. As we have seen, the first half of the present century was characterized, in the social sciences, by a widespread bias against evolutionist approaches. Kirchhoff noted that Lewis Henry Morgan and other early evolutionists had contributed in some ways to the disfavor into which "cultural evolution" had fallen. According to Kirchhoff, this was due particularly to their insistence on "unilineal" evolution—that all human societies pass through, sooner or later, the same particular set of evolutionary sequences.

Kirchhoff suggested that cultural evolution was likely to have been as "multilineal" as we know biological evolution to have been. With this concern in mind, he focussed on one particular social phenomenon of interest to evolutionists, that of "clan":

One of the tasks, therefore, which confronts us in studying the evolution of the clan and its role in the history of society is to inquire which different *forms of the clan* are found to exist, and what *their mutual genetic relationship is*. The present paper is in the main confined to this task (*Ibid.*: 372; italics his).

We see that Kirchhoff is specifically searching for answers to some of the questions raised here as a result of Lévi-Strauss' analysis of "totemic group" and "caste."

According to Kirchhoff, in societies representing the simplest (and/or earliest) condition of human existence "the concept of descent is still completely absent" (*Ibid.*). While familial relationships may certainly exist in such societies, Kirchhoff presumes that the community as a whole does not reflect organization according to any principle of descent: rather, the social body is an impermanent collectivity of families and individuals and is usually quite small in number. The members of one such group, or band, are free to stay together if they wish, or to go off and join another. In such a case, Kirchhoff argues, there are no restrictions on marriage within or between groups (apart, I would assume, from those restrictions reflecting rules against immediate-family incest): "Society here can still do without the concept of descent and consequently without the rule of exogamy" (*Ibid.*).

Kirchhoff, then, begins with a type of social organization, the simple band, that is conceptually earlier than Lévi-Strauss' "totemic group," for he sees the latter developing out of the former:

The increasing cooperative character of economic activity requires forms of kinship organization which insure greater stability of the cooperating groups (which in primitive society predominantly means groups of relatives). Greater stability of the cooperating groups of relatives requires some principle which more clearly sets off one such group from the other, and which at the same time, assures their continuity in time.

The principle of clanship, based on the concept of descent, does both. In other words, the function of the clan is to assure stable and continuous cooperation. It takes a number of different forms, but its essence appears to be the same everywhere: to group together in one permanent unit all those persons, living or dead, who can claim common descent. This group is commonly called a clan or sib (*Ibid.*: 374).

145

The reader may have concluded that there is no unbridgeable gulf between Lévi-Strauss and Kirchhoff, despite their very different theoretical perceptions and interests. Indeed, Kirchhoff's view of the "function" of clanship would probably not distress Lévi-Strauss—but of course Kirchhoff is primarily concerned with matters of sequence and causation, and he goes on to point out:

there are important, even striking differences between some of the main forms which the principle of clanship took concretely. To anticipate one of the main results of our survey: some of these forms seem to lead comparatively early to the stage of stagnation, or into a blind alley if we may say so, while others seem to possess far greater possibilities of development.

At the present stage of the investigation of the problem, I conceive of these various forms of clans not as of consecutive stages, so that one could be explained as developing out of the other, but rather as stemming from the same root, i.e., from the more amorphous type of kinship described before (*Ibid.*).

The "forms of clans" that Kirchhoff perceives are very important for this work, but before we continue with his analysis a few cautionary remarks are necessary. To begin with, Kirchhoff appears to believe that the simplest hunting and gathering societies are characterized by what he calls the "amorphous type of kinship" and therefore neither need nor know "clanship" organization. Such an assertion is certainly open to challenge, to say the least.[6]

Secondly, Kirchhoff uses the term "clan" in a somewhat ambiguous fashion. Morton Fried, in his introduction to Kirchhoff's paper, points this out:

---

[6]Kirchhoff himself notes, for example, that in aboriginal Australia, as in certain other parts of the world, complete and complex "clan" structures are found in association with what he considers to be "lower forms of the economy"; that is, "hunting and gathering." This alone should serve to alert us to the fact that not all "hunting and gathering" situations are comparable: some circumstances may permit, or require, different forms of social organization under different conditions. And it follows, equally, that not all "higher forms of economic organization" are the same, and that we must carefully avoid simplistic one-to-one equations of economic level and social form.

146

Although Kirchhoff says he is talking about clanship, he is really talking about something much broader—corporate kin groups. It is true that some of these *are* clans, but others are better classified as lineages or kindreds (Fried 1968: 370).

Fried goes on to discuss some of the differences between "clan" and "lineage" but we, bearing these cautions in mind, may now return to Kirchhoff's proposals for distinguishing types of clans. He believes that "the overwhelming majority of tribes" in the world that are in fact organized on a principle of descent exhibit one of only two types of clans (or of what Fried has called "corporate kin groups"). Kirchhoff writes:

> The first of these two types is that of *unilateral exogamous clans*, either of the patrilineal or matrilineal variety. . . . no attention needs to be paid here to this difference, since our main aim is to show what distinguished *both* of them from the other type of clan which is neither unilateral nor exogamous.
>
> The formative features of the first type of clan, in both of its varieties are: (1) The clan consists of people who are related to each other either through women only or through men only—according to the customs of the tribe; (2) every member of the clan is, as far as clan membership goes, on an absolutely equal footing with the rest: the nearness of relation to each other or to some ancestor being of no consequence for a person's place in the clan; (3) members of the clan may not marry each other.
>
> In other words, the principles underlying this type of clan are: unilateral, "equalitarian," exogamous. They constitute one indivisible whole. It is no accident that practically everywhere where we find one of them we find the other two. Neither of them would, in fact, by itself produce the same result.
>
> These principles of clanship, or rather this threefold principle, leads to sharply defined, clearly separate units, comparable to so many blocks out of which society is built. There have to be always at least two such blocks—two clans living in connubium. Usually there are more than two (Kirchhoff 1968: 375).

Before we turn to the insights—and problems—deriving from the above, let us examine what Kirchhoff believes to be the second possible type of corporate kin group:

The decisive difference between the first and the second type of clan is that what matters in the one is relationship *through* either men or women (according to the customs of the tribe), irrespective of the *nearness* of such relationship to the other members of the group or to some ancestor—whereas, on the contrary, in the other type it is precisely the *nearness* of relationship to the common ancestor of the group which matters. The first of the two principles of clanship results in a group the members of which are of absolutely equal standing, as far as this standing is determined by membership in the group (leaving aside the question of age). The second principle results in a group in which every single member, except brothers and sisters, has a different standing: the concept of the *degree of relationship* leads to *different degrees of membership* in the clan. In other words, some are members to a higher degree than others.

The logical consequence of this state of affairs is that at a certain point it becomes doubtful whether a person is still to be regarded as a member of a certain clan—a question that could never arise in a unilateral-exogamous clan. Clan membership so-to-speak shades off the farther one is from the center-line of the clan—the real core of the group. This core, the *aristoi*, consists of those who are the nearest descendants of the common ancestors of the clan.

In most tribes descent is customarily either through men or, more rarely, through women, but frequently, especially in the case of the *aristoi*, descent may be counted through either of them. That side being chosen which gives a person a higher descent, i.e., a closer relationship with the ancestor of the group. The term "ambilateral" has been coined for this system.

Genealogies, unknown and unnecessary in a unilateral clan, are here the means of establishing the "line" of descent of the nobles—this "line" being another concept unknown in unilateral clans.

A corollary of the second principle of clanship is that there is no exogamy in the sense defined above. In fact, there could be none, since there are no groups with definite and fixed "boundaries." On the contrary, we frequently find close endogamy—however, usually only for the *aristoi*. Marriage between relatives of high descent assures that their offspring will be of still higher descent (*Ibid.*: 377–78; italics his).

What I want to focus on in this chapter are the implications of the two types of social organization that Kirchhoff has distinguished: one reflecting an organizing principle of "differential descent" and the other of "common descent." Unhappily for me, there are many other issues raised in the passages just quoted

148

which are in need of clarification and emendation: the paper was written, let me repeat, in 1935. Thus, in his introduction to the next paper in his *Readings*, Morton Fried refers to one of the weaknesses in Kirchhoff's argument:

Note how Kirchhoff in the previous selection confused unilineal and non-unilineal groups; this was due, at least in part, to the failure to see non-unilineal groups in the glare of attention given the unilineal organizations (Fried 1968: 382).

Today, as Fried indicates, the issue of "lineality" is much better understood. Perhaps, had Kirchhoff had contemporary literature available to him—and had he given more attention to the implications of the Australian "clan" instead of pushing the whole subject under the figurative rug—he might not have given so much weight to "unilaterality" as a diagnostic condition.

Let us observe, too, that Kirchhoff shares with Lévi-Strauss an apparent lack of interest in the relations between societies. Does Kirchhoff assume that a society evolves in a vacuum? The subject is an important one, but discussion will have to be postponed to a later section.

If we return to the illuminations provided by Kirchhoff, we may begin by noting that Kirchhoff's first type of corporate kin group is essentially the same as Lévi-Strauss' "totemic" clan. Their concerns are very different, but both writers would draw our attention to societies composed of *equalitarian exogamous* units. Lévi-Strauss bade us consider the implications of the rule of *exogamy;* now Kirchhoff leads us to consider the significance of *equality of membership*.

Kirchhoff's contribution is, as we shall see, an important one for the development of anthropological theory about cultural evolution. The distinction Kirchhoff pointed to between types of kin groups has borne much fruit, though today, as Fried notes, we can express the distinction somewhat more sharply:

it is useful to hold the definition of clan to social units comprised of unilineally related members who trace their relationship through *stipulated descent*, that is, through ties which they cannot always explain genealogically. This contrasts with *demonstrated descent*, which involves specification of all genealogical connecting links. Unilineal groups based on this principle are better termed lineages. Both kinds of groups can exist at the same time in the same society (*Ibid.*: 370–71; italics his).

But Kirchhoff's contribution does not consist merely of noting that some social groups are organized on a principle of equal membership through common and undifferentiated descent, while other groups are organized on the basis of differential membership through lines of descent. More significantly, Kirchhoff has introduced us to some of the implications of such different organizing principles.

To begin with, he argues that *equality of membership* within the clan appears to imply a concurrent *economic* equality. That is, since no member of such a body can have a "right" to a greater share than any other member in whatever the clan corporately possesses, all members must cooperate, and share equally, in the productivity and resources of the clan. On the other hand, differential membership appears to imply differential rights to, or in, the group's corporate possessions: "it is regarded as a matter of course that all leading economic, social, religious functions are reserved to those of highest descent . . ." (Kirchhoff 1968: 379).

With this observation, Kirchhoff moves to the consideration of the problem with which he is most concerned: What are the potentials for evolutionary change of the two social types, one socially and economically equalitarian, and the other socially and economically differentiated?

With the development of production and of culture as a whole, the role of these *aristoi* within the life of the clan and the tribe becomes ever more important. The nearer in descent to the godlike ancestor a person is, the greater are his chances in the process of ever-growing economic and social differentiation. Social differentiation, at this stage of evolution of society, the *condition sine qua non* of the development of higher forms of cooperation, not only finds no obstacle in this type of clan, but on the contrary an extremely flexible medium, namely a hierarchy of relatives, based on the principle of nearness of descent.

For a long period to come this principle of clanship is able to adapt itself to the ever-growing complexity of social relations. A survey of the tribes organized into clans of this type shows a whole scale of such adaptations to the increasing degree of social differentiation within the tribes: mainly along the line of a more marked stratification of the members of one and the same group. Thus, some members of the clan may be chiefs and near-gods, while others, at the opposite end of the scale, may be slaves: yet all of them are regarded as relatives, and in many cases, are able to prove it.

The process of differentiation within the clan, while for a long time taking place within this flexible unit, finally reaches the point where the interests of those of equal standing, in *all* the clans of the tribe, come into such sharp conflicts with the interests of the other strata that their struggles, the struggle of by now fully-fledged social classes, overshadows the old principle of clanship and finally leads to the break-up of clan, first as the dominating form of social organization and then to its final disappearance. This point, at the end of one phase of human history, and the beginning of another, had just been reached when the Greeks, the Romans and the Germans enter into the light of documented history (*Ibid.*: 379–80).

So much, then, for the evolutionary potential of the clan type based on a principle of differentiation of descent and membership. What are the possibilities awaiting the type of clan Kirchhoff has labeled "unilateral, exogamous and equalitarian" when it confronts "the development of production and of culture as a whole"?

The most striking aspect of this threefold principle of clanship is its extreme rigidity. It is hard to imagine in which direction this type of clan could develop further. . . .

This type of clan makes possible a kind of economic and general cultural cooperation which in its way seems perfect. But, as the term perfect implies, it seems to be the highest type of cooperation which can be achieved along *this* line of development. The growing forces of production at a certain stage demand important readjustments in the form of kinship organization of which this type appears to be incapable. Its absolute equalitarianism, combined with the complete subordination of its members to the interests of the clan as a whole, while making possible a certain type of primitive cooperation, obstructs very efficiently the evolution of these tight forms, of cooperation which are based upon economic and social differentiation. Where, therefore, with this type of clan higher forms of economy have come into existence, as, e.g., those based on animal breeding, the development of which requires higher forms of cooperation, there this new economy has usually not gone beyond rather meagre beginnings. . . .

The form of kinship organization which the unilateral-exogamous principle of clanship creates appears definitely as a blind alley, and more than that; at a certain stage of economic and general cultural evolution as an obstacle to further development. What constitutes its greatness at the same time constitutes its limits (*Ibid.*: 375–76).

Kirchhoff has argued then, to summarize and modernize, that there are significant recurrent variations in social organization. Some societies in the world, he observes, manifest themselves in terms of small familial or shifting-band groups. Apparently the simplest ones in technological and subsistence terms, these are for Kirchhoff therefore presumably representative of the earliest human societies. While, in such societies kinship relationship may be a factor in locality-group formation and maintenance, the concept of "descent"—known or not—apparently is not significant.

Other societies, however,[7] are integrated by a principle of common membership by reason of descent. Kirchhoff points out that such societies fall into one of two categories: those in which descent, in the component "clans," is expressed in "descent lines" so that individuals are differentially descended from the common ancestors; and those in which descent is undifferentiated (common for all) and all are equal members of the component exogamous "clans."

Further, Kirchhoff argues, the type of membership to be found clearly and inescapably affects the economic standing of individuals within the group. In "common descent" societies all are equal members of the clan, so all share equally in the corporate possessions of the clan—for there is no basis for differential ownership or claim. In "differential-descent" societies, on the other hand, there is a differential degree of membership within the clan: the line, say, of "first-born" descendants of "first-born" is distinguished from other, lower-ranked lines. This creates the category of what Kirchhoff calls *aristoi:* those within any clan who are considered to have "higher" or "more important" or "greater" degrees of membership, and therefore equivalently greater rights of access to the corporate possessions of the group.

---

[7]This would not include, of course, those societies organized on principles reflecting *state* or *class* structures.

And finally, says Kirchhoff, given this difference in access, the "differential-descent" society has the capacity to evolve, in the event of propitious circumstances, into a complex, stratified state—as the *aristoi* of the clans together evolve into the *upper class*. The "common-descent" society, on the other hand, lacking an institutional framework for differentiation, is doomed—*however propitious the circumstances*—never to evolve in the direction of stratification and the state, and to remain fixed, "rigid," and unchanging, in what Kirchhoff calls again and again a cultural "blind alley."

The direction in which I am moving should be apparent by now. I would question Kirchhoff's conclusion that "common-descent" societies are "rigid" and doomed never to evolve in the direction of socioeconomic complexity. Most of all, I would argue that the South Asian caste system reflects, and derives from, a prior "common-descent" corporate kin group structure, of the kind termed "totemic" by Claude Lévi-Strauss.

Before taking up these issues, however, I think it advisable to review briefly the opinions of other writers interested in cultural evolution on the points raised by Kirchhoff. He wrote, after all, at the very beginning of the contemporary return to the problems of cultural evolution: have his arguments been accepted, rejected—or simply ignored?

A little of all three, as far as I can see. Julian H. Steward, for example, does not refer to Kirchhoff in his work *Theory of Culture Change: The Methodology of Multilinear Evolution* (1955), but he certainly gives attention to the relationship between descent type and the process of cultural evolution. He is very much aware of the two types of kin groups noted by Kirchhoff.

In Steward's view, there is in fact a genetic relationship between what we have called "common-descent" and "differential-descent" groups. Specifically, he is convinced that when the concept of descent actually attains significance in the development of human society, it *first* takes the form of descent lines or lineages. Then, over time, as the group grows larger and the lineages split into sublineages, it may happen that a given local group will be made up of people who can *no longer* "trace their relationship genealogically" but who "still preserve a sense of kinship" (*Ibid.*: 153). Thus, for Steward, a society characterized by stipulated descent,

or equalitarian membership, constitutes a comparatively late development—one possible direction that may be taken by groups organized on the principle of demonstrated descent and differentiated
membership.

Two important and somewhat more recent writers on cultural evolution are Elman R. Service and Morton H. Fried. Let us
note that both of them have been influenced by Julian Steward[8]
and both, too, cite Kirchhoff's somewhat obscure paper in their
writings.

Elman Service, in his book *Primitive Social Organization: An
Evolutionary Perspective* (1962), discusses what he calls "lineal" tribes
(apparently the equivalent of the "differential-descent" type) and
what he lumps together as "cognatic and composite" tribes, those
based on a principle of stipulated descent (*Ibid.*: 120, 133, *et passim*).

Service agrees with Steward that "cognatic and composite"
societies derive from "lineal" ones—either because, in his view, of
the impact of civilization upon "lineal" tribes, or because of certain
special circumstances such as existence in some permanently
"closed" territory, such as a South Pacific island (*Ibid.*: 134–37).
However, while "lineal" tribes have an important place in Service's
evolutionary scheme, he gives almost no attention in his work to
the evolutionary consequences or potential of "cognatic or composite" groups. Thus, while he does not use the words, it is apparent
that "cognatic or composite" societies are as much of an evolutionary "blind alley" to Service as they are to Kirchhoff.

Morton Fried, as we have seen, is explicit in expressing his
obligation to Kirchhoff, and in his own contribution to the literature on cultural evolution, *The Evolution of Political Society: An Essay
in Political Anthropology* (1967), Fried does seem to be closer to
Kirchhoff's position than he is to that of Steward and Service.

Fried's distinction between "clan" (reflecting "stipulated" descent) and "lineage" (reflecting "demonstrated" descent) is, as we
have already seen, only different in its terminology from the one
proposed by Kirchhoff. Like Kirchhoff (and like both Steward and
Service), Fried sees both "clan" and "lineage" as developing later

---

[8]Service dedicated his book to both Julian Steward and Leslie White, and
Fried dedicated a later work to Julian Steward (Fried 1972).

than "egalitarian bands." However, unlike Service and Steward, Fried gives no indication that he views "clan" as something that derives out of "lineage." Rather, he sees both as forms of what he calls "rank societies," with neither, apparently, to be accorded necessary evolutionary priority. But Fried devotes even less attention to the "clan" type than does Service, and it is clear that Fried, too, sees "clan" as an evolutionary "blind alley." Stratification, in his view, derives from "lineage"-type "rank societies" (*Ibid.*: 125–27; see also 182–84).

We see, therefore, that major contemporary writers on cultural evolution have concerned themselves with the consequences of principles of *descent*, but they have considered almost exclusively the fortunes of societies characterized by "differential descent." Societies characterized by "common descent" are either ignored or relegated to the scrap heap of special exception. That is, whether they view such societies as late developments out of "differential descent" or as concurrent emergences, they all apparently agree with Kirchhoff that "common-descent" societies constitute an evolutionary "blind alley."

This unanimity is astonishing. What is even more astonishing is that Marvin Harris has not felt compelled to take issue with any of these writers, for the "blind alley" assessment of "common descent" should remind Harris of the arguments of Harry Pearson!

It will be recalled that Pearson, when challenging the notion of "absolute surplus," also questioned whether such a phenomenon, supposing it did exist, could invariably precipitate evolutionary changes. He argued, in effect, that "absolute surplus" could never be more than an enabling mechanism, and that we must therefore look to the institutional framework of the given society confronted with "surplus" to discover how it responds, *or whether it responds at all*, to the stimulus for change.

Here we have seen Kirchhoff—and by extension Service and Fried—proposing very much in the spirit of Pearson that when a society based on differentiated membership finds itself in a condition[9] favoring evolution to a stratified stage it will make the journey, while an equalitarian society, granted the same opportu-

---

[9] The presence of an "absolute surplus"? The literature is not always specific.

nity, must and can go nowhere at all. Has Harris indeed accepted, if only tacitly, this Pearsonian view of the evolutionary potentials of societal forms?

Myself, I would argue that equalitarian clans should not be permitted to constitute a special exception, the condition under which the processes of cultural evolution grind to a halt. True, while I am convinced that "absolute surplus" in the terms proposed by Harris can occur and is the crucial factor in cultural evolution, I do agree with Pearson that such a surplus must always be considered in terms of particular societal structures. Nevertheless, even given the likelihood of different responses, in different systems, to the appearance of surplus, I fail to see why we must assume that *one* structural type—widely distributed on our planet and ingeniously variegated—must always and forever lack the capacity to take advantage of the occurrence of "absolute surplus."

I do not argue, of course, that all societies have responded successfully under all conditions to the problems posed by the occurrence of an "absolute surplus." My guess would be—and I believe it fully in line with what has been observed in studies of *biological* evolution—that some make it, and some don't. Some societies will find the avenues leading to solutions of the problems facing them, and some will not—and for the latter socioeconomic travail, or even chaos, will be precipitated. *But* neither "solution" nor "chaos" can be predicted, I would insist, *solely* on the basis of whether the society is organized into clans or lineages!

It is obvious that the question of the origins of the South Asian caste system actually encompasses two basic issues. As I noted at the beginning of this chapter, we must ask both what kind of society preceded, and developed into, the caste system and what were the circumstances of transformation from "precaste" to "caste." An adequate consideration of the latter issue—that of the circumstances of transformation—will require a review of a number of problems having to do with theories of cultural evolution. Some of these have indeed already been touched on, but all of them require more attention than I have yet been able to give and so the subject of "circumstances of transformation" must be postponed until the next chapter.

Happily, however, the conclusions arrived at in previous

chapters, coupled with the insights to be derived from Lévi-Strauss and Kirchhoff, make it possible for us to see the kind of socioeconomic environment that was most likely to have preceded, and developed into, the caste system we have been concerned with.

I suggest that, before the appearance of both agriculture and stratification in South Asia, the subcontinent was inhabited by various hunting and gathering societies. These undoubtedly occupied many ecological niches and therefore differed from each other in terms of technology and much else. Given the dimensions of the area and the natural boundaries and barriers, many of the groups probably spoke distinctive and even mutually unintelligible languages. If ecosystems were sharply different (and they must have been), then we can be reasonably certain that there were significant differences among the societies in the domains of social organization and ideology as well.

If it is agreed that there is nothing in the foregoing paragraph that is unreasonable, or even worth debating, we can go forward. Since we are postulating that all the societies at the time were engaged in one or another mode of hunting and gathering, they must have been largely independent of one another both economically and socially. If I have questioned Lévi-Strauss' assertion that hunters and gatherers do not exchange goods and services, I am fully aware that such exchange as does take place is limited to a relatively few items of uneven distribution, such as raw materials for stone tools. Such exchange could only have been reciprocal, and—given the absence of stratification—the same thing would have been true of any economic exchange between segments or units of any particular society.

Social exchange, when it occurred, also would have been only reciprocal. Such exchange—in the form of exchange of marriage partners—was likely to have been as rare *between* societies as it was likely to have been the mode *within* societies, for peoples differing in ecology, language, social organization, and ideology are unlikely to exchange spouses to any statistically significant extent. Some of these societies were undoubtedly made up of shifting bands of families; others were composed of the exogamous equalitarian segments or "clans" to which both Lévi-Strauss and Kirchhoff have directed our attention. Whether the societal endogamy

157

reflected a stated rule of the body or was a statistical conclusion, there could have been little patterned or regularized exchange of women or men between the societies—though informal genetic exchange probably took place as it does everywhere, despite all formal rules of socially permissible sexual contact.

And, if my reader is still with me, I offer one more suggestion: in this "precaste" milieu, societies characterized by differential descent—those exhibiting kin groups of the kind called "lineages" with demonstrated-descent lines—were either not present at all, or played no significant role in the transformation that was to take place.

It is impossible to know whether "lineages" were in fact present in the precaste milieu—just as we can never know whether specific totemic "clans" were actually transformed into later "gotras" or whether some "gotras" developed in response to structural needs of certain later "castes." What I do argue is this: The galaxy of societies and social groups making up the precaste South Asian milieu exhibited, to a significant degree, endogamous clusters of exogamous, unstratified, stipulated-descent, "equalitarian clans," and that it was this galaxy—this *total* social and economic milieu— that was transformed into the stratified socioeconomic system we know of as "the caste system."

I cannot "prove" any of the foregoing propositions, but I see them as reasonable and conservative conclusions to be drawn from such evidence as we have and from our present undertanding of the nature of human society.

Why "reasonable and conservative"? The present system, as we have seen, while clearly as socially and economically stratified as any in the world, exhibits no element whatever of the kind of individual or class relationship that might be associated with "aristoi" or previous "demonstrated-descent" structure. All castes are made up of marriage-circles of people claiming only stipulated descent: all persons are equal members of their marriage-circles and all share equally in its corporate possessions, rights, fortunes, and misfortunes. My proposal, therefore, does not require us to assume the presence of something in the past that has since disappeared without a trace.

After all, what other explanations are available to us? One

alternative, following all our writers on cultural evolution, would be to assume that in South Asia the progression was from "demonstrated-descent" groups to "classes" (as they have argued was the case in Europe and elsewhere) and then into "castes"—and that this final transformation was so complete as to leave no signs whatever of the two former states. The only other alternative these writers offer us is to assume that somehow the original "demonstrated-descent" groups went directly from "lineage" to "caste" without passing "class"—again without leaving any trace whatever.

I find such suppositions to be too wildly speculative to be supported. On the other hand, to assume that precaste South Asia was characterized by the presence of "exogamous," "equalitarian," "totemic" clans is to do no violence to the system we now observe. There is nothing in the present system that is incompatible with such a prior circumstance. Rather, as Lévi-Strauss has shown us, a "caste" society may be perceived as a transformation of a "totemic" clan society, exhibiting a remarkable basic structural similarity to it despite all superficial apparent difference. Given this, the transformation to stratification would have entailed no more than a shift to redistributive economic exchange as the integrative principle, with endogamy maintaining the corporate unit of the emergent system— the component "caste." That is, the marriage-circle maintains itself as a separate unit vis à vis *other* units of the system through endogamy; in many cases it continues to maintain itself *internally*, however, in the same way as does the cluster of "totemic" clans—by subunit exogamy.

Admittedly, I have not *proved* that a society of "equalitarian" clans preceded that of "castes"; I claim only that it is reasonable and conservative, and in line with all of contemporary theory, including both structuralism and neoevolutionism. My proposal has the effect of encompassing rather than disordering the data available to us from studies of caste in South Asia.

If it is accepted—not as proven, or as God's Truth, but only as the most reasonable and conservative argument yet presented—we can begin to test it. Archeological and other historical studies may be undertaken so as to transform the proposal into a true hypothesis, for surely it is specific enough to be open to verification or negation. Such tasks, of course, are beyond the scope of this book.

For us, here, one important issue remains: given the conjecture that the caste system of South Asia constitutes a transformation of a prior system of unstratified "equalitarian" groups, how did the transformation come about? I have suggested that we must assume that not all systems respond successfully to pressures for transformation. What *are* these pressures? What can we say, with any degree of assurance, about the kind of circumstances that produce such pressures, and the responses that are made to them?

8

The Emergence of the Caste System
in South Asia

One thing is clear: if you don't believe that a puzzle has an answer, you'll never find it.

Marvin Harris—*Cows, Pigs, Wars, and Witches:*
The Riddles of Culture

Under what conditions could the classic South Asian caste system have come into existence? What precipitated it? What was the sequence of events?

In an attempt to answer these questions, I propose to construct a scenario of events for a time period for which no records, historical or archeological, can presently be identified. I am aware of the dangers. Such speculation can easily slide off into fantasy, and in any case without evidence the speculation can never be tested, proved, or disproved. This is why, of course, many reputable social scientists have frowned on such efforts to reconstruct the unrecorded past.

But the efforts have their merits, nevertheless. As long as it is borne in mind that *speculation* should not be translated into *conclusion*—that *scenario* never constitutes *record*—we can at least replace outdated and erroneous explanations with ones that are more in accord with what we *do* know. By using the most informed contemporary modes of explanations, we may, if we are lucky, approach or approximate what actually happened. Best of all, our speculations may serve as guides or hypotheses for future historical and archeological researchers who will be asking: Where should we look? What might we expect to find?

161

In this chapter, then, I will offer an unsupported scenario: my suggestions as to the circumstances under which an early South Asian socioeconomic system characterized by the absence of stratification and the presence of equalitarian social groups became transformed, over time, into a complex, stratified—*caste*—system.

Certain theoretical issues require some clarification before I begin. Indeed, it could be argued that the study of cultural evolution has provided us with an almost infinite number of issues in need of clarification: there are many views and much contention. I will restrict myself, however, to issues crucial to my argument. Thus I will not deal with such pressing questions as general versus specific evolution, unilineal versus multilineal evolution, or whether "caloric ration" can ever be satisfactorily determined. This is not a work on evolution in general, but only on the emergence of the caste system. I shall concentrate here, at least to begin with, on four issues: the nature of "stratification," the implications of "absolute surplus," the significance of "population pressure," and the utility of the "pristine state" concept.

Throughout this book I have repeatedly referred to the caste system as a "stratified" one. I am sure that few social scientists would challenge that assessment, but I am also aware of basic disagreements as to what the term implies. One approach to *stratification* is exemplified by the work of Pitirim A. Sorokin:

> Social stratification means the differentiation of a given population into hierarchically superposed classes. It is manifested in the existence of upper and lower layers. Its basis and very essence consist in an unequal distribution of rights and privileges, duties and responsibilities, social values and privations, social power and influences among the members of a society (1961: 570).

This view of stratification—as reflecting "layers" of classes characterized by "status" differences—is unquestionably an important one, particularly for the study of contemporary European and European-derived societies. However certain economists—including such important theorists as Adam Smith (1793), Thomas Malthus (1798), and Karl Marx (1888)—have approached stratification solely in terms of *economic* classes (often referred to as "proprietors" and "labourers") for which the crucial defining characteristic is, as Marx would have it, the degree of "ownership of the means of production."

Many anthropologists, interested as they are in the *non-*Western world, have found the economists' approach to stratification more useful than that of the sociologists. And, in particular, many anthropologists interested in the evolution of culture have utilized this approach in their writings. The approach has been broadened in the writings of Morton Fried, who distinguished *ranking* from *stratification* in the following way:

Ranking exists when there are fewer positions of valued status than persons capable of filling them. A rank society has means of limiting the access of its members to status positions that they would otherwise hold on the basis of sex, age, or personal attributes. Rank has no *necessary* connection with economic status in any of its forms, though it frequently does acquire economic significance. The point is that rank can and in some instances does exist totally independent of the economic order.

Stratification, by contrast, is a term that is preferably limited to status differences based on economic differences. Stratification in this sense is a system by which the adult members of a society enjoy differential rights of access to basic resources. These resources are the physical things needed to sustain life, either directly (air, water, and food) or indirectly (things that cannot themselves be consumed but are required to obtain other things that are). Outstanding examples of the latter are land, raw materials for tools, water for irrigation, and materials to build a shelter (1967: 52).

The presence or absence of "differential rights of access to basic resources" can usually be determined fairly easily by the field ethnographer. Either the resources are free to all, or else certain persons or corporate groups have control of them and all others must apply to the controllers for access. It is in this sense, as I have noted, that I have termed the caste system "stratified" and it is the emergence of this kind of stratification with which I am concerned here.

It must be apparent, from the passage just cited, why the existence of "equalitarian" societies—societies in which there is no differentiation of degree of membership—can be discomfiting for students of cultural evolution. Given the above approach to stratification, the evolution of complex, stratified societies from earlier "differential-descent" groups is relatively easy to understand. Complex, class-structured societies, by definition, exhibit differential access to basic resources—and so, at least incipiently, do "differential-descent" groups.

But what if there was no differential degree of membership in the earlier society; what if the society were "equalitarian"? The step to stratification in such a case becomes a quantum jump. For some theorists, it follows, the jump seems impossible and the "equalitarian" society doomed to an evolutionary blind alley. I hope to indicate, in the pages that follow, how an "equalitarian" society might become transformed over time into a stratified one.

Harris has argued that for the emergence of stratification anywhere, the occurrence of an "absolute surplus" is necessary. As we have seen, this implies circumstances in which a society is able to provide, over an extensive time period, more energy than is needed by the population for subsistence purposes. If the population increases, furthermore, the conditions are such that the increased population can provide equivalently increased supplies of energy, at least for a long time to come.

The questions I want to consider now include: how and why, according to Harris and his associates, does the phenomenon of ever-increasing supplies of energy come about? What sources of energy appear to contribute most to this phenomenon?

Following Leslie White's lead, Marvin Harris (1975), Richard Lee (1968), and others have explored the ratio between "energy expended" and "energy returned" for a number of different human subsistence systems. They have pointed to a clear difference in ratio, expressed in terms of calories expended and calories returned.

Briefly, they have concluded that the caloric return for most hunting and gathering societies[1] is barely above the break-even point. The energy returned to the system—through the combined efforts of all adult men and women engaged in gathering wild plant and animal foods—on the average only serves to replace the energy

---

[1]A few societies of hunters and gatherers, living in particularly favorable environments in which game is plentiful and easily accessible, are considered by some to constitute special exceptions.

consumed in the food quest. A bit more, perhaps: enough additional energy must be provided to keep alive at least a small number of "nonproducers" or there would be no infants and no elderly in the group. But, even in the best of times, marginal hunting-and-gathering societies are often forced to practice infanticide and parricide.

The point is that in such a circumstance there can never be sufficient surplus to support, *over time*, specialists who can be labeled "full-time," whose administrative, technological, artistic, or other activities would leave them no time to engage actively in the food quest. Thus, the question as to whether or not the institutions permit full-time specialists is essentially irrelevant, for such a society can not maintain, for any meaningful length of time, those who do not contribute to the food supply.[2]

There appears to be a progression in efficiency, therefore, from marginal hunters and gatherers among whom the ratio of "energy expended" to "energy returned" is nearly one-to-one to various types of food producers among whom we find increasingly greater return per expenditure. True, the mere condition of "food production"—the acquisition of energy from *domesticated* plants and animals—is not in itself sufficient to provide a remarkable increase in efficiency. Indeed, sometimes those who scrabble in the field with digging sticks are hardly better off than those who scrabble in the wild with spear and dart. If the energy return of food production *is* better than that of food gathering (and on the whole it tends to be), we find that only certain types of food production are *significantly* more efficient: only certain types could have been capable of generating "absolute surplus."

---

[2]The argument has been made that in particularly favorable environments—the Northwest Coast of North America, the buffalo-inhabited plains of the same continent, and perhaps Upper Paleolithic Europe—hunting and gathering was in fact more efficient than were some forms of food production. This, perhaps, is why many Plains Indian groups in the eighteenth and nineteenth centuries seemingly "reversed evolution" and gave up sedentary life, maize horticulture, pottery, and so on. It wasn't because they were romantics seeking an earlier, purer, "noble savage" way of life, but rather because—with the introduction of the horse—they could amass more food with less effort by hunting the buffalo than by growing maize. Today, of course, we observe hunters and gatherers only in comparatively impoverished milieus such as desert, tundra, and jungle.

We are indebted to Marvin Harris for much of the illumination we have on this issue. In 1959, in his paper "The Economy Has No Surplus?" Harris suggested that "the state of nutritional science even now provides us with a basis for roughly calculating the minimum subsistence level of activity for a specific population" (*Ibid.*: 189). In that same work, moreover, he questioned the likelihood of exceptions to "rational" economic behavior, and he sidestepped the question of the nature of the "initial context" in which some members of a society gain control over food production (*Ibid.*: 194, 198).

A great deal of work and thought has since been devoted to these matters, particularly by Marvin Harris and his students and associates. His analysis of "sacred cow" ecology was, as we have seen, an attack upon those who would claim that human ecosystems can be "irrational." Further, on the knotty question of the sociopolitical circumstances of the emergence of stratification, Harris has suggested (1975: 374–76, *et passim*) that a "big man" emerges with the appearance of a surplus, develops over time into a "redistributor," and thus sets the stage for the emergence of a "governing class" and stratification.[3] And, finally, in this same work, he provides us with a detailed comparison of a number of societies in terms of food energy returned versus the factors of production (*Ibid.*: 233–55).[4]

At the beginning of the progression of examples of "techno-environmental efficiency" Harris places the !Kung Bushmen, hunters and gatherers of the Kalahari Desert of Africa. Using the findings of Richard Lee (1968), Harris reports that: "the technoenvironmental advantage or labor productivity of the Bushmen's mode of production" has a value of 9.6 (*Ibid.*: 234). At the other

---

[3]Harris utilizes the contemporary literature on "big men" in societies around the world. From his discussion, however, it is not clear, at least to me, the extent to which his category is meant to encompass leadership in both demonstrated-descent and stipulated-descent societies (see also Kolenda 1978: 23–24).

[4]Actually, Harris provides a formula: $E = m \times t \times r \times e$, or "food energy ($E$), or the number of calories that a system produces annually, equals the number of food-producers (m) times the hours of work per food producer (t) times the calories expended per food producer per hour (r) times the average number of calories of food produced for each calorie expended in food production (e)" (*Ibid.*: 233).

end of Harris' progression we find a village in China in which, through intensive irrigation agriculture, energy in the form of a rice crop was produced with a "technoenvironmental efficiency" factor having a value of 53.5. Thus, some 700 Chinese villagers produced over 3 billion calories more than they themselves required (*Ibid.*: 245–46).

Whatever questions may be raised about the details of the analysis of food production and energy return, it is clear that there is a truly great and obviously significant difference in efficiency between hunting-and-gathering and intensive irrigation agriculture. In the latter case—one that also characterizes South Asia—we are dealing with a system in which *one* production unit (a farm, a family, a village, or whatever) can produce enough energy to support, in addition to itself, a *large number* of equivalent but *non-foodproducing* units. Harris has demonstrated this, at least to my satisfaction.

Such an efficiency of productivity, one might argue, must surely precipitate massive population increase, whatever else it precipitates. What, then, is the role of population increase in the emergence of stratification? Can one speak of "population pressure" or "population density" as an evolutionary factor? This is a much-debated issue. Indeed, Harris warns us: "There is no simple correlation between technoenvironmental efficiency and population density" (*Ibid.*: 248). The economist Ester Boserup disputes the view she attributes to Malthus and others that food production and agricultural development govern the rate of population growth. Her study, instead:

is based throughout on the assumption . . . that the main line of causation is in the opposite direction: population growth is here regarded as the independent variable which in its turn is a major factor determining agricultural developments (1965: 11).

But Boserup, we must note, is primarily concerned with agricultural development and related factors in the twentieth century—for her, "medical invention" is a variable of equivalent importance—and we are concerned here with developments at the beginning, in the murky distant past. More relevant for our needs, therefore, is the work of Michael J. Harner, who examines the role of

167

population pressure in cultural evolution in his paper, "Population Pressure and the Social Evolution of Agriculturalists" (1970).

Harner, as does Harris, gives great emphasis to the postulate of "scarcity." In other words, he is convinced that population growth leads inevitably to increasingly scarce resources, particularly of cultivable land, and that this in turn leads to the emergence of stratification. As he sees it, the sequence from the appearance of agriculture to the appearance of stratification is characterized by two particularly significant stages:

(a) An early one of plenty, marked by the increase of population and the movement of the population into hitherto uncultivated land. This availability of land—either entirely unoccupied, or converted from hunting-and-gathering territory—in his view serves to weaken or "undermine" an existing unilineal kin structure, for with "free" land available there would be no need for warfare, or control and protection of the group's territory.

(b) A later stage, one of scarcity, in which all available land has been occupied, and there are now people in need of land. With the absence of "free" land, population pressure becomes a factor. Control of resources and protection from enemies become important once again—but since earlier unilineal kin groups have weakened or disappeared, new forms of groups will emerge, and most particularly *lineages*.[5] These, in turn, lead to stratification, "based upon unequal inheritance of subsistence resources" (Harner 1970: 69, 84–85).

Harner states explicitly that his analysis of the relationship between population increase and the emergence of stratification is intended only for situations in which the progression is from hunting and gathering to "class" stratification, noting: "for theoretical reasons which will not be gone into here, slavery and caste stratification are not dealt with in the present paper" (*Ibid.*: 80). His decision was unfortunate for us, since our concern here happens precisely to be with the emergence of "caste stratification," but he has given us an important insight: if increase in food supply does

---

[5]When he uses this term, Harner appears to be referring to nonequalitarian kin groups, those characterized by demonstrated descent and differential degrees of membership.

indeed precipitate a substantial increase in population, then, since arable land in any area is likely to be finite, population pressure in its turn is likely to lead to competition for scarce land and other resources. Harner appears to suggest that in the case of differential-descent societies, aristoi emerge as war leaders and develop into resource controllers. It will be our task to see what might happen, under similar circumstances, in the case of equalitarian societies.

Let us note, finally, that in his analysis Harner appears to give little attention—at least for his first stage—to the implications of culture contact and of the interpenetration of peoples. For his second stage, of course, there is rivalry for scarce land, and this may be between different groups or among the component units of one original society. Thus, while culture contact *may* constitute a factor, it does not appear to be a crucial or inevitable one for Harner, even for his second stage. Like Lévi-Strauss and Kirchhoff, Harner is really asking us to consider the society in a vacuum. Along with most contemporary writers interested in cultural evolution, Harner appears to be focussing on what has come to be called a "pristine" situation: one in which the population of a given area develops food production *on its own* and makes the progression to stratification *on its own*, both without significant influence or contamination from other areas of the world where such events might have occurred earlier.

It is impossible to avoid this issue, since it will be argued, by those who hold that only pristine emergences warrant consideration, that no important plants or animals are believed to have been first domesticated in South Asia, and that therefore food production and concomitant socioeconomic change must have "diffused" into the area from outside. If this be true, it follows that we must search elsewhere for at least some of the conditions and events that led to the emergence of caste!

There are two ways of responding. One could accept the validity of the "pristine/nonpristine" distinction and go on to argue that important plant domestication—particularly that of rice—might very well have occurred "first" in South Asia. If that were the case—and there is some support from paleobiology—then we could claim that our hypothesized early population represents a "pristine" situation of absolute surplus and consequent cultural evolution.

169

An alternative response, and one I propose to espouse, is to challenge the assumptions underlying the "pristine" issue. I do not believe that the distinction between "pristine" and "nonpristine" is significant for the analysis of cultural evolution, and I am also increasingly dubious that a "pristine" situation can be said *ever* to have occurred!

To begin with, the issue is an old one, deriving from controversies over a hundred years old. In the early days, there were those scholars who believed that all cultural phenomena "evolved" in exactly the same way as—in their view—biological phenomena did. Thus, just as you had to explain the occurrence of wings among both bats and birds as similar but totally unconnected events, so the presence of fire or pottery among two separated human groups had to be seen as similar but unconnected human evolutionary developments. The basic assumption, apparently, was the equation of culture trait and genetic trait: just as one cannot "borrow" genes from another species, it was assumed that one cannot "borrow" traits from another culture.

This assumption was challenged early, of course, and theoretical purists, as is their wont, moved swiftly to new extremes. Some appeared to believe that *all* cultural developments can only have occurred *once each* in all of human history. Thus, the appearance of similar traits in different groups—however widely separated in time or space—can only reflect "borrowing" or, as such scholars would have it, *diffusion*. Some scholars, at the beginning of the present century, opted for a third explanation: there was neither "diffusion" *nor* "independent invention." Instead, cultural similarities merely reflected *migration* of peoples, each group carrying its cultural baggage to new localities.

Let us not mock these earlier views: taken together, they were *all* right. On the basis of all we have learned about human behavior in the past century, we may say that humans everywhere are capable of "independent invention" of cultural items; that human groups have indeed migrated throughout human history, and over enormous distances; and human groups do indeed borrow, and with remarkable facility and celerity, the practices—and particularly the technological innovations—of their neighbors.

These disorderly propensities of humans still seem to pose

problems for some who would theorize about cultural evolution. Particularly, if two separated groups can be determined to have exhibited the same sequence and set of responses to the presence of food production, does this mean that both groups have responded separately but in the same way to "evolutionary forces"? Or does it merely mean that one group copied, after the fact, everything the first group did? From this perspective, diffusion becomes a threat, a contaminant of samples.

Marvin Harris has dismissed as a "myth" promulgated by "diffusionists," the argument asserted above that early evolutionary theorists tended to ignore the implications of cultural borrowing (1968: 173–74). Let us observe, however, Harris' obvious delight in what he calls "the second earth," a reference to the implications of separate cultural evolution in the New World:

At last, it could be seen through archaeological data that American Indian populations, starting with paleolithic tool kits and restricted to a life of hunting and gathering, had slowly advanced through various degrees of complexity in a direction fundamentally similar to that taken by racially and culturally separate populations in the Old World. There was no longer any possibility that either area had depended on the other for any of the vital steps in the sequence. The New World in other words had finally emerged as the equivalent of a second earth; and on that second earth, due to the fact that in the psychocultural realm, as in all others, similar causes under similar conditions lead to similar results, hominid cultures tended to evolve along essentially similar paths when they were confronted with similar technoenvironmental conditions (*Ibid.*: 682–83).

We can understand, of course, that Harris' jubilation relates to his continuing debate with those who would deny cultural evolution, or at least its occurrence in any regularized fashion. The problem is that an overriding concern with the processes of evolution can lead to a kind of impatience with the equally important processes of diffusion. For example, where in the passage from Harris just quoted do we detect *any* consideration of the possibly *necessary* role of diffusion *in* cultural evolution?

I would argue that this constitutes a weakness in contemporary cultural-evolution theory: the *occurrence* of diffusion is acknowledged, but the *implications* of diffusion are largely overlooked.

Elman Service, for example, glances at the beginnings of both ancient Egyptian and early Indus civilizations. He concludes that both came later than the Tigris-Euphrates civilization, and this seems to make them almost unusable:

There is no doubt that the whole of the fertile crescent from Mesopotamia to the Nile was heavily influenced by diffusion from and emulation of Mesopotamia. The rise of civilization in Egypt, therefore, may well have been related in some respects to that of Sumer; it was nearly contemporaneous. Keeping this in mind, it will still serve some purpose to treat Egypt separately. . . (1975: 225).

And, for the Indus Valley, Service can only observe:

as in the case of Egypt, there is evidence of trade with Sumer, so again there is the problem of how to assess the degree of independence of the Indus civilization (*Ibid.*: 239).

Similarly, Morton Fried is aware of the occurrence of diffusion, and he finds it necessary to distinguish between "pristine" and what he calls "secondary" situations for cultural evolution. A "secondary" situation is, for Fried, one in which events are occurring in a context of stimulation or influence from the outside, presumably from groups that have themselves already made the progression from stage to stage. In such a situation, the group undergoing change presumably is not responding to events and forces by developing its own solutions, but is simply "borrowing" or "copying"—or even having conditions imposed upon it. Thus, for Fried, the "pristine" situation is very different:

To the extent that no society exists in a superorganic vacuum, but is necessarily surrounded by other sociocultural entities, part of its developmental process will result from and be influenced by interaction with those external entities. However, there are situations in which none of the external cultures are any more complex than the one being considered, and these situations can be regarded as pristine (1967: 11).

Clearly, Fried is aware of "diffusion"—or, to get away from this somewhat old-fashioned term, the notion that all human societies exist, and have always existed, in conditions of constant and structured interaction with other societies around them, involving constant interpenetration of cultural elements. Therefore, when Fried writes: "A pristine situation is one in which development occurs *exclusively* on the basis of the indigenous factors" (*Ibid.*: Italics mine), he does not mean to imply that no culture contact whatever has taken place, but only that he is ignoring it as a factor.

We see, therefore, that Harris' dismissal of the "myth" promulgated by "diffusionists"—that evolutionists tend to ignore the implications of culture contact and borrowing—was a bit too casual.[6] The issue is not that evolutionists—from Morgan through Harris, Fried, and Service—are unaware of the phenomenon of culture contact, but simply that they make no provision for it in their efforts to explain cultural evolution.

What I am arguing for here, in a typical eclectic way, is an approach to cultural evolution that is flexible enough to incorporate the ubiquitous human propensities for invention, borrowing, and migration. I propose to do just that in my scenario for the emergence of stratification in South Asia. I propose, further, to incorporate the factors of "absolute surplus" and "population pressure" as they have been advanced respectively by Harris and Harner.

To begin, I urge that cultural evolution not be conceived of as an arrow moving upward. Rather, a more accurate representation might be of horizontal arrows, pointing and interpenetrating every which way, massing into a vertical mound.[7] The implication is that small innovations occur, spread to contiguous areas, and in turn spark new innovations, some of which return, and so on. In favorable circumstances, and over time, the cumulative effect of this interaction between separated groups results in that

---

[6]In *Cows, Pigs, Wars, and Witches* (1974), Harris cites Fried's position on the exclusive nature of the pristine situation with every indication of approval!

[7]I derive this image from the writings of A. L. Kroeber on the formation of "culture areas" (1939).

appearance of "upward" movement that we perceive as "cultural evolution."[8]

We must go back, then, to a point just before the appearance of food production in South Asia; to a time when hunting and gathering was the sole source of energy acquisition for the entire population of the area. No one will argue, I am sure, that there never was such a time, despite the fact that we cannot pinpoint it with certainty.

We can make some guesses, however. Judging from the archeological record, it is possible that the cultivation of rice in the lands bordering the Bay of Bengal may go back as much as five to six thousand years, if not indeed more.[9] Hard grains, such as wheat, rye, and barley, were known in Southwest Asia, on the other side of the subcontinent, by about the same time (Richardson and Stubbs 1978: 77). It is reasonable to assume, therefore, that both rice and hard grain cultivation—along with other associated domesticated plants and animals—had spread throughout favorable ecological zones of the South Asian subcontinent during the next thousand years.[10] By about four thousand years ago, therefore, it is likely—and the likelihood is supported by such archeological evi-

---

[8]We know, for the New World, of the circuitous route taken by maize from its origins to its final form (Mangelsdorf, MacNeish, and Galinat 1964). Sociopolitical developments for the New World exhibit a similarly complex interweaving. The only truly "pristine" situation in "Nuclear America" is the entire area—from what is now northern Chile to what is now the southwestern United States, encompassing most of the area in between. This is because an innovation in one area, spreading to a second, precipitated an innovation in a third. When the innovations found their way to the original area additional changes were precipitated—but ones that could not have taken place had it not been for the intervening developments in distant areas!

[9]See the writings of Carl Sauer (1969), and the report of W. G. Solheim (1972), as well as the recent summary of contemporary opinion on the wheres and whens and hows of agricultural origins by Richardson and Stubbs (1978).

[10]I am probably being much too conservative in all this. The archeological evidence for the spread of the hard grain complex throughout Southwest Asia and North Africa, and for the movement of the maize complex throughout nuclear America, points to a much more rapid diffusion of technological innovation. And this human propensity for the rapid acquisition of usable technological innovations is confirmed, more recently, by the spread of horse domestication throughout aboriginal North America and of tobacco cultivation throughout the world.

dence as we have—that wheat and other hard grains were being cultivated at least in the northwestern part of the subcontinent, while rice cultivation was being practiced in many parts of the eastern and southern regions, most particularly in areas that are today part of such political units as Assam, Bangladesh, West Bengal, Bihar, Tamilnadu, and Kerala.

In which of these areas am I suggesting that the caste system originated? In any of them—or, more probably, in all together. Which production complex played a greater role in the emergence of caste—hard grains or rice? I have no idea: perhaps social developments interpenetrated, perhaps one food-complex area was more significant. If the latter, I would lean, personally, toward rice cultivation. I suspect, among other things, that it was of greater antiquity and provided, even at an early date, more efficiency of energy returned over energy expended.

However, from the theoretical position I have espoused these issues are not really important ones. From my perspective, only two things are important:

(a) At the time under consideration South Asia *as a whole* became characterized by spreading rice and hard-grain cultivation in certain ecological zones, while other zones (as today) were characterized by hunting and gathering, shifting agriculture, herding, and so on. This *totality* is the arena for sociocultural change, for the events with which we are concerned did not—could not, in my view—have happened in any one place. Thus, I propose that the caste system came into existence *not* in Bengal or the Malabar Coast or the Indus Valley, but over the entire subcontinent. Different regions and peoples participated in different and unequal ways, sometimes making a contribution and at other times remaining peripheral to developments.

(b) At the time under consideration, as I have argued earlier, I suggest that the subcontinent was inhabited in all or most ecological zones by nonstratified hunters and gatherers who were acquiring the new technology wherever conditions permitted, and whenever the hunters perceived the new technology to be capable of providing a better way of life. The social systems of these various peoples were characterized, as I see it, by what Lévi-Strauss has called "totemic" structures, and Kirchhoff has called "equalitarian"

175

organizations. Very possibly, there were shifting bands in some areas, but I do not believe that groups reflecting "demonstrated descent"—if any were present at all—played important roles in the development of stratification in the subcontinent.

The new technologies, then, appear in the favorable regions of the subcontinent and spread swifty to the limits of each ecozone. That is, in a given geographic region, wet rice (or hard grain) crops are quite soon produced on the total land area on which such a crop is possible, given the environmental conditions and the technological sophistication. Beyond, inevitably, lie marginal or unfavorable regions, inhabited by less fortunate folk, still constrained to hunt and gather. And still further, of course, lie other favored—and unfavored—regions, the populations of all of them more or less aware of one another, and more or less in contact.

For those groups able to practice agriculture, an "absolute surplus" has come into existence: more food can be produced than is needed by the food producers, and this continues to be true over time, despite occasional poor crops and even despite population increase.

In the beginning, as Harner has pointed out, there were probably not enough cultivators to occupy all the suitable land in the favorable ecozones, and so a good portion of the land lay unused. Slowly, Harner suggests, the population must have expanded to fill up the unused land.

But we are striving for a multidimensional perspective. Let us therefore not forget the peoples all around the favored ecozone, the groups residing on "unsuitable" land, all of them aware of the new technology and its advantages but unable to use the technology in their own ecozones. We must assume, then, that as many of these who desired to, and as could possibly manage it, would crowd into the more favored areas, seeking land or some degree of share in the crop. Within a relatively short period, therefore, what with natural population increase and the immigration of groups seeking land for cultivation, all of the "best" land—the land most suitable for cultivation—will have been occupied, and "population pressure" will have become a factor.

Obviously, I am incorporating into my scenario the factor of "diffusion," the implications of communication between groups.

We do not have to wait for one single "pristine" group to expand sufficiently by natural increase for land pressure to be felt. Marginal or "unsuitable" land is not necessarily uninhabited land; we are speaking only of unsuitability for agriculture, not for hunting and gathering. For any given region, therefore, once agriculture and its productivity make an appearance, there must be many groups— internal as well as external—eager to move from land that is suddenly "unsuitable" to land that is cultivable. And behind them, inevitably, press still others.

Furthermore, it is probable that in such circumstances internal pressures and problems come into existence long *before* all suitable land has been exhausted. The fact that there is good land somewhere on the distant periphery—on the outer marches or frontier—hardly diminishes the desirability of possessing land in the center of things. Thus, when population increases in a region where all cultivable land is already occupied, the population is likely to be divided into three distinct categories: those who inherit or otherwise obtain possession of the cultivable land, those who are willing to establish new settlements somewhere else, and those who prefer to remain in the familiar territory and to seek some other way of sharing in the harvest.

With this, of course, we are back to the problem posed in the first chapter. If "absolute surplus" means that one productive unit will have the capacity to provide the energy needs of a substantial number of nonfood-productive units, why should the productive unit do so? Why shouldn't the members of the unit limit their production to that which satisfies their own needs?

It is pointless to suggest, as others have, that given time "big men," descent lines, military specialists, or whatever, will emerge on the scene, because there does not appear to be time to give. Almost from the beginning of the new technology, there will be more people present than are needed for actual food-production activities—people for whom there is, or could be, more than enough food, if there were only a reason for sharing it with them. I am suggesting, in other words, not only that the pressure for land develops more swiftly than Harner has allowed for, but also that the pressure of the landless to share in the harvest develops even more swiftly!

I have postulated the presence of "equalitarian" groups: the population is composed of social groups characterized by full and undifferentiated membership in internal units. Prosperity or misfortune must, in such a case, be shared by all, for there can be no aristoi to put forth a claim to a greater share of the wealth of the unit. From one perspective—that of Kirchhoff, Fried, and others—the absence of the aristoi element is disadvantageous for cultural evolution, for neither individuals nor descent lines can separate themselves from the rest of the pack. From another perspective, however, the "equalitarian" society may be seen to enjoy certain advantages. What belongs to one member of any group belongs to all the members; therefore good fortune in the form of a line of access to basic resources must quickly become the property of the entire corporate group.

Since ancient times, South Asia has exhibited innumerable examples of this situation: caste groups continually penetrate, and then assume effective local monopoly over, some new occupation, trade, or skill. From soldier to taxi driver to college professor to scribe to doctor—once a few members of a marriage-circle have stumbled onto a good thing they swiftly draw an ever-widening circle of brothers and castemates into the new adventure. The existence, all over the subcontinent, of specialist marriage-circles—from scavengers to priests—attests to the antiquity of the phenomenon. I suggest, therefore, that it is in fact a necessary, inherent, and advantageous feature of equalitarian social structure, and that it is reasonable to conclude that it was as much in evidence during the period of the emergence of the caste system as it was later, and as it is now.

Further, in a society made up of equalitarian social groups, if we say that some people have access to land and others do not, we must mean that some *corporate groups* have access and some *corporate groups* do not, since in equalitarian corporate groups all share equally. Individuals who were members of groups without access must have sought to share in the harvest—as, we have seen, they still do in South Asia—not as individuals, or as descent lines, but as representatives of corporate bodies.

In other words, as in the case of Kumbapettai, individual members of landless corporate bodies contracted with other individuals, who in principle represented corporate bodies with land and crops, to provide the latter with something desirable in exchange for grain or land. The offered item could not reflect any *individual* skill or resource, but rather the common property of the offerer's respective corporate group, and it had to be acceptable not just to one individual but in principle to the recipient's own corporate group. Since group, in effect, dealt with group, there does not appear to have been any structural role for "big men," even if they were present.

What might have been offered in exchange for a share of the crop, or for access to land? Obviously, anything that offerers could think of, or the receivers could ask for. What emerged over time was a situation in which a variety of services was being offered, each by a corporate equalitarian group. Some services provided a degree of autonomy and variety to the offerers, as in the case of animal husbandry: others were as narrow and limited as ear cleaning. Some services permitted the offerers to prosper, comparatively speaking; others could keep the corporate group alive only in want and privation.

An obvious and important service would be that of labor in the fields, those who have no land being constrained to do the work of producing the crop for those who do, in return for a barely adequate share of the crop. Of course, this occurs in stratified societies everywhere in the world, but the difference is that in the caste system of South Asia—as it emerged and as it is—the field labor is done not by landless individuals who in sum compose an agricultural proletarian *class*, but by *corporate groups* who engage in agricultural labor for landed corporate groups.[11] Gough's account, cited earlier, of how the Kōnāns of Kumbapettai became adimai may constitute only one example, but it is sufficient to illuminate both process and relationship.

---

[11]Though I speak of such labor as "offered" I am of course aware that it was not only arduous and unrewarding, but also often involuntary in the bargain: those engaging in it usually surrendered a large measure of their freedom. Thus, the landed/landless relationship exhibited a substantial measure of "exploitation" (see Mencher 1974)—but so, of course, does any stratified society. What I am concerned with here, therefore, is the difference between "caste" and other forms of stratification-exploitation.

Another obvious category of service to be offered in exchange for shares of the crop is that of artisans. Craftsmen, representing specialized corporate bodies, could offer to make or repair a wide variety of tools, implements, and other items. In short, one hardly needs to speculate about the origin of carpenters, blacksmiths, potters, and so on, or about the attractiveness of what they were offering in exchange for grain shares.

But one might ask why the land-controllers accepted these services: why did they not prefer to make their own pots, or do their own carpentry—or even perform all their own labor in the fields—and thus produce less of a crop and keep it all for themselves? We are raising the issue of values: is it "better" to do it yourself, or have someone do it for you? There is no universal rule; cultures differ on the value of self-sufficiency and self-reliance. If some find it hard to believe this about "field labor," there are other services to which we can point for which culturally derived differences in values are obvious. I refer to services of a personal nature, whatever is seen as easing or enhancing or maintaining the human condition. Should a man shave himself, or a woman cut her own nails?

For South Asia, we observe a remarkably long list of personal services offered by corporate bodies. These include, and extend far beyond, the activities of barbers, midwives, scavengers, latrine cleaners, and so on and on. The value system then, as it apparently developed—and I will return to the question of why it developed—determined which personal activities individuals preferred not to perform for themselves, and preferences varied from group to group. Further, the value system determined which of the services—such as washing menstrual cloths—was to be considered demeaning and degrading, and which of the services—such as that of priest, or intercessor with the divinities—was to be considered ennobling or transfiguring. In none of the cases, however, is the occupation open to any individual as such. Rather, it is the monopoly, jealously guarded and controlled, of a particular marriage-circle or cluster of marriage-circles.

Thus, while Ibbetson, Nesfield, Weber, and others have variously proposed that castes came into existence when those engaged in specific occupations banded together into marriage-circles,

and Risley and others suggested that the marriage-circles or
in some effort to ensure group purity and only *later* adop
tinctive occupations, I am proposing something entirely di

We assumed the presence of societies in the first stage
ing systems of equalitarian corporate groups, each group
distinction of degree of membership, and each society lackii
nificant economic specialization and therefore exchange of s
ized goods and services. From such a structure, with the intr
tion of "absolute surplus," I suggest the emergence of a syst
corporate groups still separated socially but no longer econom
equivalent, a system in which one or a few groups (but no l
all) control access to basic resources, and the other groups
offer services for shares in, or access to, those resources. The g
and services thus offered move, in reality or in principle, to
marriage-circles controlling land and crops, and the member
such groups redistribute crops, goods, and services to all
others.

At the beginning, we saw a galaxy of equalitarian endo
mous societies, many of them composed of equalitarian exogam
segments, or clans. Now, though there is exchange of goods a
services among marriage-circles that are arranged in a hierarch
endogamy still characterizes the marriage-circle, and exogan
often characterizes the subunit. Further, absolute equality of men
bership still characterizes both the subunit and the marriage-circ
in most cases—but not the total galaxy, for each marriage-circ
exhibits a different degree of access to the basic resources. Wit
this, we have the classic *caste* socioeconomic system, as we hav
observed and analysed it.

There is no quantum jump in all this, but only the easiest
progression, seemingly the most minimal of transformations, but it
takes us from the "bear" to the "barber," from unstratified "equalitarian" hunters and gatherers to the complex and stratified agricultural production system that is "the caste system."

* * *

I have offered an alternative explanation for the emergence of
the caste system in South Asia, an explanation reflecting a synthesis of the insights and formulations of a number of leading contemporary schools of anthropology. Inevitably, a new explanation

leads to new questions and new problems. I cannot answer all of these, but happily they take us beyond the purview of this work. There are a few questions, however, that I would like to consider before bringing this chapter to a close.

Why should such a unique development occur—and why, if it did occur, should it happen in South Asia and nowhere else?

We have already noted that Fried, Service, and others have given little attention to "equalitarian" societies, preferring for their own reasons to concentrate on "differential-descent" societies and their presumed progression to class stratification. I might therefore counter the above question with some others: Was "differential descent" in fact as important in the emergence of class stratification as some have assumed? Was it really that ubiquitous, at least for the stage in evolutionary sequence with which we are concerned? And, if "differential descent" was really all the rage almost everywhere, why could South Asia still not be the one place where "absolute surplus" met up with a rare example of "equalitarian" social structure, thus precipitating a variety of stratification different from that produced in all the other cases?

My own suspicion is that equalitarian clans were in fact not all that rare, but that their presence in history and their evolutionary potential have both been largely overlooked. Poor vision, brought about by theoretical blinkers, has plagued the discipline of anthropology before: how long did students of social organization ignore the presence and the implications of nonunilineal descent systems?

Perhaps Africa would be a good continent on which to begin a search for the presence of original equalitarian structures and the emergence of castelike forms of stratification. I am not referring to the customary analogue, that of the contemporary South African "racial" or ethnic hierarchy—in my use of "caste" I am concerned not so much with social hierarchy as with corporate control of resources and services—but rather to the circumstances that may have produced certain "tribal" formations in both West and East Africa. I am particularly intrigued by the existence of so-called

"pariah" tribes in the eastern portion of Africa. From the available literature, it would appear that these "tribes" exhibit many of the characteristics of "caste," but we need to know more about them and about the total socioeconomic system.[12]

Southeast Asia might well prove another fruitful area for investigation. Moving right along, I would by no means exclude all areas of Southwest Asia, Europe, and the New World from consideration. The issue I would raise, in all these cases, is whether in fact stratification always emerged as a "class" phenomenon, or whether there were sometimes corporate "equalitarian" bodies contending for access to basic resources.

However, lest the cry of theoretical imperialism go up, I had better return to a safer position. In this essay I am merely arguing that "absolute surplus" coupled with "equalitarian" clan-structured societies, led—in *South Asia*—to the emergence of a caste-stratified society, and I leave the issue of what did or did not happen elsewhere in the world to other students.

How did the structural transformation take place: what motivated the actual individuals involved to make all the changes necessary to take them from "bear" to "barber"?

With this, we return to the question, first raised by Pearson, of why food-producers would want to continue to produce, over a long period of time, far more food than they needed for their own subsistence, thus making possible that continued and sustained support of nonfood-producers necessary for the emergence of a stratified society.

I take my lead in this matter from the writings of Fredrik Barth (1963, 1967), a student of social change on the microcosmic rather than the macrocosmic level. Barth urges us to remember that in any society individuals vary in response to seemingly similar pressures and events, as they do in their perceptions of needs and advantages, and in their allocations of time and effort:

---

[12]I refer here specifically to the endogamous "hunting and artisan castes" in Ethiopia and the Horn described by Herbert S. Lewis (1962) and others.

People make allocations in terms of the pay-offs that they hope to obtain, and their most adequate bases for predicting these pay-offs are found in their previous experience or in that of others in their community. The kinds of new ideas that occur can no more determine the direction of social change than mutation rates can determine the direction of physical change. Whatever ideas people may have, only those that constitute a practicable allocation in a concrete situation will be effected. And if you have a system of allocations going—as you always must where you can speak of change—it will be the rates and kinds of pay-offs of alternative allocations *within that system* that determine whether they will be adopted, that is, institutionalized. . . .

I do not wish to minimize the complexity of the dynamics of such change and adjustment. My main point is that most of the salient constraints on the course of change will be found to be social and interactional, and not simply cognitive. They will derive from the existing social and ecological system within which the change is taking place. And finally, they can most usefully be analyzed with reference to the opportunity situation of social persons or other units of management capable of decision-making and action: the mechanisms of change must be found in the world of efficient causes. It should follow from this that though it may be a convenient and illuminating shorthand of culture history to differentiate between "emergent" and "recurrent" change, the mechanisms involved seem to be essentially the same. . . (1967: 668; italics his).

If I cannot identify and delimit all the mechanisms and circumstances of change in the situation I have proposed, still it seems to me that the situation itself fits quite comfortably within the boundaries of Barth's strictures. I have suggested that in the period of the emergence of the caste system corporate marriage groups controlled the basic resources as they do to this day: land and the crops grown on it. Individuals, as well as the corporate groups, may certainly have varied as to whether they wished to produce for subsistence only, or in a quantity beyond subsistence. If the latter choice was made, those who made it probably varied greatly as to the quantity beyond subsistence they were willing to produce. There were pressures: nonfood-producers—some familiar, some potentially threatening and worrisome—desperately pressed for land or for shares in the crop.

Manifestly, those who produced beyond their immediate

needs were rewarded in many immediate and substantial ways. The burdens of labor were taken over by others; there was access to manufactured items that were beyond the capacity of those who must spend their time in agricultural pursuits; the pressures from the have-nots upon the food-producers were alleviated. Those, on the other hand, who opted *not* to produce "surplus" and *not* to develop exchange relationships with nonfood-producers must, over time, have perceived their choice to be less practical and less desirable.

Note that the alternatives derive, as Barth (and Pearson) have said they must, from "within the system." We can even perceive "likely units of management capable of decision-making and action." Not any hypothetical "chief" or "big man," but the assembly of the whole that is an almost inevitable feature of both equalitarian structure and of the marriage-circles of the *present* South Asian caste system.

Barth tells us that cognitive changes follow upon the social and interactional changes, and Lévi-Strauss has pointed to the different kinds of names, or self-identifications, used by caste groups as against "totemic" ones. Indeed, changes may be expected to occur throughout the symbolic or ideological system, from notions of purity and pollution to categories of divinities, from feelings about the relative superiority of giving over receiving to conclusions about the structure of the universe. And stratification implies *hierarchy*, so the ideological system must account for, as well as encompass, that too, as Louis Dumont has taught us (1970).

I do not mean to imply that all of what I have described *had* to happen; only that, in this case, it apparently did. People were faced with the tensions and contradictions attendant upon "absolute surplus"; solutions were stumbled upon and tried out, and as new problems emerged still other responses were made. It is perfectly possible to imagine, however, that there were similar situations—in South Asia or elsewhere—where *no* solutions were found at some particular point in the sequence. Such as impasse would have resulted, at best, in continuing social discomfort. At worst, it could have precipitated the dissolution of the society.

This brings us to a final question:

Caste

Does the case of the emergence of the caste system in South Asia represent an example of technoenvironmental determinism, or does it demonstrate the absence of causality in cultural evolution?

I am immediately made uneasy by the limitations of such a Manichaean "either/or" formulation. Rather, echoing Harris, I prefer to say that similar social systems, in similar kinds of situations of pressure for change, will likely arrive at similar solutions. For Harris this may demonstrate *determinism;* for me it indicates only "possibility" or at most "likelihood"—for it may well be that the society will arrive at *no* solution at all.

Failure to find a solution usually spells some kind of disaster for the group; solutions, by definition, constitute continued existence. But is this what is meant by "causality"? I suspect not, so I am on the whole more comfortable with the approach advocated by Jonathan Friedman in his dispute with Marvin Harris:

> There is evolution because societies, species (as populations), etc. come into contradiction with their "environments". . . . History is built upon the failure of social forms as much as on their success. If social forms fail, it is because they have laws of their own whose purpose is other than making optimal use of their techno-environments (Friedman 1974: 466).

I am not even sure we need go as far as that: if the social forms fail, perhaps it is for the reason suggested by Friedman, or perhaps it is for some other reason. In any event, for South Asia, history was built upon success, not failure, and the caste system emerged, definitely if not inevitably.

9

Conclusions and Final Thoughts

We are at the end of our inquiry, but as so often happens in the search after truth, if we have answered one question, we have raised many more. . . .

Sir James G. Frazer—*The Golden Bough*

I really do not see any need for a comprehensive and detailed summary of all my arguments as to the nature of caste and the caste system, my reasons for discarding the explanations for the origin of that system proposed by other scholars, or my own explanation of the emergence of the caste system in South Asia. Surely the preceding chapters are sufficiently prolix that one is entitled to say that they speak for themselves.

In brief, then, I have proposed that the emergence of the present structure should be traced to some specific time, four or more millenia ago, when the techniques and rewards of agricultural production became available to the populations of South Asia. I have suggested that these fortunate people were at the time primarily organized in "totemic" or "equalitarian" social groups. With the rapid dispersal of the new agricultural techniques to all favorable ecological areas of the subcontinent, contradictions inherent in a situation of "absolute surplus" came to the fore equally rapidly, and throughout the subcontinent. Whatever the total range of responses, the solution that apparently achieved the greatest support and success was the one entailing the exchange of the services of nonfood-producing corporate groups for shares of crops or access to land controlled by food-producing corporate groups. Given time, I have argued, this resulted in the full emergence of what—in all its social, economic, and ideological manifestations—we know as the South Asian caste system.

I have tried to demonstrate that such an argument is in accord with (or at least not in conflict with) the perceptions and findings of historians, archeologists, and paleobotanists who have concerned themselves with South Asia. Further, in my presentation I have endeavored to incorporate and synthesize the insights and arguments of a wide array of contemporary anthropological theorists, including Morton Fried, Fredrik Barth, Marvin Harris, and Claude Lévi-Strauss. Works reflecting such diverse theoretical schools as ecological anthropology, structuralism (of both the "pure" and the "Marxist" varieties), and substantivist economics have been consulted. I can only repeat that, in comparison, all other explanations of the origins of caste reflect hopelessly outdated theory and data.

The details of my arguments, as I noted above, need not be repeated here: at this point they have convinced my reader of either their merit or their worthlessness. For the rest of this chapter, therefore, I would prefer to turn from the issue of the origins of caste to a few other, and perhaps peripheral, issues.

I wish to associate myself most emphatically with those who have argued the need to search for an explanation of origins. Those of my readers who are themselves well aware of the importance of efforts to penetrate into that enormous portion of the history of our species for which we will never have written records may wonder that I find it necessary to make such a statement. After all, is it not true that, despite the hiatus in anthropology during the first half of the present century, an increasing number of scholars now devote themselves to the issues of cultural evolution? True enough, but you would never know it if you confined yourself only to the anthropological literature, both theoretical and substantive, relating to South Asia!

For South Asian anthropology, alas, apart from a few unreconstructed followers of *Kulturkreislehre*, the apostles of synchrony or even achrony still rule supreme. Here, almost invariably, the issue under discussion is: What *is* the caste system? Very occasionally, one may also hear the question: What is it changing into? Elsewhere, anthropologists may be asking: What might have brought about the present socioeconomic conditions? Elsewhere, indeed, there may be much healthy, if at times ferocious, debate about origins, sequences, consequences, and such—but not here.

Therefore, while others, long before this writing, have advanced the reasons for resuming and continuing the search for origins, it is necessary for me to repeat some of the arguments, since word of them has apparently not reached the purlieus of the Indological anthropologists.

Written records, delightful as they are when one has them, are by no means the only source of information about the past, although that may have been the assumption of earlier scholars such as Max Weber and A. R. Radcliffe-Brown. Happily, anthropological archeologists and physical anthropologists, though bereft of a shred of documented evidence, have been able to push our understanding and knowledge of the events of human history back thousands, then hundreds of thousands, and finally millions of years.

Oddly, the implications of what they are doing sometimes diffuse most slowly to their "cultural" colleagues across the corridor. Can one, in all seriousness, continue to refer contemptuously to "conjectural history" or even to "pseudohistory" in the presence of students who have just come from a class in which events in human history taking place five million years ago were under consideration? Surely if it is respectable and important to reconstruct what *must* have happened to our ancestors during the Pleistocene Epoch, it is equally respectable, and just as important, to try to determine what *probably* took place four or five millenia ago, when most of the societies we see around us today were becoming recognizable.

And, apart from all the reasons the neo-evolutionists have advanced, it seems to me that students of South Asia have a particularly pressing reason for attending to the question of origins. As we have seen, this question was a favorite one throughout the early decades of modern South Asian study, and the assumptions and conclusions of that period of inquiry have found their way into a large portion of the literature.

To my Indologist colleague, therefore, I say: You may come up with evidence or insight enabling you to dismiss my proposals as hopelessly improbable, but you cannot in good conscience ignore the issue of origins itself. For if you do, if you continue to tell

189

your students that the origins of the caste system are and must forever remain a mystery, you are in effect leaving the field, by default, to Risley and Ibbetson and other proponents of what are, at this point in our discipline, both factually and theoretically incorrect positions. Further, if your students—and you yourself— absorb errors about how caste came to be, might this well not threaten the trustworthiness of views about what caste *is?*

It must be clear that I am by no means advocating any return to simplistic evolutionism. But I am also not advocating a reliance upon contemporary culture-materialism, or any other single theoretical approach. Rather, at the deepest level, this work should be read as a plea that my colleagues in anthropology cast off all dogmatic, single-theory fetters.

I am not prepared to argue that the study of human society will never arrive at that happy state in which one comprehensive theory system manages to encompass all the issues of importance in the discipline. As far as I can see, however, we are nowhere near that state at the moment. Such a situation can be frustrating, I suppose, and one can see the attractions of some of the approaches that have been advanced.

At one extreme there are those who insist that, since no present theory is all-encompassing and all-satisfying, *all* of them are time-wasting and dubious. Such scholars, and I think their numbers grow smaller, advocate only the accumulation of data according to traditional categories, and insist that the interpretation of this data, when it is necessary at all, should take place only on the most basic and pragmatic of levels. Proponents of such a position have been attacked by others, and most particularly by Marvin Harris, as "Boasian" and "eclectic."

At the other extreme are those who argue that if no theory can deal satisfactorily with all problems of interest to anthropologists there is nevertheless *one* theoretical framework—their own, of course—that can deal with the "important" or "meaningful" problems of anthropology. Thus, to such scholars, the investigations of others interested in different kinds of problems—whether they be of evolution, transformation, kinship, symbol, economy, or whatever—are bluntly a waste of time.

It is easy to understand why such single-theory proponents

spend a good deal of their time, whatever their favorite theory, casting out devils. Sometimes the devils are opponents who propose to waste good money and good paper on "unimportant" problems pursued for "worthless" theoretical reasons. And sometimes the devils are colleagues who were formerly of the "right" persuasion but who have now unfortunately strayed from the one and only true path.

I urge a reassessment of what "theory" is and what it is not. For example, while I would not presume to speak for Boas, my own reading of his works has caused me to doubt assertions that he was resolutely nontheoretical. Whether he was investigating the color of sea water or the distribution of Eskimo needlecase patterns, he was clearly and consciously utilizing the advanced theoretical formulations of his own time—though not necessarily mutually compatible ones.

What Boas objected to, as far as I can see, was untested and untestable speculation, particularly when it derived from questionable but unquestioned assumptions and limited or even dubious evidence. Well, so do we all, from Radcliffe-Brown to White to Harris to Lévi-Strauss to Kirchhoff, to you and to me. And, if I am right about Boas, then—paradoxically—anyone who insists on limiting himself to the problems studied by Boas, or the categories utilized by Boas, is in fact *not* following in the footsteps of Boas!

I do not intend, however, to pose the issue in terms of whether this or that approach is "Boasian" or not: I have no desire to be charged with advocating a "neo-Boasian" school of anthropology. Rather, my position—and I admit I suspect it was also his—is that, given the limitations of our present knowledge, we should be wary of "theories" that are professed as all-encompassing and all-important. On the other hand, however, we must maintain at all times a clear understanding of the theoretical underpinnings and consequences of the research we are engaged in. In practice, this means viewing theoretical frameworks pragmatically, in terms of their individual effectiveness in dealing with the particular problem at hand. Given other problems, we turn to other theories.

Does that constitute an attempt to anoint "eclecticism" and raise it up on a throne of its own? I don't think so, not if that implies equating it with "culture-materialism" or "structuralism" or

191

"symbolic analysis" or whatever. As I tried to indicate earlier, what I am advocating is nothing more—*nor* less—than established scientific methodology and procedure, in which theories derive from tested and confirmed hypotheses, but are still never more than the *best available* explanation, subject always to modification, or even supplanting. Over time, and with good fortune, the various types and levels of explanation may begin to fit together into one overarching system. But until some anthropological Unified Field Theory emerges, if it ever does, we should not expect to study anthropological protons using the formulations we have found suitable for the study of anthropological quasars.

I have wandered far from the consideration of the origins of the caste system of South Asia, so let me retrace my steps. I note again that I found it necessary, for this work, to utilize the perceptions and findings of many supposedly warring schools. Harris has given us important insights into the nature and workings of the South Asian socioeconomic system, but so has Lévi-Strauss, and I really do not see how one could expect to arrive at meaningful conclusions about the origins of caste without attempting, as I have, a synthesis of the many conflicting but nevertheless related arguments.

But what of the fundamental oppositions between the contending theorists? One might argue, for example, that while Lévi-Strauss perceives transformations as reflective of the Hegelian dialectic process, Harris perceives only a straight "causal arrow" reflecting a determinism derived from Marx. Must I, in order to make use of their contribution to South Asian ethnology, first determine which of them is right on this matter?

I think not; the issue is a philosophical one, and not amenable to pragmatic research and analysis. I am happy to leave the problem to the growing body of "structural Marxists," for I have every confidence that they will locate that point behind the paradox where seeming contradictions turn out not to be contradictions at all. It has happened before, of course: we saw in an earlier chapter how Leslie White brought the seemingly separated environmentalist and sociological theorists together in one seamless "ecological-functionalist" whole.

Rather than ponder the ultimate implications of the term "causality" I prefer, in my own efforts to understand major cultural changes or transformations, to rely on the insights we derive not from philosophical inquiry but from biological investigations into the evolution of species. In this, I am not referring to mutation and the other factors contributing to the differential selection of individuals *within* a species, but rather to the issue of why some species survive and proliferate, and even occasionally radiate into new species, while other species of the same genus dwindle and die out.

On this level of biological evolution, the significant term is *adaptation* (see Alland 1967: 221–26). In other words, throughout the long history of life on this planet, species—or major component breeding populations of total species—have continually faced serious threats to the survival and perpetuation of the group. Individuals come and go, they die or survive long enough to pass their genetic material on to the next generation, but the group—the sum total of the individuals within it—must as a *body* (as Leslie White reminded us) replace the total energy needs of the group with sufficient regularity so that sufficient individuals survive to ensure a next generation. At any time, a hitherto "successful" population may come upon significantly changed conditions and the population will respond to those conditions in ways that will lead to the continuation and expansion or the disintegration of the group.

Thus, when we speak of the expansion or contraction of a population, we are actually referring to the sum of successful or unsuccessful responses to the new circumstances on the part of the component individuals of that population. Since, in any biological population, individuals normally vary in genetic endowment, the totality of responses may be seen to reflect the enormously complex interaction of, on the one hand, the nature of the changed situation, and on the other hand the range of responses possible to the population given its gene pool. Two populations exhibiting slightly different gene pools may face identical challenges, and one of the populations may survive while the other succumbs. Two "identical" populations may face different challenges, with the same results.

Actually, of course, it is unlikely either that two populations of the same species will exhibit identical gene pools, or that the circumstances facing even closely contiguous populations will ever be exactly the same. Invariably, we find that we cannot go beyond the word *similar*.

Given that, prediction and analysis can deal only with *probability*, and really can be of service more for explaining the past than for predicting the future. We conclude that, given seemingly similar challenges, the seemingly similar responses of seemingly similar populations lead sometimes to success and sometimes to failure. True, meticulous investigation may sometimes reveal the significantly different in the "seemingly similar," but to speak of "causal arrows" or even of "inevitability" would be to simplify the processes involved to the point of meaninglessness.

Faced with challenges, new conditions, threats to existence, and "contradictions," biological populations of all kinds will make their responses, each in a particular set of ways. After the fact, we can note that for some the challenges turned out to be prohibitive and disastrous, while for others they proved not to be. After the fact, we note that one population responded successfully in one fashion, while a second population (seemingly similar) responded successfully but in a totally different way, while a third population (seemingly equally similar) died off without issue.

This would appear to be as true of human populations as it is of other biological groups. Further, it is true whether they are responding in *biological* terms, as in the case of the challenge of malaria,[1] or they are responding *culturally*, as in the case of "absolute surplus."

There are of course no one-to-one correlations on the individual level between biological change and cultural change. However, there do appear to be some on the group level. That is, in both types of change the group exhibits a variety of individual responses. There is a gene pool that governs biological response, and in any situation of culture change there will be a set of culturally derived perceptions of both the situation and of conceivable responses. This "response pool" is conceptually as finite as the gene pool, although—as in the case of gene pools—there is always the possibility of the appearance of a new response, either from outside or by internal generation. Thus, the total cultural response reflects, as Pearson suggested and as Barth argued, both the external stimu-

---

[1]Some populations die out, some move away, some develop sickle cell anemia, some develop protective but malformed spleens, and so on and on.

lus—which may or may not be identical from group to group—and the internal structure, which if not completely unique is at least peculiar to the group.

We cannot say, therefore, that all unstratified societies, when faced with the challenge of "absolute surplus" will inevitably respond by developing class stratification. *Some* may, but others may develop *caste* stratification, and others may develop in a direction not involving stratification—and still others may well collapse into chaos because the society was unable to "find" a solution to the contradictions.

Must we say, then, that all we can do is merely report that some survive and some do not? No: we can probe, as others have done and as I have tried to do in this book, into the mechanisms and processes by which those who did survive were able to do so. More difficult, but still perhaps possible, would be an investigation of why the failures failed—if, of course, we are able first to identify them in the crowded cemetery of the past.

One thing we need *not* do, however, is introduce the pointless issues of "causality" and "inevitability" into our discussion of why some survive and some do not, of why and how some adapt and others do not. "Absolute surplus," the capacity continually to produce more than the producers need for themselves, raises problems and must constitute a crisis of major proportions for the members of any society faced with it. Why should they produce more than the producers need for themselves? Why should they give that additional productivity to those who may want it but who play no role in the production? Some cultures will find answers to these questions, and in the process transform themselves into new structural systems. Some cultures in the past, quite probably, could not find solutions and so became what Kirchhoff called "blind alleys."

But we need not look only to the past to see this process at work. It is all happening around us at this very moment, and in much the same way as I suggested it happened in ancient South Asia! Within the past few centuries the entire human species—and not just an isolated population in one region—has acquired techniques for energy acquisition, production, and utilization on a scale undreamed of by any society in our entire history.

Thus, we have a new situation of "absolute surplus," but

with the same old problems. Again, it is possible with the technology readily available, such as that of automation, for a small group of producers to provide for the food needs of a much greater population. Given full utilization of presently available technology, how many people are really needed to provide all food and other requirements of the total human population of the planet? How many for, say, *three times* the present population?

Remember: we have seen that once the *possibility* of providing for nonfood-producers occurs, the *necessity* follows hard upon it: internal population increase is quickly compounded by the demands of external groups who want to share in the productivity. And the cry goes up: Why shall we feed those who do not produce? Why not satisfy our own needs and forget about those in or out of our society who have the need but not the means? Why *should* we produce for them? What will we get in return?

Again we see that a hitherto successful social system is seemingly not equal—socially, economically, and ideologically—to the task imposed by the new condition of surplus. National sovereignty, supply-and-demand economy, the work ethic—all these and more pose seemingly insurmountable obstacles to the solution of the contradictions.

But it may be that we will surmount them nevertheless. It may be that, through the interplay of different responses already occurring in different places, successful patterns of response will eventually emerge. In that event, our planetary system of social systems will undergo structural transformations comparable to that of unstratified society to stratified society.

And it may be that no solution will appear in time, and we will collapse under the weight of the contradictions.

Let us devoutly hope, therefore, that the solution does emerge, for clearly we cannot assume that it *must*—and *will*.

Bibliography

Abū Tāleb Khān, Mirza
1814   *The Travels of Mirza Abū Tāleb Khān.* 3 vols. London: R. Watts.
Alland, Alexander, Jr.
1967   *Evolution and Human Behavior.* American Museum Science
         Books. Garden City, N.Y.: Natural History Press.
Allchin, Bridget, and Allchin, Raymond
1968   *The Birth of Indian Civilization: India and Pakistan before 500 B.C.*
         Baltimore: Penguin.
Arensberg, Conrad M.
1957   "Anthropology as History." In *Trade and Markets in the Early
         Empires: Economies in History and Theory,* edited by K. Polanyi,
         C. M. Arensberg, and H. W. Pearson, pp. 97–113. Glencoe,
         Ill.: Free Press.
Baden-Powell, Baden Henry
1908   *The Origin and Growth of Village Communities in India.* London:
         S. Sonnenschein.
Barth, Fredrik
1963   *The Role of the Entrepreneur in Social Change in Northern Norway.*
         Bergen: Norwegian Universities Press.
1967   "On the Study of Social Change." *American Anthropologist* 69:
         661–69.
Basham, A. L.
1954   *The Wonder That Was India: A Survey of the Indian Sub-continent
         before the Coming of the Muslims.* New York: Grove Press.
Bateson, Gregory
1958   *Naven.* Stanford, Calif.: Stanford University Press. (First
         printed in 1936.)
Beidelman, Thomas O.
1959   *A Comparative Analysis of the* Jajmani *System.* Monographs of
         the Association for Asian Studies, no. 8. Locust Valley,
         N.Y.: J. J. Augustin.

197

Bista, Dor Bahadur
  1976   *People of Nepal.* 3rd edition. Kathmandu: Ratna Pustak Bhandar.
Boas, Franz
  1966   "Some Problems of Methodology in the Social Sciences." In
          Race, Language and Culture by F. Boas. New York: Macmillan.
          (First printed in 1930 in *The New Social Sciences*, edited by L. D.
          White.)
Boserup, Ester
  1965   *The Conditions of Agricultural Growth: The Economics of Agrarian
          Change under Population Pressure.* Chicago: Aldine-Atherton.
Bouglé, Célestin
  1971   *Essays on the Caste System.* Translated and with an introduction
          by D. F. Pocock. Cambridge: Cambridge University Press.
          (Originally published in 1908.)
Childe, V. Gordon
  1957   *New Light on the Most Ancient East.* 4th edition. New York:
          Grove Press.
Cohn, Bernard S.
  1955   "The Changing Status of a Depressed Caste." In *Village India:
          Studies in the Little Community*, edited by McKim Marriott.
          American Anthropologist Association Memoir no. 83, pp. 53–
          77.
  1971   *India: The Social Anthropology of a Civilization.* Englewood
          Cliffs, N. J.: Prentice-Hall.
Columbia Encyclopedia, 3rd edition
  1963   S. V. "Caste." New York and London: Columbia University
          Press.
Cox, Oliver C.
  1948   *Caste, Class, and Race: A Study in Social Dynamics.* Garden City,
          N. Y.: Doubleday.
Dales, G. F.
  1965   "New Investigations of Mohenjo-Daro." *Archeology* 18.
Dandekar, V. M.
  1969   "Cow Dung Models." *Economic and Political Weekly* (Bombay)
          8/2/69, pp. 1267–71.
de Bary, William Theodore (editor)
  1958   *Sources of Indian Tradition.* New York: Columbia University
          Press.
de Gobineau, Arthur
  1967   *The Inequality of Human Races.* Translated by Adrian Collins.
          New York: H. Fertig. (Reprint of 1915 edition.)
Dubois, Abbé J. A.
  1906   *Hindu Manners, Customs and Ceremonies.* 3rd edition. Translated
          by K. K. Beauchamp. Oxford: Clarendon Press.

Dumont, Louis
1970   *Homo Hierarchicus: An Essay on the Caste System.* Translated by Mark Sainsbury. Chicago: University of Chicago Press.
Dutt, Nripendra Kumar
1931   *Origin and Growth of Caste in India,* vol I. London: Kegan Paul, Trench, & Trubner.
Encyclopaedia Britannica, 11th edition
1910   S. V. "Eclecticism." New York: Encyclopaedia Britannica.
Fairservis, Walter A., Jr.
1971   *The Roots of Ancient India: The Archaeology of Early Indian Civilization.* New York: Macmillan.
Frankfort, Henri
1961   *Ancient Egyptian Religion.* New York: Harper and Row.
Frazer, James G.
1958   *The Golden Bough: A Study in Magic and Religion.* Abridged edition. New York: Macmillan.
Freed, Stanley A.
1957   "Suggested Type Societies in Acculturation Studies." *American Anthropologist* 59: 55–68.
1963   "An Objective Method for Determining the Collective Caste Hierarchy of an Indian Village." *American Anthropologist* 65: 879–91.
Fried, Morton H.
1967   *The Evolution of Political Society: An Essay in Political Anthropology.* New York: Random House.
1968   editor, *Readings in Anthropology,* Vol II: *Cultural Anthropology.* New York: Thomas Y. Crowell.
1972   *The Study of Anthropology.* New York: Thomas Y. Crowell.
1975   *The Notion of Tribe.* Menlo Park, Calif.: Cummings.
Friedman, Jonathan
1974   "Marxism, Structuralism and Vulgar Materialism." *Man* n.s. 9,3: 444–67.
Geertz, Clifford
1973   *The Interpretation of Culture.* New York: Basic Books.
Ghurye, G. S.
1950   *Caste and Class in India.* Bombay: Popular Book Depot.
Gough, E. Kathleen
1955a   "The Social Structure of a Tanjore Village." In *India's Villages,* edited by M. N. Srinivas. Calcutta: West Bengal Development Department.
1955b   "The Social Structure of a Tanjore Village." In *Village India: Studies in the Little Community,* edited by McKim Marriott. American Anthropological Association Memoir no. 83, pp. 36–52.

1956   "Brahman Kinship in a Tamil Village." *American Anthropologist*
        58: 826–53.
1962   "Caste in a Tanjore Village." In *Aspects of Caste in South India,
        Ceylon and North-West Pakistan*, edited by E. R. Leach. Cam-
        bridge: Cambridge University Press, pp. 11–60.

Gould, Harold A.
1971   "Caste and Class: a Comparative View." *Module 11*. Addison-
        Wesley Modular Publications.

Harner, Michael J.
1970   "Population Pressure and the Social Evolution of Agricultural-
        ists." *Southwestern Journal of Anthropology* 26: 67–86.

Harris, Marvin
1959   "The Economy has no Surplus?" *American Anthropologist* 61:
        185–99.
1966   "The Cultural Ecology of India's Sacred Cattle." *Current An-
        thropology* 7,1: 51–66.
1968   *The Rise of Anthropological Theory: A History of Theories of Culture.*
        New York: Thomas Y. Crowell.
1971   "Comment" on "An Approach to the Sacred Cow of India,"
        by Alan Heston. *Current Anthropology* 12: 191–209.
1974   *Cows, Pigs, Wars, and Witches: The Riddles of Culture.* New York:
        Random House.
1975   *Culture, People, Nature: An Introduction to General Anthropology.*
        New York: Thomas Y. Crowell.

Herodotus
1954   *The Histories.* Baltimore: Penguin.

Herskovits, Melville J.
1952   *Economic Anthropology: A Study in Comparative Economics.* New
        York: Alfred A. Knopf. (Originally published in 1940 as *The
        Economic Life of Primitive Peoples.*)

Heston, Alan
1971   "An Approach to the Sacred Cow of India." *Current Anthropol-
        ogy* 12: 191–209.

Hocart, Arthur M.
1950   *Caste: A Comparative Study.* New York: Russell & Russell.

Homans, George C., and Schneider, David M.
1955   *Marriage, Authority and Final Causes: A Study of Unilateral Cross-
        Cousin Marriage.* Glencoe, Ill.: Free Press.

Horowitz, Michael M.
1971   "Comment" on "An Approach to the Sacred Cow of India,"
        by Alan Heston. *Current Anthropology* 12: 191–209.

Hutton, J. H.
1969   *Caste in India: Its Nature, Function, and Origins.* Bombay: Ox-
        ford University Press. (First printed in 1946, Cambridge Uni-
        versity Press.)

Ibbetson, Denzil C. J.
 1883   *Report on the Census of the Panjáb*. Lahore: Superintendent of the Central Gaol Press.
 1916   *Panjab Castes*. Lahore: Superintendent, Government Printing, Panjab.
Kirchhoff, Paul
 1968   "The Principles of Clanship in Human Society." In *Readings in Anthropology*, Vol. II: *Cultural Anthropology*, edited by Morton H. Fried, pp. 370–81. New York: Thomas Y. Crowell. (Originally written in 1935; first published in 1955 in *Davidson Journal of Anthropology*, University of Washington.)
Klass, Morton
 1961   *East Indians in Trinidad: A Study of Cultural Persistence*. New York: Columbia University Press.
 1966   "Marriage Rules in Bengal." *American Anthropologist* 68: 951–70.
 1978   *From Field to Factory: Community Structure and Industrialization in West Bengal*. Philadelphia: Institute for the Study of Human Issues.
Kolenda, Pauline Mahar
 1963   "Toward a Model of the Hindu Jajmani System." In special issue of *Human Organization*, vol. 22, no. 1: *Contours of Culture Change in South Asia*, pp. 11–31.
 1978   *Caste in Contemporary India: Beyond Organic Solidarity*. Menlo Park, Calif.: Benjamin/Cummings.
Kosambi, D. D.
 1969   *Ancient India: A History of its Culture and Civilization*. New York: Meridian.
Kroeber, A. L.
 1939   *Cultural and Natural Areas of Native North America*. Berkeley: University of California Press.
Lambrick, H. T.
 1967   "The Indus Flood-Plain and the 'Indus' Civilization." *Geographic Journal* 133: 483–95.
Leach, E. R.
 1962   "Introduction: What Should We Mean by Caste?" In *Caste in South India, Ceylon and North-West Pakistan*, edited by Edmund R. Leach, pp. 1–10. Cambridge: Cambridge University Press.
LeClair, Edward E., Jr., and Schneider, Harold K. (editors)
 1968   *Economic Anthropology: Readings in Theory and Analysis*. New York: Holt, Rinehart and Winston.
Lee, Richard B.
 1968   "What Hunters Do for a Living, or How to Make Out on Scarce Resources." In *Man the Hunter*, edited by R. B. Lee and I. DeVore, pp. 30–43. Chicago: Aldine.

Lévi-Strauss, Claude
1963   "The Bear and the Barber." *The Journal of the Royal Anthropological Institute of Great Britain and Ireland* 93,1: 1–11.
1969   *The Elementary Structures of Kinship.* Boston: Beacon Press. (Originally published in France in 1949 as: *Les Structures Élementaires de la Parenté.*)
Lewis, Herbert S.
1962   "Historical Problems in Ethiopia and the Horn of Africa." *Annals of the New York Academy of Sciences* 96: 504–11.
Lynch, Owen M.
1969   *The Politics of Untouchability: Social Mobility and Social Change in a City of India.* New York: Columbia University Press.
Maine, Henry Sumner
1887   *Village Communities in the East and West.* 5th edition. London: John Murray. (Originally published in 1871.)
Majumdar, D. N.
1961   *Races and Cultures of India.* New York: Asia Publishing House.
Majumdar, R. C.
1960   *The Classical Accounts of India.* Calcutta: Firma Mukhopadhyay.
Malthus, Thomas A.
1798   *An Essay on the Principle of Population.* London: J. Johnson.
Mandelbaum, David G.
1970   *Society in India.* 2 vols. Berkeley: University of California Press.
Mangelsdorf, Paul C.; MacNeish, R. S.; and Galinat, W. C.
1964   "Domestication of Corn." *Science* 143: 538–45.
Marriott, McKim
1959   "Interactional and Attributional Theories of Caste Ranking." *Man in India* 39: 92–107.
1960   *Caste Ranking and Community Structure in Five Regions of India and Pakistan.* Deccan College Monograph Series no. 25. Poona: Deccan College.
Marx, Karl
1888   *Manifesto of the Communist Party.* Chicago: Charles H. Kerr.
Mayer, Adrian C.
1970   *Caste and Kinship in Central India: A Village and its Region.* Berkeley: University of California Press.
Mencher, Joan
1971   "Comment" on "An Approach to the Sacred Cow of India," by Alan Heston. *Current Anthropology* 12: 191–209.
1974   "The Caste System Upside Down, or The Not-So-Mysterious East." *Current Anthropology* 15: 469–93.
Mitford, Jessica
1963   *The American Way of Death.* New York: Simon and Schuster.

Nag, Moni
1971   "Comment" on "An Approach to the Sacred Cow of India,"
          by Alan Heston. *Current Anthropology* 12: 191–209.
Neale, Walter C.
1957   "Reciprocity and Redistribution in the Indian Village: Sequel to
          some Notable Discussions." In *Trade and Market in the Early
          Empires: Economies in History and Theory*, edited by K. Polanyi, C.
          M. Arensberg, and H. C. Pearson, pp. 218–36. Glencoe, Ill.:
          Free Press.
Needham, Rodney
1960   *Structure and Sentiment: A Test Case in Social Anthropology*. Chi-
          cago: University of Chicago Press.
Nesfield, John C.
1885   *Brief View of the Caste System of the North-Western Provinces and
          Oudh, together with an Examination of the Names and Figures Shown
          in the Census Report, 1885*, Allahabad: North-Western Provinces
          and Oudh Press.
Odend'hal, Stewart
1972   "Gross Energetic Efficiency of Indian Cattle in their Environ-
          ment." *Journal of Human Ecology* 1: 1–27.
Oxford English Dictionary
1961   S. V. "Caste." Oxford: Oxford University Press.
Pearson, Harry W.
1957   "The Economy has no Surplus: Critique of a Theory of Devel-
          opment." In *Trade and Market in the Early Empires: Economies in
          History and Theory*, edited by K. Polanyi, C. M. Arensberg,
          and H. W. Pearson, pp. 320–41. Glencoe, Ill.: Free Press.
Piggott, Stuart
1950   *Prehistoric India to 1000 B.C.* Harmondsworth, Middlesex: Penguin.
Pitt-Rivers, Julian
1971   "On the Word 'Caste.' " In *The Translation of Culture: Essays to
          E. E. Evans-Pritchard*, edited by T. O. Beidelman, pp. 231–56.
          London: Tavistock.
Polanyi, Karl
1957   "The Economy as Instituted Process." In *Trade and Market in
          the Early Empires: Economies in History and Theory*, edited by K.
          Polanyi, C. M. Arensberg, and H. W. Pearson, pp. 243–70.
          Glencoe, Ill.: Free Press.
Polanyi, Karl; Arensberg, C. M.; and Pearson, Harry W. (editors)
1957   *Trade and Market in the Early Empires: Economies in History and
          Theory*. Glencoe, Ill.: Free Press.
Raikes, R. L.
1964   "The End of the Ancient Cities of the Indus." *American Anthro-
          pologist* 66: 284–99.

Raj, K. N.
    1971   "India's Sacred Cattle: Theories and Empirical Findings." *Economic and Political Weekly*, 3/27/71, pp. 717–22.
Richardson, William N., and Stubbs, Thomas
    1978   *Plants, Agriculture, and Human Society*. Reading, Mass.: W. A. Benjamin.
Risley, Herbert H.
    1892   *The Tribes and Castes of Bengal*. 2 vols. Calcutta: Bengal Secretariat Press.
    1908   *The People of India*. Calcutta: Thacker, Spink and Co.
Rosman, Abraham, and Rubel, Paula G.
    1971   *Feasting with Mine Enemy: Rank and Exchange among Northwest Coast Societies*. New York: Columbia University Press.
Sauer, Carl O.
    1969   *Agricultural Origins and Dispersals: The Domestication of Animals and Foodstuffs*. 2nd edition. Cambridge: M.I.T. Press.
Senart, Émile
    1930   *Caste in India: The Facts and the System*. London: Methuen. (Originally published in 1896 in France as *Les Castes dans l'Inde*.)
Service, Elman R.
    1962   *Primitive Social Organization: An Evolutionary Perspective*. New York: Random House.
    1975   *Origins of the State and Civilization: The Process of Cultural Evolution*. New York: W. W. Norton.
Slater, Gilbert
    1924   *The Dravidian Element in Indian Culture*. London: Ernest Benn.
Smith, Adam
    1793   *An Inquiry into the Nature and Causes of the Wealth of Nations*. 7th edition. London: Strahan and Cadell.
Solheim, Wilhelm G.
    1972   "An Earlier Agricultural Revolution." *Scientific American* 226: 34–41.
Sorokin, Pitirim A.
    1961   "Social Stratification." In *Theories of Society: Foundations of Modern Sociology*, Vol. I, edited by Talcott Parsons, Edward Shils, Kaspar D. Naegele, and Jesse R. Pitts, pp. 570–73. Glencoe, Ill.: Free Press.
Srinivas, M. N.
    1954   "A Caste Dispute among Washermen of Mysore." *Eastern Anthropologist* 7: 149–68.
    1955   "The Social System of a Mysore Village." In *Village India: Studies in the Little Community*, edited by McKim Marriott. American Anthropological Association Memoir no. 83, pp. 1–35.
    1959   "The Dominant Caste in Rampura." *American Anthropologist* 61: 1–16.

Steward, Julian H.
   1955   *Theory of Culture Change: The Methodology of Multilinear Evolution.* Urbana: University of Illinois Press.
Weber, Max
   1958   *The Religion of India: The Sociology of Hinduism and Buddhism.* Glencoe, Ill.: Free Press.
   1964   *The Theory of Social and Economic Organization.* Glencoe, Ill.: Free Press.
White, Leslie A.
   1973   *The Science of Culture: A Study of Man and Civilization.* New York: Farrar, Straus and Giroux. (First printed in 1949.)
Wiser, W. H.
   1936   *The Hindu Jajmani System.* Lucknow: Lucknow Publishing House.
Yalman, Nur
   1962   "The Structure of Sinhalese Kindred: A Re-examination of the Dravidian Terminology." *American Anthropologist* 64: 548–75.
Zinkin, Taya
   1962   *Caste Today.* London: Oxford University Press.

Index

206

1 2 3 4 5 6 7 8 9 10 11 12 13   89 88 87 86 85 84 83 82 81 80

a novel by
COLBY RODOWSKY

P.S.
WRITE
SOON

Franklin Watts
New York/London/1978

Library of Congress Cataloging in Publication Data

Rodowsky, Colby F
  P. S. write soon.

  SUMMARY: A physically handicapped girl uses
her letters to a pen pal as an outlet for daydreams
about her family and herself.
  [1. Physically handicapped—Fiction. 2. Pen pals
—Fiction. 3. Family life—Fiction] I. Title.
PZ7.R6185Paf   [Fic]   77–16436
ISBN 0–531–01474–6

for my husband Lawrence
and for our children
Laurie
Alice
Emily
Sarah
Gregory
and Katherine

P.S. WRITE SOON

Dear Jessie Lee,

I'm going to write fast because Courtney-the-zilch is getting home today and I want one more day on her skateboard before she gets here. Guess what—I finally learned to do a 360 and now I'm up to 4 in a row. My skateboard career is probably over because she (Courtney) is not the most generous sister in the world (and she doesn't even use it anymore) unless I can figure a way to get my own—except I'm broke.

I'm *almost* glad that school starts tomorrow, what with softball over and all. I got the picture from the championship game (with me sliding into home plate) and I would send it to you but there's only one.

Last night I went to an Oriole game with Jody. They (the Orioles) are in first place and if they win the pennant and are in the World Series I'm going to get to go because Jody's father is a real fan and has tons of tickets and says he'll give us two. I can't wait.

Write and tell me about school and your teacher and everything. I used to think sixth grade was really old. I wonder why once you get there things always feel the same? Do they for you too?

Walter's waiting so I have to go. We take turns

[1]

on the skateboard and I'm as good as he is. (Maybe better.)

love,
Tanner

p.s. write soon.

Chapter 1

It was a Saturday morning in September.

School had started again and already it seemed to Tanner that there had never been any vacation at all, as if time had just gone swooping along hooking June onto September. And the McCleans were busy being involved.

McCleans were always involved.

It was bad enough being the youngest, thought Tanner as she watched the sun splotching through the long kitchen windows. But being the youngest McClean just made it all the more awful: like being the tail of the kite, or the caboose that was never, no matter how hard it tried, going to be the engine.

Sometimes Tanner sat back and pretended to look at her family as if she'd never seen them before.

Sometimes she wished she were a Brown, or a Johnson, or better still, an only child.

Sometimes she gathered the bits and tatters of overheard conversations and tried to string them all together, then push and slide them like beads on an abacus.

It seemed as though people were always talking about the McCleans.

. . . all so bright . . . honor societies . . . good athletes . . . and leadership . . . look at the parents—Alice, an architect, and into city planning . . . and Frank, his classes at Hopkins always the first to fill up . . . the oldest boy—going into law . . . and the other boy—13 or so—just like the rest . . . amazing family . . . outstanding . . .

And then always that little tag end: the afterthought.

. . . wait a minute, isn't there another one? Ummmm, you may be right . . . let me see, a girl, I think. Oh yes, isn't she the one . . .

Tilting back on two legs of the kitchen chair Tanner tried to nudge her way back into the conversation. "Hey, who wants to go to the Oriole game? They're still in first place and we could . . ."

But Courtney-the-zilch was prattling on as usual, totally missing the point.

"But mo-ther, do you realize that makes you almost a mother-in-law? You can't be. You're not the type, I mean not like in cartoons and all."

Their mother tucked a piece of gray-brown hair

[4]

behind her ear and said, "Oh well, I really think you have to think like a mother-in-law to be that kind. Sort of like menopause, it requires thought. I don't have time."

Walter popped Oreo cookies in half and licked off the icing. When his mouth was stuffed, he said "Hey you guys, I'm going to play lacrosse."

Chocolate crumbs splattered across the table.

Tanner decided now was the time. She gave a hardly noticeable push on the underside of the table and caught the edge of the cloth as she hurtled backwards.

Crash.

For a minute she had a funny kaleidoscopic view of the kitchen turning topsy-turvy: the clock on the wall jerking sideways then back again; the ceiling dipping crazily; cups in the air; the plastic paper-napkin holder in space; yellow napkins drifting gently down; her mother's face only mildly alarmed; Walter popping another Oreo creamy; the "zilch" staring, open mouthed.

She landed in slow motion, arms out, her left leg in the clunky metal brace called Fenhagen resting on the dog's back. Sandy, the dog, looked mournfully at Tanner then moved up to lick her face. The brace clanged onto the floor. For a minute everything was silent.

"She did it on purpose, Mo-ther. She's always do-ing that: It's an attention getting device. We learned in psychology . . . Honestly, first thing you know she'll smash up her other leg. I mean you'd think . . . And she's letting that dog lick her face and his breath positively reeks . . ."

"Courtney, do be quiet. Walter, help your sister up."

"Don't need help," said Tanner as she struggled to a sitting position, draping her arms around Sandy's neck. "And I didn't do it on purpose, and I *never* smashed my leg—a car did. And your psychology teacher can take that book and . . ."

"Mary Tanner McClean, that's enough," said her mother.

"Tanner Mary. It's Tanner Mary McClean. I changed it last year when that creepy teacher wanted everyone to use their really first name and no nick-names allowed."

"I'll bet that makes you illegitimate then," said Walter reaching down to give Tanner a hand.

Alice McClean laughed, and pushed her hair back. "Illegal, maybe, but not illegitimate. I can attest to that. Clean up this mess, Tanner, and then tell us what you think about Jonathan's news."

Tanner ignored Walter's hand, then wished she hadn't. She flopped herself over on one knee and hoisted herself up, trying not to notice the bruise on her elbow that was already turning purplish-blue.

"It stinks. Jonathan getting married I mean. It stinks."

"She just says that because Jon's her favorite.

It's some kind of Oedipus thing only with brothers. Freud would say . . ."

"Freud–smeud," said Tanner.

"What's Jon want to get married for anyhow, for pete's sake," said Walter. "I'm going outside."

"Don't forget the garbage," called his mother automatically. "And it's cleaning day."

"Tell us again what Dad said that Jon said on the phone," asked Courtney. "Every word."

"I should have taped it, or taken shorthand at least," said Dr. McClean, coming into the kitchen. "By the way, did someone drop his watch? I thought I heard something."

Tanner looked up and met her father's eyes briefly, then ducked her head as she pulled a baseball cap out of her jeans pocket and jammed it down on her head.

"But why's he getting married? I mean . . ."

"Because he wants to I guess. Jon's twenty-two. Young but . . ."

"It's not Jon so much, but that girl he's marrying," said Courtney. "She's only a year older than I am and she hasn't even gone to college . . . and . . . I mean could you see me getting married?"

"Oh yech," said Tanner.

"All right, now wait a minute," said Alice Mc-Clean, pouring her husband a cup of coffee and putting the pot in the middle of the table. "I'm sure Cheryl's a very nice girl. You have to have enough

[7]

faith in Jon to know he'd marry someone we could all love."

"Well, I don't love her and nobody's named Cheryl anyway. People are named Ann and Joan or stuff like that," said Tanner.

"There is someone named Cheryl and she's on her way here with Jon and soon she'll be Cheryl McClean so . . ."

"But why's she getting married here?" asked Courtney. "Brides get married in their own home I thought."

"That's a stereotype," said their father. "Who said brides had to get married at home?"

"But that's just it," said her mother. "Cheryl doesn't have a family. She was raised by her aunt, and the aunt recently died. So Jon thought . . . married here . . . his family . . . oh dear, a wedding."

"A wedding?" Tanner spun her baseball cap around on her head, peak toward the back, and looked up. Her dark blond hair hung limp and scraggly down her back, and from her ears dangled red starfish earrings. She tugged at the brim of her cap and said, "A real wedding? Here? With flowers and a cake and me a bridesmaid? Jessie Lee was one when her sister got married and she wore a blue dress that itched—Jessie Lee, I mean, not her sister."

"Wait a minute," said her mother. "When Jon said wedding, I think he had in mind something very simple, plain—just the family at home."

"I would wear pink, I think," Tanner hurried on.

"Long and fluffy, with a big floppy hat and . . ."

"And those red starfish earrings?" asked Courtney, not unkindly.

"What's wrong with my starfish?" Tanner prickled. "They're my best earrings. Jessie Lee sent them to me last year—for Christmas—that's how come Mom let me get my ears pierced."

"Boy, Mom," Courtney looked up, "remember how I had to be in high school to get my ears pierced, and you let Tanner do it in grade school—that's almost obscene."

"It's because I'm precocious. Everybody knows that the youngest child is precocious, especially with a working mother and a career-oriented family situation."

"Mo-ther," wailed Courtney.

Alice McClean scarcely looked up from the copy of *Architect's Journal* that had come in the morning mail. "Tanner, feed the dog. And speaking of Jessie Lee, here's a letter from her—after you feed Sandy."

It always amazed Tanner that her mother heard everything that was going on, no matter how engrossed she was in something else. Even now, Tanner was pretty sure that her mother was planning Jon's wedding on some level of her mind, while totally absorbing the article on urban planning in St. Louis, Missouri. But still, Tanner thought, a pink dress, long and with ruffles.

The "zilch" started to clear the table, unloading the dishwasher and loading it again.

[9]

"Come on, Sandy," Tanner pushed her chair away from the table. As she walked across the kitchen, her brace scraped on the linoleum with a funny lisping sound. Tanner walked with an almost hop of a limp, her left leg held straight by the heavy metal brace that went from her waist to the bottom of her sturdy, built-up shoe. In the long hospital months after the accident, Tanner had named the brace Fenhagen after a particularly oozing day nurse. And in the years that followed, Fenhagen had become as much a part of her as her good leg, or her elbows or her toes.

"You want an egg today?" she asked the Golden Retriever who waited while she dumped dog chow into the bowl.

"Hey Tanner," said Courtney, wiping off the kitchen table around her mother and father and their coffee cups and newspapers and journals and morning mail. "D'you still get letters from that girl in Virginia? That pen pal?" She held the letter up to the light.

"That's Jessie Lee and you leave my letter alone." Tanner plopped the dog's bowl on the floor and lunged across the room.

"That's mine and you give it to me."

"Oh for pete's sake," said Courtney, still holding the letter. "I was only kidding. But how come you're still writing to her?"

"Because she's my friend—my best friend in the

[10]

whole world except for maybe Jody and Marikate and sometimes except for just Jody cause Marikate's so . . . yuk. And we've been writing since way back last year in the beginning of fifth grade when the creep couldn't think of anything else for us to do, and we're friends, and you put that letter down."

Tanner made a grab as Courtney waved the letter over her head. She paused for a moment then carefully brought her left leg down on her sister's foot, the metal bar on the bottom of the brace digging into Courtney's instep.

"Mo-ther! She kicked me with Fenhagen. Here, take your rotten old letter. Who'd want to read it anyway."

Mrs. McClean looked up mistily. "Uh, Frank, girls, now about this wedding. I mean we have to do something. Tell me what you think of this—just us and the grandparents and chicken salad. And after the wedding Jon and Cheryl can have those two rooms on the third floor if they want. I think that's what Jon said on the phone . . . money, you know . . . and Jon starting law school. Almost like a little apartment—even a key somewhere I think—except of course they'll have to share a bathroom with Walter." She paused to scribble a few notes on a piece of paper.

"And till after the wedding, we'll just have to put Cheryl in with Tanner."

Dear Jessie Lee,

You'll never guess what is going to happen. My brother Jon (my very favorite McClean) the one who's been away at college in Virginia and whose graduation we all went down to in May but then he stayed because he had a job for the summer—well, anyway, Jon is on his way home with his girl (only we didn't meet her in May cause she was taking care of her sick aunt) (who died), and then (in May) we didn't know she was anything special so we didn't know we were missing anything by not meeting her. But I guess she was (special, I mean) cause now Jon's bringing her home and guess what? They're getting married, and we're going to have a wedding. A HUGE WEDDING. Right here, and I'm going to be a bridesmaid. (I guess the "zilch" will be too). Jon really only asked for me, but since she (Cheryl—the girl) doesn't have any family (the aunt died), I guess they'll use Courtney. Then afterwards they (Jon and Cheryl) will live in this really neat apartment on our third floor, and Jon will go to law school. I can't wait!

School started last week and our new teacher is Mrs. Tyson. She's okay, and I guess compared to the creep last year she's terrific. Who's your teacher and do you like her?

Did I tell you that Cheryl (Jon's girl) is from Virginia too—but the mountain part not the Eastern Shore part like you are. I wonder if she'll like Baltimore?? She'd better, cause where we live is real city city. It's Saturday and I have to stop and clean my room and do other yukky stuff.

love,
Tanner

p.s. write soon.

Chapter 2

It's bad enough that Jon's bringing some dumb girl
home to marry, thought Tanner, but why does she
have to sleep in my room?

Tanner yanked the spread off the extra bed and
threw it on the floor. She shook out the clean bottom
sheet and put it on the bed, not bothering to smooth
out the mattress pad underneath.

A few lumps will be good for her. Bet she's not
a princess who'd feel a pea through twenty mattresses.
Whoever heard of a princess named Cheryl, anyway.

Tanner stood back and looked at the bed. For
a minute she had a wildly dancing vision of worms
and snails, egg shells and slimy orange peels, and that
unknown Cheryl-person reaching her toes down into
the bed. She shook those thoughts away and settled
for five rocks and three shells from the collection on

the top of her bookcase. Tanner quickly tucked them under the bottom sheet and made up the rest of the bed, carefully smoothing the spread over the top. She kicked a pile of dirty clothes under the bed and swept an empty Sprite can into the top drawer. She fed a half-eaten doughnut to the dog.

"There," she said, sitting down on the window seat. "It's clean."

Tanner had a lot of serious thinking to do. She could feel a "think" coming on the way other people could feel a headache or a sore throat. But first, everything had to be just right.

"Stay here, Sandy, and I'll be right back." Tanner went down the long second floor hall, through the den at the back, out through the upstairs backporch that was mostly filled with extra coathangers and stacks of newspapers, and carefully worked her way down the steep backstairs. Ever since her accident Tanner knew that her parents had been very conscious of never saying "be careful," "watch out," "don't do that." But she also knew that her mother held her breath everytime Tanner started down the backsteps, because of Fenhagen, and the funny metal treads on the edge of each step. Tanner used the backstairs a lot.

Down in the kitchen she put together a peanut butter and banana sandwich and a glass of chocolate milk. She put it on a tray and gathered up a hunk of bologna and three biscuits for Sandy and an extra banana for herself. Slowly, carefully, she managed to

[15]

work her way up the stairs and to her room without seeing anyone. After all, it was cleaning day and there was no point in letting anyone know she had finished her room already.

Settling back on the window seat, she bit into her sandwich and listened to the distant sound of the vacuum cleaner. One of the things Tanner really liked about the McCleans' house was that vacuum cleaners and her older sister and brothers could be distant.

Everything about the house seemed tall and narrow. Ceilings that reached up, up, up, and windows that reached up with them. Long halls that stretched from front to back on all three floors. Funny jumbly storerooms at the back of the third floor, the two rooms that had been Jon's at the front (soon to be Jon's and Cheryl's), with Walter's room and a bathroom with a claw-footed tub wedged in between. There was a skylight in the hall and one of the things Tanner liked best was to sit at the bottom of the steps and listen to the rain.

Guess I'm a real city mouse, thought Tanner, looking out at the backs of the houses across the alley. Tanner went to school in the suburbs with pine trees and elms and onion grass in the spring. She went to visit friends in look-alike developments with new sprouty trees and power mowers. But she was always glad to get home.

I wonder what she'll think of our house, this she-Cheryl, thought Tanner. Bet she'll hate it, it and

[16]

all the other houses on the block, and the white marble steps, and the halfway park in the middle of the street—and—and our backyard all made of bricks with bushes in wooden tubs, and the cellar that's just a cellar with mice and pipes that clang. And Amber the cat. I know she'll hate Amber and Amber's kittens when she has them. She's probably the kind who's allergic, and she'll get all itchy and say "take that cat away."

Tanner felt the anger choking inside of her. "She'll hate everything, Sandy," she said, throwing her arms around the dog's neck. "She'll hate everything . . . and Baltimore . . . and living in the city . . . and we'll hate her . . . and then Jon'll hate us . . . and . . . and . . ."

Tanner burst into tears. For a minute she cried into Sandy's coat, then she pushed the big dog away and wiped her eyes with the backs of her hands. Tanner pushed herself up off the window seat and grabbed the banana peel. Stumping across the room she pulled back the bottom of the covers and shoved the banana peel in between the clean white sheets.

Then she stood back. "Okay Cheryl, smeryl. Come ahead. We're ready for you, right Sandy?"

Jon and Cheryl didn't come on Saturday, or on Sunday, or even on Monday.

Tanner didn't want them to come, ever, but she spent most of her free time at the tall front win-

[17]

dows peering around the inside shutters and pretending to read.

The rest of the family seemed to go on much as usual.

"Jon said expect them when we see them."

"Have to settle things in Virginia."

"Mo-ther, Tanner's room smells funny. Are you sure she cleaned it?"

"Maybe tomorrow . . . ?"

Tanner was in the cellar that was just a cellar, looking for Amber who was looking for a place to have her kittens. It was after dinner and the rest of the family was lingering over coffee and end of the day conversation.

Suddenly Tanner heard a difference: doors slammed; the sound of laughter; chairs scraping overhead; Sandy's bark; the rumble of her father's voice; another voice—Jon's.

Starting up the cellar steps Tanner stopped and spit on her fingers. She rubbed cobwebs off her nose and straightened her baseball cap. Hanging onto the railing to keep her leg from shaking, she pushed her way up, one step at a time.

The door at the top of the steps was open.

"Didn't want any fuss . . . a little overwhelming for Cheryl . . . married Sunday in Harrisonberg . . ."

Tanner came up into the kitchen. All at once her eyes took in the girl across the room: the thin pale girl in the wrinkled cotton dress and the ankle strap sandals; the girl with the frightened face and the fingers that twisted and knotted their way around the handle of her white plastic handbag.

Jon swung around and let out a yell. Wonderful, sunburned, laughing Jon.

"Tanner, baby, come here and meet my wife."

Dear Jessie Lee,

We had the *most beautiful* wedding in the whole world. (Well, I guess your sister's wedding was just as pretty.) I wore a pink dress that was long—down to the floor and white shoes and a pink hat that was all floppy just like something out of "Gone With The Wind," and carried a basket of really pretty roses. The "zilch" wore blue with a blue hat and carried white drippy kind of flowers. And Cheryl wore a beau–ti–ful white dress that was her great, great somebody's wedding dress and she looked just like a princess. Jon was so handsome. My father gave the bride away (because she doesn't have one—father, I mean), and Walter took my mother down the aisle and sat with her except that his jacket was too small and his wrists stuck out.

The wedding was at a church around the corner called Corpus Christi, and the aisle was about a mile long, and I had to go first, and I was so scared, but I just sort of glided all the way down, and Cheryl said I was the most graceful one there.

And afterwards there was champagne and little sandwiches and mints and a cake about ten feet tall with a bride and groom on top. And then Jon and

Cheryl left to go on their honeymoon but nobody knows where. It was so exciting I could burst, and I still get goose prickles when I think about it.

There isn't much of anything else to say cause the wedding took up most of our time. Your this year's teacher sounds neat, especially being a man and all. Wish we had one, but Mrs. Tyson's okay (and we don't even have boy students).

Amber is still looking for a place to have her kittens. Courtney fixed up a box on the upstairs back-porch, but I think that's only so she won't have them in her room. I hope she has them soon—and a lot. I wonder if Cheryl will have a baby soon?

love,
Tanner the bridesmaid

p.s. write soon.

Chapter 3

"Thank God for the crock pot," said Alice McClean, giving it an affectionate pat as she came into the kitchen.

"Hi girls. Walter not home yet? How's the math going Tanner? Better?"

"Ummm. What's for dinner?" said Tanner, pushing aside the math book.

"Spanish chicken," her mother said vaguely as she flipped through the mail—sorting, opening, discarding with one quick motion. "Where's your father?"

"In the den," said Courtney. "He came in all scowling and muttering about freshman students and non-English majors and positively never again."

Her mother laughed and picked up a package from the table. "Oh, he says that every year, and by the end of the term he swears he'll never limit himself to English majors, makes a point of asking for a freshman class. It just takes a while for your father and the freshmen to stop feeling tentative with each other. Court, run tell him I'm on my way in with a drink."

A door slammed far in the front of the house, and Walter came into the kitchen dropping soccer equipment along the way.

"Hi everybody. I'm starved."

"Dinner'll be a while yet," his mother answered. "I need a chance to unwind and talk to your father. Get yourself a glass of milk. Courtney, how about setting the table?" Mrs. McClean looked down at the package she seemed to have forgotten in her hand. She shook it and turned it over.

"A package from Hutzlers. Now what could . . . oh, this isn't for me. It's for Jon and Cheryl. Must be a wedding present."

"Do you get wedding presents when you elope?" asked Courtney.

"Ummm, some, I guess."

Walter dropped the lid back on the crock pot. "Hey, there's olives in that chicken."

"You'll love it," said his mother, putting ice into glasses and a wedge of cheese and some rice crackers on a tray. "Hey Tanner, run this package up to Cheryl will you please. Oh, and here's the key to those rooms on the third floor. I found it last night, and you may as well give it to her. And tell her we're in the den if she wants to join us. This is Jon's night at school, I think."

Tanner started through the shadowy back hall. The sounds from the kitchen were warm and jumbled, and for a moment she stood alone. She shivered, then punched the light switch. The hall was flooded with light: shadows and bugaboos pushed back into corners. The enormous coatrack on the wall dripped with coats and jackets, funny wool hats and broken umbrellas. An empty binocular case dangled from one hook. Passing into the front hall Tanner could still hear her mother talking to Walter and Courtney.

"The luncheon speaker was excellent, urban planning commission, usually deadly dull. He was all into 'scatter site housing.' What I've said for years . . . to get away from those vertical ghettoes . . . imaginative planning . . . housing modules . . ."

Everything's so perfectly horribly normal, thought Tanner as she shoved the package under her arm and started up the stairs. Mom just goes right on with her "Urban Sprawl," and Dad with his freshmen, and Walter has his soccer and the "zilch" does whatever is zilchiest. They don't even care that that girl's upstairs and that Jon married her and . . . and . . .

Tanner swung along the upstairs hall, the bottom of Fenhagen whispering against the carpet. She turned onto the steep third floor steps and took a tighter grip on the package.

It's as though, Tanner stopped for a minute and

looked up at the dark skylight, it's as though, oh, when you dig a hole with your finger in the wet sand and it all fills up with water and you can't even see the hole anymore and it's back to being part of the beach again. As if Cheryl were the hole and now she's part of our family. AND SHE'S NOT.

Tanner reached the last three steps where they right-angled sharply. She banged the side of Fenhagen against the riser as if to punctuate her thoughts and lost her balance. She gave the package a shove over the top step and caught the spindles to keep from falling. Twisting slightly, she managed to sit down with a thud on the second step from the top.

"My goodness, Tanner. Are you all right?"

Tanner looked up at Cheryl's pale, slightly mottled face looking over the bannister.

"I always come up the steps this way, it's better than knocking," said Tanner, blinking back tears of surprise and anger.

"Can I help you up?" Cheryl asked hesitantly.

"Help? Help? I don't need help, ever, never, whatever it is. My mother just asked me to *run* this package upstairs, and you ask me if I need help. There's your dumb old package anyway."

Tanner watched Cheryl as she ducked down to pick up the box, then saw her jump back quickly. She looks as though she's afraid somebody'll come along and grab it away from her. Bet she's even afraid of the dark and water bugs, too, thought Tanner as she got up off the step.

[25]

"I'm not afraid of anything," Tanner announced, climbing the last two steps to the third floor.

"Oh, uh, well, that's nice. I mean, well, thank you for bringing up the package. I mean . . . all those steps. You didn't, well, what I mean is . . . it must be hard for you coming up here. You didn't have to."

"I always come up here," shouted Tanner. "I come up here any time I want to. I come up here to poke around in the storerooms and to see Walter and to go to the bathroom, and I used to come up here to see Jon. And Sandy comes up here too and maybe Amber'll even decide to have her kittens up here. And it's not a little bit hard. Nothing's hard for me and Fenhagen. We can do anything we want—run or jump or anything!"

Cheryl took another step back. "But Tanner, I didn't mean . . . well, what I mean is . . . well, what's wrong with saying something's hard if it is. I mean, what's the big deal?"

"Deal, smeal," Tanner spat back.

Cheryl took another step back. "Well, uh, that's nice. Look Tanner, now that you're here why don't you come in . . . and sit down or, or, whatever you want. I've been unpacking the boxes I brought with me."

Tanner stepped over the threshold and into Jon's room. She caught her breath and sat down quickly on the studio couch. Even after her brother had left for college, even after four years and this summer thrown in for good measure, the room had always stayed Jon's. It was the large front room on the third floor with a row of windows across the front and a fireplace on the outside wall and a safe no one ever opened tucked away in the corner. The room still had its faded green wallpaper, water-stained; and funny crooked bookcases that oozed and bulged with books and old school notebooks and soccer shoes. The same scruffy tan rug was on the floor—ink-stained, paint-stained, shoe-polish-stained. Almost a whole life marked out by blots on the floor, thought Tanner, rubbing her foot over a burn mark on the rug and remembering her father's anger when he found Walter and her sneaking smokes on the third floor when Jon was away.

It was Jon's room, but it wasn't.

It was like a chocolate ice cream cone that someone had sprinkled sparkles all over. Red, green, pink, and silver sparkles. Cheryl's sparkles.

"W-well what do . . ." Cheryl hesitated then sat down on a lumpy armchair across the room.

"We want to really fix it up when we can, and the bedroom too," she nodded her head at the next room. "But anyway, I thought I'd brighten it up by putting some of my things around." Cheryl kept pushing the words out like an ant with a crumb. She cracked her knuckles and twisted a piece of thin blond hair. "What do you think?"

Tanner looked around wildly. She felt as though she were in a honky tonk shop at the end of the boardwalk in Ocean City. As though she would any minute smell french fries and candy apples, and hear the music of the merry-go-round. A row of little girls made of shells and red net marched across the top of Jon's bookcase. Cheryl had put her trunk in front of the studio couch, a pink ruffled doily turning it into a coffee table. On the center of the doily rested a shiny brown cedar box with "Greetings from Virginia Beach" burned into the lid. A nest of green glass ashtrays with fluted edges sat next to it.

On a small gilt shelf hung over the couch stood a herd of plastic-look-like-glass animals and a china ballerina poised on a pin cushion.

"Well," said Cheryl, going over to an open cardboard box on the floor. "Well, what do you think? I mean, maybe we can paint the walls. Your mother said we could. It would be okay, but this is a start. Sort of makes it more homey, don't you think?"

Tanner watched the girl kneeling by the box, carefully unwrapping a china plate with a picture of Queen Elizabeth on the front. Words tangled themselves inside of her.

"We don't go in much for doodads. Least our clutter's important," she said, looking up at the ceiling. "How come you're not sunburned? We all get dark. Don't you even know how to swim?"

Cheryl put the plate carefully on the floor then reached back in the box. "I can swim some, but not much. When I go in the sun I turn pink and spotty.

Anyway, with my job I was inside most of the time."

"What job?" asked Tanner, all the while trying to fit this unsunburned nonswimmer into Jon's life. Jon who loved every sport in the world and who got so dark in summer he was tan almost until Thanksgiving. "What kind of job?"

"I was a waitress at the Dinner Bell. That's where I met Jon," said Cheryl, polishing a plate on the hem of her skirt.

"While you went to college?"

"No, with Aunt May so sick by that time . . . well, I figured she'd need me at home. So after I finished high school, I went to work at the Dinner Bell, part-time. Jon was washing dishes there. Now tell me about you. What grade you're in and who your friends are, and what you do, and oh, everything."

Tanner breathed in deeply. "Well, I'm . . . didn't Jon tell you about me? I bet he told you a lot of stuff."

"Sure he did. He told me a whole lot, but I want to hear it from you."

"Well, yeah, I'm just me, and in the sixth grade, and even . . . even . . . well, you know," Tanner put her hand down on her left leg uncertainly. "Even with the hospital and all I didn't have to repeat cause everybody tutored me, specially Jon when he got home . . . and Mom and Daddy . . . and Walter sort of, and even the 'zilch'."

"Why do you call her the 'zilch'?"

[29]

"Cause she is. Like nothing. And I'm not afraid of anything in the world, and I have tons of friends, mostly Jody and Marikate and Jessie Lee."

"Do they live near you? In Bolton Hill?" asked Cheryl.

"Nope. Jody lives in Guilford, and Marikate lives in a development in the county. I think you have to be really discriminating to live in the city, don't you?" Tanner flopped back on a pine-scented satin cushion and hurried on.

"Jody's neat. And Marikate's okay, but sometimes she's so cute she makes you want to puke."

"Huh?" said Cheryl.

"You know, puke, vomit, barf. You'd love her."

"Well," Cheryl hesitated, not sure whether to go on. "Well, who's Jessie Lee?"

"She's my best friend. We're pen pals, and we tell each other everything. *Absolutely everything.*"

Tanner leaned forward suddenly, tracing the letters on the top of the brown cedar box with her fingers.

"Is this all you have? This stuff?"

"Oh no," said Cheryl, balancing a plate on top of her sewing machine. "I have a whole house in Virginia. A little house. What you'd call a bungalow, I guess, but it's mine. My aunt willed it to me. I rented it out for a year. Jon helped me and all, till we can decide what we want to do, whether we want to go back and settle down there."

Tanner stood up as quickly as she could. "Down

there? Down there? What for? Jon would never go there to live. Never. Never. Never."

"Well, we might," said Cheryl, looking startled. "We just haven't made up our minds. But meanwhile, the house is rented for a year so we have nothing to worry about. And that's why I brought my pretty things with me. So I'd have a bit of home."

"They're not pretty. They're cheap and tacky and ugly, and I hate them, and I bet Jon hates them too, and . . . and . . ."

Tanner headed for the door. "And I can climb these steps whenever I want to. So there."

As she got to the door Tanner stopped, remembering the key her mother had given her for Cheryl. She dragged the key out of her pocket and dropped it on the rug, right on the green ink stain.

"There. My mother sent that to you. You might want to lock up your precious heirlooms."

Tanner saw Cheryl's face go from white to red to pink, then back to white.

"Oh no," she said. "We won't need that. You don't need keys with family around."

Dear Jessie Lee,

The honeymooners are back. Where they went was New York City. I think that's really neat, and they brought me this really terrific book from the Hayden Planetarium which is where I'm really dying to go. The planetarium, I mean. I've been to New York when I was little and saw the Bronx zoo and Chinatown and all that. Jon and Cheryl said that next time they go, they'll take me and then we'll go everywhere and see everything.

We have a planetarium here now—down by the harbor where everything's all new and rebuilt. It's one of my favorite places to go, but I still want to see the one in New York. (Planetarium, not harbor—I've seen that).

Anyway, you wouldn't believe how Jon and Cheryl have fixed up their apartment on the third floor—painted it and everything—all blue and white like you see in Williamsburg. And Cheryl has her antiques sitting out—real heirlooms—old and all—a slipper made of blue glass that's old as anything and candlesticks, and a lamp that used to be oil but is now electric. They have been in her family for ages and ages. And GUESS WHAT? She owns this really big house in Virginia that belonged to her aunt. Cheryl showed me pictures of it—like some kind of plantation or something and a winding driveway and everything. But of course now it's rented cause they're here forever and ever.

Your letter about the girl scout trip was funny, but I guess all that rain wasn't (funny) especially with you all in sleeping bags. My father says we're going camping some summer—and mountain-climbing too.

I have to go now and do my homework. After school Courtney picked me up, and then we went to Walter's soccer game and then took three of his friends home. Interesting observation: 13-year-old boys smell. Courtney had the windows down all the way. Another interesting observation: sometimes the "zilch" isn't bad. (She even got us ice cream at 31 Flavors).

love,

Tanner

p.s. Amber hasn't had her kittens YET.
p.p.s. write soon.
p.p.s.s. And guess what! Jody's father did get us tickets for the World Series. My mother said "no" because of school but she just *has* to change her mind. For somebody who's sort of smart (my mother) she doesn't know *anything* about sports.

Chapter 4

Tanner plucked a Kleenex out of the box and held it up to her mouth as she lay back on the flattened pillow. She let her left arm dangle over the side of the bed, and tried to make herself look pale and wan.

She heard someone coming down the hall and quickly shut her eyes, managing a slight flutter of the lashes as her mother came into the room. She gasped faintly.

"How are you feeling, Tanner?"

"Oooo, a little better I guess," said Tanner, peeking out of half-closed eyes. "But Mom, I think I really ought to have the yellow basin, the one for throwing up in, you know, in case . . . and my stomach . . ." She let her hand hover in the air then settle lightly on her middle.

"Oh, I think you're better now, probably just the twenty-four-hour virus. The worst is over."

"I don't know. My stomach's doing flip flops, and what if I get sick again? Last night . . . almost didn't make it to the bathroom, dropped the crutches, and then . . ."

Alice McClean put her cool hand on her daughter's forehead. "I wish you'd called me. I could have done something, held your head or kept you company, or something."

"It was all right," said Tanner weakly. "Didn't want to disturb you." She turned her head away trying to keep the edges of her mouth from twitching into a smile. "But the basin . . . if you could . . . and something to drink . . ."

"Okay, I'll go rummage up the yellow throw-up bucket, and bring you a little ginger ale."

Tanner's head popped up. "Maybe a chocolate milk shake."

Her mother swung around and looked at her. "A milk shake? Heavens no. Not on an upset stomach. Just ginger ale."

Dropping her head back quickly, Tanner sighed. "Yes, you're right, a little ginger ale." Her stomach made hungry growling noises.

As soon as she heard her mother going down the steps, Tanner hoisted herself over to the edge of the bed and pulled open the drawer on the night table. Shoved all the way to the back was her diary, and out from between October 6th and 7th, she took the ticket.

The beautiful, shiny, crispy ticket for today's game of the World Series.

Tanner flopped back, holding the ticket overhead. THE BALTIMORE ORIOLES vs. THE ATLANTA BRAVES. Then she rubbed it gently against her cheek and tucked it under her pillow.

Every bit of Tanner wanted to get up and dressed and go out to the stadium where she was supposed to meet Jody. Jody, who had given her the ticket, and who didn't have to gasp and gag and pretend to be deathly ill. Jody, whose parents never said "no excuse for missing school. Baseball games only on weekends." As if it were any old everyday kind of ball game instead of the *World Series.*

Her stomach growled again, and she smelled bacon cooking downstairs. She thought of eggs and orange juice and raisin toast and then of the nasty, pallid ginger ale her mother had promised to bring.

Listening carefully, Tanner swung herself out of bed and onto her crutches and across the room. She found her baseball cap and put it on, then hurried back to bed. She hooked the cap onto the bedpost and settled herself limply under the covers. It would never do for her mother to see her moving around: Alice McClean had been known to bundle a child off to school at noon if she looked at all healthy. McCleans weren't sick very often.

"Here Tanner, here's the ginger ale. Just take little sips, and drink it slowly." Her mother put the glass on the table and the basin on the floor next to the bed.

Tanner moaned softly.

"Oh dear," said her mother, settling onto the foot of the bed. "Do you feel that awful? You are a little peaked. Maybe I shouldn't leave you in the house all alone, but I have a meeting at twelve thirty . . . let's see, if I called the office and . . ."

Tanner propped herself up on one elbow and tried to keep just the right amount of quiver in her voice. "Feel a little better . . . if I just drink the ginger ale I'm sure I'll be okay."

It's like walking on a tightrope, she thought picking up the glass. If I'm too well, I'll land in school and if I'm too sick, Mom'll stay home with me.

"Try and sleep now, Tanner. I'm going down for another cup of coffee. See you later."

Tanner heard Courtney leave for school, yelling back something about a hockey game and being home late. She heard Walter thumping up and down the steps, looking for his math book and saying what Mr. Gibbs would do to him if he were late. Doors slammed. Cars started. She knew her father and Jon had left.

She thought of the ticket underneath the pillow and of the buses she would have to take to get to the stadium and of Jody waiting for her at the west

[37]

side gate. She tried to finish a book and read the last chapter over twice. Still the thoughts jiggled around inside her head. She planned what she would do if anybody got home before she did—out for a little air . . . feeling better. She thought about how for once she was really glad her mother was so "out of" sports that she didn't even remember about the game. The tiny itch of guilt at having deceived her parents was quickly eased by the thoughts of the game: the wonderful fourth game of the Series with the Orioles already ahead by three. This could very well be *it*. And she, Tanner, was going to be there.

She read the last chapter of her book a third time and watched the clock and twitched her good leg underneath the covers. She waited for her mother to leave.

Finally, Alice McClean came into the room carrying another glass of ice and a bottle of ginger ale. "You do look better, Tanner. Think you'll be all right this afternoon? I cancelled everything this morning but have to make that meeting . . . if you're sure you'll be okay."

"Mo-ther, I'm not a baby, and I feel lots better." Tanner worked for just the right tone of voice: better, but not quite well. Weak, but not too sick. "Maybe if I eat something . . ."

"You stay right in that bed. Give your stomach a rest. Maybe a little soup for supper."

"But I have to go down and see Amber and the kitten. Make sure they're all right."

"Don't be silly, Tanner. Amber's fine and taking good care of the kitten." Her mother poured the ginger ale and folded Tanner's robe across the foot of the bed. Then she went over and adjusted the venetian blind, almost as if she were dragging her feet, as if she were not quite ready to go.

Tanner watched her mother as she puttered around the room: thin almost to the point of being lanky, with her hair brushed back away from her face and great huge glasses that gave her a rather questioning look. Her mother dressed casually, mostly in skirts and blouses and loafers and enormous, bulging shoulder bags. What Tanner liked about it was that it was the kind of casual that said "This is the way I am. Take it or leave it."

But today Tanner didn't care how her mother looked. She just wanted her to leave. Hurry up, hurry up, hurry up raced inside her head.

Pushing herself up into a sitting position, she looked at the clock. "Hey, Mom, you're going to be late. Thought you had a meeting."

Alice McClean folded the robe one more time. "You're right, I have to run. If you're sure you're all right. I won't call you. Don't want to make you come to the phone, but you know the office number."

She kissed her daughter on the cheek and was gone. And Tanner lay still for a few minutes and savored the perfect silence of the house.

Struggling up as quickly as she could, Tanner

scooted across the room on her crutches and dragged Fenhagen over to the side of the bed. Then she went back to the dresser and rooted around for pants and a shirt.

She was suddenly aware of a presence.

A silent, staring, watching someone.

Cheryl.

"What are you doing in this house?" asked Tanner, swinging around and dropping a crutch. She caught herself on the edge of the bureau and glowered at Cheryl. Cheryl, who was so unimportant that Tanner hadn't even thought of her when she was planning her day. Cheryl, who shouldn't be here—married to Jon and living on the third floor and who had appeared at the door of Tanner's room. Cheryl, who had moved across the room and was smoothing the sheets and getting dangerously close to the pillow where the ticket was hidden.

"Don't do that," screeched Tanner, balancing herself and bending to retrieve the other crutch. "Get away and leave it. I like it lumpy. Like it the way it is. What are you doing here?"

"I, uh . . . well . . . uh . . ." Cheryl jumped back. "I met your mother outside. She was sort of worried leaving you here alone. Said I'd stay with you. Finished my business this morning and I'll be here all afternoon. Now get into bed."

"You can't," wailed Tanner.

"I don't mind a bit," said Cheryl, closing the

[40]

bureau drawers and picking up the clothes that Tanner had dropped on the floor.

"Nursed my Aunt May for ages. Now come along. Into bed."

"Don't touch that bed," said Tanner. "And I don't need a nurse for pete's sake. Just because I threw up, people throw up all the time. I might do it again if you don't leave me alone."

Cheryl stood by the bed holding the top sheet pulled back. "Come on now." And Tanner noticed a new sureness in her voice, as if this were a different Cheryl, not the usual sniveling pink-spotted girl with the sweaty palms. Hmmph, thought Tanner as she stumped across the room and got into bed, who's she think she is—super nurse or something?

Tanner touched the ticket under her pillow and looked at the clock. Cheryl pulled a chair up to the side of the bed and sat down. Tanner closed her eyes, but she could still feel someone sitting there. Sitting, breathing, waiting, staring.

It's like being in the hospital again, thought Tanner, with yukky old Miss Fenhagen there. And for a minute she was back in the second grade, back in the year of the accident and the long months in Wyman's Hospital. Back to the days of the slow awareness that her left leg was useless, atrophying and was in fact paralyzed; to the endless stream of doctors, nurses, and therapists. To the family in typical McClean fashion, getting her through the second grade—scooping her up by the corners, as it were, and hurrying her along with them.

"Aren't you going to say anything?" asked Tanner, opening her eyes. "You just going to sit there like a blob?"

The hands of the clock inched around.

"Well," said Cheryl, "I'll tell you about my business this morning. I got a job starting tomorrow."

"What kind of job?" asked Tanner, in spite of herself.

"In the drugstore over on Park Avenue. Savage's I think it's called, a real neighborhood store. It reminds me a lot of back home."

Doc Savage's drugstore was one of Tanner's favorite places. The kind of place she thought of as "hers." The store was small and cluttered with Kleenex boxes and hairspray cans making pyramids in the aisles. It had a warm licorice smell, and a soda fountain with real milk shakes that ran all smooth and chocolatey and didn't cave your cheeks in when you tried to drink them with a straw. Doc Savage was little with white bushy hair. He called everybody by name, and Tanner loved him dearly.

Now old Cheryl's going to push her way in there too, thought Tanner, crunching loudly on the ice and slamming the glass down on the table.

She glared at the clock. By now she should be on the bus on her way to meet Jody, and instead she was trapped with a watchdog of a Cheryl sitting beside her.

"Why don't you go out?" she asked.

"Don't have any place to go," said Cheryl. "And besides . . ."

"You could go to the library, or don't you read books? Or to the museum, or the planetarium," said Tanner, jamming the baseball cap down on her head.

"Oh no, heavens no, I'm just fine. I want to stay here with you."

"Well then, I'm hungry." Tanner kicked at the covers with her good leg.

The hands of the clock had inched further along. By now Jody would be waiting—looking out over the crowd and waiting. Tanner touched the ticket and kicked the covers again.

"I'm hungry."

"Okay," said Cheryl, getting up and moving Fenhagen from the side of the bed back to the corner. Tanner's face burned, and she slid down lower in the bed, as if by touching the brace Cheryl had seen into her very innards.

"More ginger ale? Or how about some chicken bouillon?"

"Yech—it'll make me throw up. I want a bologna sandwich with mustard and pickles and chopped onions and a banana and cookies and a coke in a yellow glass." And all the while she was saying it, Tanner felt the means and uglies sticking out all over her like a huge porcupine.

"Chicken bouillon," said Cheryl firmly. She turned as she got to the door. "Oh, and Tanner, while I'm downstairs I'll peek in at Amber and the kitten. It's so cute—uh—if you don't have a home well, I mean I'd just love to have it—when it's big enough. I mean I just love cats."

"My kitten? You want my very only one special kitten that Amber had? I have thousands of people who want that kitten. There's Jody and Marikate and Doc Savage and . . ."

"Oh well, never mind. I just thought, kittens are sometimes hard to get rid of and all, but never mind. I'll get the soup."

Tanner folded her arms across her chest and closed her eyes. She heard the gentle whir of the clock on the bedside table and could almost feel the ticket, as if it burned like a red hot coal through her pillow.

She felt Cheryl put the tray on her lap but kept her eyes tight shut until she heard her sister-in-law move across the room.

When she opened her eyes she looked down on a lonely bowl of chicken bouillon and a spoon and one white paper napkin.

The clock said one o'clock.

In the inside reaches of her mind Tanner heard the umpire yell "Play Ball."

Cheryl hurried out into the hall to answer the phone.

Tanner took one of the crutches leaning against the table and poked the yellow basin out from under the bed. She upended the bowl of soup into the basin then set the empty bowl carefully on the tray.

"Hey Cheryl, come quick! I just threw up. I told you I would and I did. Oooo, I'm sick."

Dear Jessie Lee,

Boy, do you know what? Amber only had one kitten after all that. One. O-N-E. Can you imagine—an only child cat? But it's (the kitten) really cute, all amber colored like Amber. I don't know what I'll name it, but I thought maybe pumpkin (with a small p) in honor of Halloween, except that's a while yet. I bet my mother'll let me keep it, especially since there's only one. I hope.

Guess what else. My mother made me stay home from school the other day and take care of Cheryl because she was sick. And you know how my mother is about school. I had to take her (Cheryl) cokes and ginger ale and fix her soup. I spent all day running up and down the stairs. My mother said virus but it's my own considered opinion that she's pregnant and had morning sickness only she had it all day and she doesn't have it anymore. Do you think that's how it works with morning sickness? I'll have to observe carefully cause that would make me an aunt.

And I did go to the World Series. With Jody and sat in a box and saw the Orioles win the Series—four straight games. It was really terrific.

Write and tell me what you're doing for Hal-

loween. I think I'll be a gypsy unless I'm a hobo. Your
sister Sally sounds a lot like the "zilch."

love,
Tanner

p.s. write soon.
p.s. jr. I'm not sure how Sandy'll like the kitten. Whenever he goes to look, Amber just sort of prickles all over.
I feel that way, too, sometimes but cats can prickle better than people. Maybe if we had tails.
love,
me

Chapter 5

"And the Constellation, can we go to the Constellation and the planetarium? Can we have lunch—a hot dog from one of those little carts and . . ."

"Wait a minute, Tanner. I do have to work a little bit tomorrow, you know," said her mother.

"Boy, does she have another holiday tomorrow? Wow, wish we got all those days off," said Walter, lying on the floor copying football statistics from the newspaper into a marble-back copybook.

"Oh it works out," said his mother. "You all seem to get the same number of holidays. It's just that they're on different days."

"Yeah, smarty," said Tanner to her brother, "and tomorrow I get to spend the whole day with Mom at work and you have to go to dumb old school."

"So what," said Walter, chewing the end of his pencil. "Besides, Mom doesn't work at the Constellation anyway."

"But we're going there and to the planetarium and . . ."

"Slow down, Tanner. Maybe not the Constellation, you've been there plenty of times, and in the morning I have to run a set of blueprints over to Liz's and then I have a surprise for you."

"What kind of a surprise and how come you have to go to Liz's and are you going to talk for ages and ages?"

"No, not ages," her mother smiled. "But then instead of a hot dog from a cart, I thought we'd eat lunch at the restaurant in the inner harbor—then maybe the planetarium, if there's time."

Tanner looked up from brushing Sandy. "What restaurant?" she asked. "Do they have chili dogs?"

"It's an old ferry boat that's tied up down in the inner harbor and has been turned into a restaurant. Now go take a bath and wash that hair if you're going out with me tomorrow."

"Hey, if she gets to do all that on her holiday, I get to do something next time I get one too, something decent I mean, not a dumb old floating restaurant, but something like McDonald's and . . ."

"Okay Walter, I don't exactly think you're underprivileged," laughed his mother. "Now how about the homework?"

The next morning Tanner was up and dressed before seven o'clock. She put on her tan corduroys, a red and green plaid shirt, and her baseball cap. Tying a brown and white ski sweater around her waist, she stepped back and looked at herself in the mirror. She pinched her cheeks and examined herself backwards and forward. Going back to the dresser, she added her red starfish earrings and a squirt out of the Eau de London bottle she had salvaged from Courtney's trash can.

"There," said Tanner, "that's better." And she went downstairs to make French toast, feed Sandy, check on Amber and pumpkin, read the paper, watch cartoons, and wait for her mother.

As Mrs. McClean maneuvered her yellow Volkswagen through downtown Baltimore, Tanner peered out the window. "Hey, there's the Shot Tower," she called.

"Umm," said her mother. "I hope I don't get lost. I never remember which streets are one way going which way."

"Where's Liz live and how come we're going to her house instead of her being in the office?"

"Because she had her gall bladder out. Anyway I thought you'd like to see Stirling Street where she lives. Liz is an urban homesteader."

"A what?" asked Tanner as her mother slowed to read a street sign.

[50]

"I think it's up here past Old Town Mall. An urban homesteader is someone who bought a house from the city for a dollar and . . ."

"A dollar? A whole house for a dollar? Wow, why didn't we get one?"

"It's part of a renewal project, sort of an antidote to urban blight. The city sells certain houses for a dollar to people who agree to fix them up within a certain period of time and to live in them for a while. It sort of goes back to the Homestead Act of 1862 where the government gave land to anyone who'd live on it for five years."

"Hey, that's neat. Are they dumpy?"

"Well, pretty dumpy to start with," said her mother, turning left onto Monument Street. "And it takes a lot more than a dollar to do the work. Everything has to be done according to code, but the results are pretty terrific. See for yourself."

Her mother pulled up in front of a gray-green formstone church. "This way," she said, locking the car. "Through the fence."

Tanner stepped through the tall wire-mesh gates and caught her breath.

"Hey, neat. Oh boy, wow."

They stood in the center of a narrow street that was only one block long. Both sides of the street were lined with tiny houses. Each house was two stories high with a dormer on the third floor. Each house was the same, yet each was different.

"Look Tanner," her mother said, "I'm going on

[51]

over to Liz's. I have to explain these blueprints to her. You look around for a while then come on over. It's the house across the street with the gold trim."

After her mother had left, Tanner stood alone on Stirling Street. She felt as though she had wandered onto an empty television set; as though she should step carefully over cables and around wires; as if any second the lights would blaze on and the scene would come alive. A brown and white cat rubbed against her leg. Picking the cat up absently, she started down the left side of the street.

Tanner walked slowly, rubbing the cat's ear and looking up at the houses. Hardly more than twelve feet wide, the houses at the north end of the street were finished and obviously occupied. The outside brick was the live red color of fire, and the ridges in between were newly painted. Carriage lamps, window boxes, brass door knockers. Tanner stepped off the curb, standing in the middle of the narrow street to get a better view.

"Hey neat. Look Cat, do you live around here?"

The houses were trimmed in muted colors —golds, greens, blues, browns. The large front doors were sanded down and burnished.

It's as though I'm the only one here, she thought. Like one of those Playschool toys I used to have when I was little—"Tanner's Neighborhood."

Tanner scrunched her eyes together and imagined a whole family of roly-poly wooden dolls for her Playschool world. There were mother and father dolls, a Walter and a Jon, Courtney, a Tanner, Sandy, Amber, and pumpkin. And, Tanner thought grudgingly, even a Cheryl doll.

And we'd all have our own little houses. We'd work on them and paint them and rewire and re-everything and sand and polish and . . .

Tanner grabbed her arms tight across the front of her. The cat yowled and jumped onto the ground. She opened her eyes in time to see him run down a narrow arched passageway between two houses.

From somewhere across a vacant field stubbled with brick foundations and old tires, from across the silence that edged the downtown streets came the sound of the church bells from St. Vincents.

Tanner shook her head and the toy people vanished. Feeling suddenly alone, she cleared her throat several times. "Hey Cat, come back here. Where is everybody?"

Going closer to the house at the end of the street, she pressed her nose up against a windowpane. Smudged putty and plaster dust covered the window. Cupping her hands on either side of her eyes, Tanner peered inside.

The interior of the house was gutted except for walls and studding. An old bathtub standing by the front door was filled with plaster chunks and curls of faded wallpaper. A paint splattered ladder was in the middle of the floor with a red plaid thermos and two mugs on the top step.

Tanner spit on the glass and rubbed it with her

elbow. She blinked her eyes. For a minute she saw Jon sitting on the ladder drinking coffee, with Cheryl scraping wallpaper, and herself sanding the stair rail. Tanner twitched her fingers, almost feeling the grittiness of the sandpaper in her hand. She rubbed the glass again—the picture switched:

the walls smoothly plastered . . .

Jon and Cheryl with rollers and blue paint . . .

Tanner waxing the mantle . . . polishing the brass of the andirons . . .

Jon working on an electrical outlet . . .

Cheryl hammering molding . . .

Jon and Tanner by the built-in bookcase . . .

a fire in the fireplace . . .

Tanner put her head back on the red plush seat in the planetarium and waited for the show to start. The circular room was shadowed, almost dark, and the projector in the middle of the floor cast shadows on the walls. Music that sounded of nighttime and country and bird song filled the room.

The lights went out suddenly, and Tanner grabbed for the arms of her chair. For a minute a feeling of panic engulfed her, but then the narrator's voice took over, steady and calm. And the first stars began to appear in the "sky" overhead.

Tanner listened with half an ear, the way she felt she had paid attention to lunch at the restaurant with only half of her mind. She had really liked the floating restaurant, an old ferry boat with the dipping-down gangplank and the funny "at sea" feeling it gave her even though it was snugly docked. She knew that any other day she would have been thrilled with the view of the harbor: the edge of boats, Federal Hill, the McCormick building that sent its breath of warm cinnamon over the whole area.

But then, as now, Tanner had been back on Stirling Street. Back in the little house with the shambled insides, back to Jon's house. Jon's and Cheryl's.

Tanner watched the arrow dart across the "sky" as the announcer pointed out the zodiac constellations. The dark gently paled and "morning" came. The music faded, and the show was over.

Following her mother out into the lobby, Tanner stopped by the diorama of the city set on a green wooden platform. She spotted the Science Center where they were now; her mother's office in Charles Center; the walk around the inner harbor.

"Is Stirling Street on here?" she asked her mother, leaning across the green railing.

"Yes, look Tanner, over to the east, but not too far. There it is. You really liked that, didn't you?"

"Ummm, it's neat," said Tanner, walking around to the other side, "but Mom, you know what I was thinking, I mean, those houses and all. Well, Jon not having much money, and, well, why couldn't he and Cheryl buy one and then they could fix it all up and everything and . . ."

"But all those houses are sold, people are already working on them." Mrs. McClean started to walk away. "Come along now, I have to stop by the office."

"But Mom, wait. Those houses are taken, but there must be more. I mean there wouldn't be one little block of houses. I mean that's not going to do much for the city."

"Well, yes," said her mother, coming back. "There are other dollar houses in other parts of the city but . . ."

"Oh good, then it's not too late. Jon and Cheryl can get one of those and we can . . ."

Mrs. McClean leaned on the railing next to her daughter. Her voice, when she spoke, was low and probing.

"It's a great idea, Tan. The whole urban homesteading kind of thing is exciting really. That's why I wanted you to see Stirling Street. I knew you'd feel that way about it," her mother paused, looking over the white and blue diorama, searching the model city as if for words. "But Tanner, it's wonderful for you, or for me, or Liz, but you have to be very careful not to put someone else in your own daydreams."

"But, but it would be . . ."

"What I mean is, this might not be the thing for Jon and Cheryl. Their lifestyle might not be yours, just as it might not be ours. Come on, let's walk up to the office, I've got a bunch of work to do at home tonight."

Tanner followed her mother to the elevator.

Suddenly her good leg ached, and Fenhagen felt heavy and draggy. The whole wonderful day felt as though it had turned to soot around her.

I can't walk another step, thought Tanner as she dawdled behind her mother through the lobby, past the book stand and out the turnstile. But she also knew she would not tell her mother she couldn't go another step, the same way she wouldn't admit she couldn't climb a tree or run to the third floor. A McClean can do anything, thought Tanner grumpily as she looked up at the leaden sky.

"It's starting to rain," said her mother, "so we may as well drive. We can park under the office and run up for a few minutes. I want to check my mail and gather up my stuff for tonight. Did you have a nice day?"

"Oh great. It was great, Mom. Thanks."

Tanner leaned her forehead against the car window and closed her eyes. She felt the smudgy window of Stirling Street and saw the tattered pictures of the wonderful, wonderful house.

November 4

Dear Jessie Lee,

Today we had a holiday for teacher's meetings, and my mother sort of took the day off, and we spent it all together (the day, I mean).

First we went to see this friend of my mother's who lives in this house she got for a dollar and then fixed all up and it's great. And the really neat part is that Jon and Cheryl are getting one, and then they're going to start working on it, and they want me to help. Boy—will we have to do everything—like new plaster and paint and wiring and pipes and everything. The houses that are done are cute—all tiny with window boxes and stuff like doll houses sort of I guess. It'll probably take pretty long, but with everybody helping it'll be fun. I did watch Cheryl like you said, but she looks the same to me so how can I tell if she's pregnant or not, but if she is we'll have to work even faster on the house, except that they can stay here as long as they want. Wish I didn't have to go to school. I think I'll be a carpenter.

Your Halloween sounds like fun with the party and all. We (Jody and Marikate and a whole bunch) went trick or treating except we had to go to Marikates because her mother gets really hyper about the city and saying it's not safe and all and that's really dumb because it is (safe). We balanced eggs on doorknobs and rang the bells and ran—and this one man was so mad he and his dog chased us for seven blocks. Boy, were we scared.

Guess I'll stop and do my homework. Why do teachers always make you write compositions called "How I Spent My Holiday"?

love,

Tanner

p.s. write soon—
p.p.s. I wrote this as soon as I got home even before dinner so I could tell you about Jon and Cheryl's house.

Chapter 6

"They're overpriced at a dollar. You couldn't give me one of those places, or all the headaches that go with them, or the rats either," said Jon, reaching back to get an ashtray off the sideboard.

Tanner held a bite of cupcake in her mouth, not sure whether to try and swallow it or to spit it out in her napkin. She felt the chocolate turn to acid under Jon's words.

"Oh, it was really a good day." Alice McClean poured herself another cup of coffee, "and Tanner was really impressed with Stirling Street." Tanner felt her mother looking at her; felt her mother almost willing her not to pay attention; not to listen to Jonathan's words.

"I don't blame Tanner for being impressed,"

said Dr. McClean. "One of our young instructors at the university has one. He and his wife have slaved on it—real yeoman's service. But fortunately, like Thomas Dekker, they feel that 'Honest labor bears a lovely face.' "

"Well, lovely face or not," said Jon, pushing his dishes aside and folding his arms on the table, "I think I need a little more breathing room, right Cheryl?"

Hmmph! What's the matter? Cat got your tongue, thought Tanner as she looked across the table at Cheryl. Almost before her eyes she watched her sister-in-law spotting and blotching all over her face. Watched her shred her paper napkin, then upset a tumbler of water on the table. The water dribbled into a blobby amoeba shape on the light green cloth.

Wow, trust Cheryl-smeryl, thought Tanner. Can't even spill her water with a big swoosh like any normal person. There she is all mumbly mouthed, and I just positively absolutely know that she's brainwashed him. Jon's always loved the city.

"Hey, anybody want the last cupcake?" said Walter.

"You've had two already," said Tanner, reaching out. Then she shrugged and dropped her hand, turning to Jon. "Anyway, you ought to go to Stirling Street. You ought to see these houses. They're really neat—all sort of old and new at the same time. How about Sunday? Could we go on Sunday? I even told Jessie Lee about them, and I know she'd love them, and she lives in a really little small town."

"Terrific, Tanner, get Jessie Lee to come look at them with you. You can even buy one. I'll chip in the dollar, but not me. I'm up to my eyeballs what with work and law school and trying to study. And Cheryl's working so hard, I never even get to see her. Okay?"

"Oh Courtney," Mrs. McClean hurried into the conversation, "how about hockey? Isn't the season almost over? How's it going?"

"Just one game left, and I've started every one. Right now we're 6 and 1, but tomorrow's the really big game—we play Greenridge, and they're 7–0."

"Hockey's a dummy game," said Walter, "unless it's on ice with a lot of fights. Hey, can I go to more ice hockey games this year and skate afterwards? I only went to one last year. And besides, do I get to go to the Colt game Sunday?"

"Oh Dad, speaking of going places, can I borrow a car Sunday? Some of us from school want to go up near Harper's Ferry to look at a college. I've only applied to two. The guidance counselor says we have to apply to three, and it's supposed to be neat up there," Courtney smiled.

"Hey Mom, we got back a bunch of papers—tests and stuff—they have to all be signed, and tomorrow's the last day. They're good and all—they just have to be signed and guess what? I got an A on my *Kidnapped* book report—the highest in the class," Walter pulled a wad of papers out of his pocket, "and I didn't even use a cheater. Vincent didn't give it to me in time, and I had to read the whole book 'cept it was good. Next I'm going to read *Treasure Island* even if we don't have to, except I bet we will."

"How're the tutorials going, Dad?" asked Jon. "You got some pretty good writing out of those one to one sessions last year, didn't you?"

"Yes, very good. There's one this year—the kind of student who makes it all worthwhile."

"They all make it worthwhile for you Dad, deep down, I bet, and you for them. Oh, I was supposed to ask you if you'd speak at school. There's career day, and they need people from every field. I told Mrs. Whelan you'd probably . . ." Courtney's words stretched on and on.

All around her Tanner felt the swell of words building to a crescendo—point and counterpoint.

"Why don't we all . . . Honor's Assembly . . . my Torts professor . . . the class in seventeenth-century lit . . . private housing . . . intergenerational living . . . touchdown in the fourth quarter . . . early admissions . . ."

And I don't have one almighty blasted thing to say, thought Tanner. Not one thing that everybody else can't do better or faster or smarter or something-er. Why can everyone in this family do everything? Tanner twirled her baseball cap 360 degrees and stuffed her orange T-shirt into her jeans. She looked around the table.

Everyone was talking. Across and backwards, catty corner, and up and down.

Everyone but Cheryl.

Oh that's great, thought Tanner. There I am lumped together with blobby old Cheryl. Next thing you know, I'll probably absolutely erupt with hives or something horrible, maybe even leprosy, or even the bubonic plague.

"The trouble with this family is that no one ever takes time to daydream, they just do things . . . the trouble with this family is that no one ever takes time to daydream, they just do things . . . the trouble with this family is . . ."

Somewhere in the edges of her mind Tanner heard her own voice boring steadily; saw everyone talking—mouths opening and closing, hands gesturing. Still, she intoned . . .

"The trouble with this family is that no one ever takes time to daydream. . . ."

She saw Cheryl looking at her. She heard a lull in the storm of dinner table conversation.

"Tanner's right." Cheryl's voice sounded louder than anyone had ever heard it before. She tried to gulp it back, then went on, "Everybody needs time to dream. I think . . . I mean, I guess." She looked at Tanner and smiled weakly, as if they were some kind of allies.

Jon jumped up from the table and grabbed Cheryl's hand. "Come along beautiful dreamer. You can dream your way through the library while I study, that is, if the girls will do the dishes tonight." He reached in his pocket and dropped a dollar bill on the table in front of Tanner.

"There you go, Tan. There's your house money. Be my guest."

Tanner jumped up as quickly as Fenhagen would let her.

"THE TROUBLE WITH THIS FAMILY IS THAT NO ONE EVER TAKES TIME TO DREAM AND I'M GOING TO BECOME A BUDDHA AND JUST SIT AND CONTEMPLATE MY BELLY BUTTON," she shouted at the top of her lungs.

Flipping the light switch in Jon's and Cheryl's living room, Tanner leaned against the doorframe and rubbed her leg. She looked around at Cheryl's array of gewgaws and antimacassars and shuddered. Tanner wasn't exactly sure what she was doing on the third floor except that all during the dishes while the "zilch" babbled on about school and boys, college and boys, sports and boys, she had thought about Jonathan. Had had a sort of inside conversation with herself about Jon.

He must be really really tired . . .
all that work and night school . . .
otherwise Jon would have never . . .

he always wanted to go places with me . . .

Tanner had had to do a lot of inside talking to keep from crying when Jon had thrown the dollar on the table in front of her. And as she scraped away at the casserole dish, she pretended that every swipe at the crusty inside of the bowl was a swipe at Cheryl.

It's all her fault. I mean, I bet if he weren't married to *her*, he could even go to day school—people do. And the way he talks about poor overworked Cheryl, I mean it's enough to make you puke or something.

But it was this pretend conversation that had sent her to the third floor, leaving Courtney to wipe the counters and sweep the floor.

I'll do something terrific for them, that's what I'll do. Something really great, and it'll be so much help that Jon and *she* will have to do something for me. They'll take me to Stirling Street, and they'll see the houses and they'll fall madly in love with them. They'll want one and then they'll get it. We'll really work on it and make it super—just like I told Jessie Lee in my letter.

Tanner stepped further into the room and looked around. She ran her fingers over the table tops looking for something to do, some way to help.

I have to give it to her, I mean it's plenty clean, thought Tanner, remembering her own hodgepodge room on the second floor. Probably too clean, everybody needs germs, for pete's sake.

She wandered into the bedroom. On Jon's orange corded bedspread Cheryl had piled fluffy blue and white pillows with a stuffed angora kitten in the middle.

Oh yuck and double yuck, gagged Tanner.

On the edge of the dresser Tanner saw a box of Tide and a pile of clothes. Moving quickly across the room she picked up the clothes: two blouses, one red and the other white with ruffles; and a white knit sports shirt of Jon's.

That's it. I'll do the wash even if some of it is *hers*. I'll wash it in the bathroom and hang it up and when they come home they'll . . .

Tanner filled the old-fashioned bathtub with scalding water and sprinkled it with Tide. Bubbles swarmed over the top and down onto the cracked linoleum floor. She dropped the clothes into the tub and pushed them under water with the toilet brush. Up and down, around and around she swirled them. Steam rose out of the tub, and sweat trickled down her face. Balancing herself on the edge of the tub with her left hand she leaned forward, sticking Fenhagen out in back.

Pink.

Suddenly everything was pink. Pink bubbles slushing over the top of the tub. A pink toilet brush. Pink water.

Pink clothes.

Tanner speared Cheryl's ruffly white blouse on the end of the brush and held it up in the air. It hung dripping and straggly. It hung pink. She dug

[67]

into the tub again, feeling for Jon's shirt. Jon's handsome new white sports shirt with the tennis emblem on the pocket. PINK.

Yanking the chain that was attached to the stopper, Tanner listened to the water gurgling out. She leaned on the sink and tried to stop herself from shaking, inside and out. The drain made one final slurping sound, and Tanner looked down at the sodden mess in the bottom of the tub. The red shirt (still plenty red, she noticed), and the two pink monstrosities; pink bubbles that popped and faded while she watched. Even the ring around the tub was pink.

What'll I do? Oh my gosh, what am I ever going to do in the whole forever world. They'll kill me, one hundred percent kill me, and I was only trying to help.

Tanner scooped each piece out of the tub with the toilet brush and dripped it over to the sink. She wrung each one out as hard as she could, then stood in the middle of the floor holding the sopping bundle and looking around wildly. Somewhere far down on the first floor she heard a door close.

Oh my gosh! I bet they're home, and they're gonna catch me, and . . .

She looked quickly around the room, then bending over as far as she could she threw the wet clothes under the bathtub. As she started out of the room, a little stream of pink water was already starting to dribble out from under the tub and across the floor.

Downstairs, Tanner climbed into bed without even getting undressed. She pulled the covers up over her head and stayed there. Sometime later—hours, maybe minutes, eons, or forever, she heard Jon. Jon on the third floor. Jon on the stairs. A perfunctory knock on the door then Jon in her room, next to the bed.

Jon angry; and somewhere in the background Cheryl, all whimpery and pleading.

"For God's sake, Tanner, what are you trying to do?"

Tanner clutched the sheets in her fingers. Sweat dripped into her ears. The air under the covers felt hot and stifling.

"Why can't you leave things alone . . . Cheryl's good blouse . . . my new shirt . . ."

"Jon, leave her alone . . . she meant well . . . only trying to help . . ."

"We'll have to lock that door . . . whatever possessed you. . . ."

The door slammed and Tanner felt the silence hovering all around her. She climbed out of bed slowly and began to get undressed.

November 20

Dear Jessie Lee,

I would have written before, except I was fantastically busy. We had basketball tryouts at school, and I made the sixth grade team (I'm a forward, by the way), and we have been practicing and practicing, and there hasn't been much time except that I wrote a play for Thanksgiving, and we're doing it in assembly on Wednesday, and I'm an Indian (I like the Indians better than the pilgrims anyway, how about you?).

What have you been doing? Are you going to your grandmother's farm for Thanksgiving? We're having about a million people here.

Jon and Cheryl have started work on their house. I help them a lot. First comes all the yukky work with all the awful old plaster. I can't wait till the pretty part.

Write and tell me about your Thanksgiving and I will too. Sandy ran away, but we got him back. (He didn't exactly run away—he has a girl friend a couple of blocks away.)

love,

Tanner

p.s. write soon.

[70]

Chapter 7

"Oh, she's the cutest thing. I just love kittens." Tanner watched Marikate as she ran the tip of her index finger gingerly down pumpkin's back. "I wish I could have one, but my mother says pets are germy and buggy."

Tanner bristled as she watched Marikate wipe her fingers on a Kleenex then stand up so the kitten couldn't settle in her lap.

"She's not buggy or germy or anything else-y," said Tanner, tugging on the peak of her baseball cap. "And besides, you couldn't have him anyway, 'cause Jon wants me to give her to Cheryl and I'm going to."

Marikate opened her pocketbook and took out a comb and mirror. "Oh, you're just doing that so you'll get to keep the kitten here for your very self. Honestly Tanner, I mean everybody knows that."

Tanner watched Marikate comb her blond hair with a small comb with flowers painted on it. Watched her fluff her hair out around her shoulders, then run her tongue over her lips and smile into the flower-trimmed mirror. Watched her with almost loathing as she replaced her things in the pocketbook, then flung the strap over her shoulder and flounced across the room.

"Okay Tanner, what shall we do?"

That's the trouble with having Marikate over for a Saturday or a half holiday like today, thought Tanner. I mean, it always seems like a good idea and then all of a sudden there you are actually stuck with her.

"Well, *come on* Tanner. You wanted me to come. You said there was stuff to *do*."

"Want to play Monopoly?" asked Tanner, rubbing pumpkin against her face.

"That's not *doing* anything. When you give that kitten to John and Cheryl, will it stay up there—where they live, I mean?" Marikate curled her lip slightly when she spoke, as if she smelled something not quite clean.

"Oh no, I mean, it'll run up and down and everywhere. They couldn't lock it up for pete's sake," said Tanner. Inside herself she gave a sigh of relief, remembering how Jon had threatened to lock the doors the night she washed the clothes and made the pink awful mess. She smiled to herself, remembering Jon coming down the next morning and giving her a quick hug and a "sorry Tanner, I was really a pain last night. You were only trying to help I guess—in your own funny way." And even when Jon had gone on to say how much Cheryl would like to have pumpkin. Maybe it would be a nice thing to do. It had only taken Tanner a few seconds to make up her mind. "Okay Jon, just as soon as I'm absolutely positive that Amber won't mind."

"Tanner McClean you come on," said Marikate. "You invited me over here and I want to do something, not just sit and moon over a dumb cat."

"Let's go to the store," said Tanner, getting up slowly. "To Savage's where Cheryl works, and you can meet her. She'll give us something. She always gives me anything I want. Positively anything. Come on."

Outside the day was clear and cold with a definite December bite in the air. Tanner burrowed deep into her parka and followed along behind Marikate.

Yech, does she have to skip, for pete's sake, thought Tanner as she watched Marikate in her pink ski coat skipping along the street in front of her; jumping up onto steps and under railings, then back to circle around Tanner. Suddenly Tanner felt slow and clumsy.

"Come on," said Marikate, hopping up onto a marble mounting block and spinning around. "Come on Tanner. You're the tortoise and I'm the hare," she said, hopping off the block and skipping around the corner.

"Yeah," yelled Tanner. "And remember who won

that race too. And for pete's sake DON'T SKIP."

When they got to the drugstore, Cheryl was behind the counter waiting on a woman with a tote bag on her arm and a long list.

"She's busy now," said Tanner. "Want to get something at the fountain? Some cocoa or something?"

Marikate looked over at the fountain and patted her pocketbook.

"Do we have to pay?"

"Sure we have to pay."

"But you said . . ."

"Not at the fountain, for pete's sake. Cheryl doesn't work at the fountain, but she'll give us some candy or something—you wait and see." As Tanner said the words, she looked anxiously over her shoulder at Cheryl and gave her a little wave. She began to have a deep down wish that she was back home playing *Monopoly*, or even back at school.

"Come on, I want a hot chocolate."

The girls sat at the fountain, drinking hot chocolate and eating Lorna Doones. Tanner rubbed her fingers along the black marble counter. The chocolate had warmed her all the way through, and she suddenly felt more like the hare than the tortoise— as if she could hop and spin like Marikate. She sniffed the smell of coffee and egg salad and licorice candy, and spun around once on her seat.

"I just love this drugstore. It's so . . . so neat."

"Well, I guess," said Marikate, playing with the

lid of the large glass jar filled with graham crackers. "But it's so sort of old fashioned—I mean those tables and the funny pointed chairs and all." Marikate looked around scathingly, then pushed her empty cup across the counter.

The girls counted out their money and put it under the saucers.

"Come on," Marikate bounced off the stool. "Introduce me to her."

Tanner eased her way down, Fenhagen clanging against the tile floor.

"Hi Tanner, you got off early today I see. Having a good time?"

"Okay I guess," said Tanner, going to the back of the store. "Cheryl this is Marikate from school," she mumbled.

"Hi Marikate. Having a good day?"

"Oh yes, first we stayed home playing with that adorable kitten that's going to be yours, but then Tanner insisted we come up here because she said . . ."

"Uh—you been busy today Cheryl? Many customers, I mean?"

"Ummm, not too. What can I help you girls with today?"

"Oh, nothing much," said Tanner, looking hard at the display of candy and gum then back again at Cheryl.

"Do you live near here, Marikate?" asked Cheryl.

"Oh no. I live in the county, and next year my father's putting in a swimming pool."

"Just a minute, girls. I have a customer." Tanner pulled Marikate out of the way while Cheryl sold Kleenex and nosespray and rang up the sale.

"Well," said Cheryl, "what are you girls going to do now? I mean it was nice of you to stop in and all but . . ."

Tanner watched Cheryl turn pink and splotchy. She wants us to leave, wants to get on with her big deal job I guess, she thought.

"Oh we don't have anything special to do—nothing at all."

"Hey Tanner," whispered Marikate, "how about the you know what?"

Tanner punched her in the ribs, through the pink ski coat and all. She walked over to the candy rack and stood staring down at it.

"Boy, look at all that candy," she said. Just then the bell on the door jangled, and a woman with a child in a stroller came in. She talked at the counter with Cheryl for a few minutes buying baby shampoo and Pampers.

Tanner stepped back to make room for the stroller. She found herself pressed against the metal of the candy rack. Suddenly the M & M's loomed large in front of her. Yellow packs. Brown packs. Growing. Growing. GROWING.

She looked quickly over her shoulder at Cheryl, then scooped two bags of peanut M & M's into the sleeve of her parka.

The woman left, easing the stroller between tables and display cases.

"Come on, Marikate. Let's go home."

"But the ca—. I mean you said she'd . . ."

Tanner gave her a nudge with her shoulder. "Come *on*, let's go. Bye Cheryl. See you later."

Tanner turned towards the door.

"So long girls. But Tanner, don't forget the candy."

Tanner swung around. "The what?"

"The M & M's. You forgot to pay for the M & M's."

Reaching into her pocket, she found a quarter and flung it down on the counter. Her face burned and her legs felt as though they wouldn't move beneath her. Tanner pushed herself away from the counter. Halfway across the store she slammed into a pyramid of hairspray cans and sent them clattering across the floor. She looked back over her shoulder and shouted above the noise:

"I didn't forget at all. I STOLE THEM."

The bell jangled as the door swung shut behind them.

"You said she'd give them to us. You said she'd give us candy. You're nothing but a liar, Tanner McClean. A liar and a thief." Marikate pranced up and down in front of her, swinging her pocketbook.

Tanner pushed her fists down into her pockets as hard as she could.

"Oh Marikate. You're the dumbest thing I've ever seen. I mean, honestly. It was all part of a plan. Doc Savage wants me to do that every once in a while —you know, to see if the clerks are paying attention and all. It's like the FBI or the CIA or something, espionage and all. How dumb can you get. Don't you know anything?"

After Marikate left to go home, Tanner took pumpkin two blocks down the alley where a group of children was playing in the last shreds of daylight.

"Who wants a kitten?" she called. "Her name is pumpkin with a small p. She's really neat and whoever wants her can have her if you promise to take really good care of her forever."

Tanner handed the kitten over to a boy in a red knit cap with a runny nose.

All the way home she kicked a Tab can and said, "I will not cry, I will not cry, I will not cry."

Tanner waited outside until it was all the way dark. Until the tears in the bottom of her throat were an icy lump, and her fingers were stiff inside her mittens; and her left leg ached with a faraway ache that wasn't quite a pain, but more like a terrible heaviness.

Inside, the kitchen was warm and bright and smelled of goulash. From the den came the sound of her father practicing his bagpipe—the whine of the pipe sharply different from the Scott Joplin record on

[78]

the stereo. Alice McClean was at the sink draining noodles. Cheryl was making the coffee. The "zilch" was setting the table.

"I just gave pumpkin away," said Tanner quickly, rubbing her nose on her sleeve. "I gave her to this cute little boy down the alley who just begged and begged me for her. He's so pathetic—the kid I mean. He hardly has anybody to play with, and he wanted her more'n anything in the whole world. So I did. I gave her away." Tanner sniffed loudly and went to hang her parka on the hall rack.

All during dinner Tanner felt as though she were sitting on a volcano waiting for it to erupt. She waited for Cheryl to say something about the peanut M & M's and her trip to the store. She waited for Cheryl to say something about her giving pumpkin away.

Nothing.

Tanner paid Walter fifty cents to do her share of the dishes so she wouldn't have to be alone with Cheryl. And still she waited. All through her homework and her shower and her bedtime snack, she waited. Waited for her mother or father to call, "Tanner Mary McClean come here." But no one called.

Tanner went to bed and lay rigid and cold under the covers. She thought of pumpkin and the kid with the runny nose and Marikate skipping in her pink ski coat and giant bags of peanut M & M's. She thought of Cheryl all splotchy-faced in the store saying, "Tan-

[79]

ner, you forgot to pay for the candy." She thought of the look in Cheryl's eyes when she heard Tanner say she'd given pumpkin away.

Tanner heard Jon go up the third floor stairs, tired from law school. And still she waited.

Nothing.

When she woke up the next morning, her fingers ached from clutching the covers. Her first thought was "I wonder why she didn't tell?"

Dear Jessie Lee,

The day before yesterday we had a half day at school. (Walter says we have a million holidays, but I think he has as many). Anyhow, Marikate came over. Sometimes I think she's really a louse, but sometimes she's okay. Right now I think she's a louse. She skips a lot and always combs her hair. I've never even met you, and I know one hundred percent for certain that you don't skip. And from your picture your hair's so short you couldn't always be combing it or you'd be bald. Anyway, we went over to Savage's drugstore where Cheryl works. First we had hot chocolate at the fountain, and Marikate's so cheap she only left a penny tip. (I left a dime). Then we talked to Cheryl a while, and she gave us a whole bunch of candy and gum. She always gives me stuff every time I go in there, and sometimes she brings me stuff home like eye makeup and perfume samples and everything. It's really neat, and she doesn't *steal* them cause Doc Savage says it's okay.

Well, anyway, after Marikate left I was walking pumpkin up the alley (well, actually I was walking and carrying pumpkin), and I met this really pathetic little boy with a red hat and a snotty nose. He just begged and begged me for the kitten, so I just had to give it to him even though I promised it (the kitten) to Cheryl. But Cheryl said since the kid was so lonely and pathetic, what I did was okay. What she really said was noble and stuff like that.

What's new with you? That's really neat about your team winning all the games. We won all but one so far.

write soon,

love,

Tanner

p.s. Cheryl is only working in the drugstore part-time. Then she's going to night school same as Jon—but not law.

p.s. jr. I guess that means she's not pregnant if she's going to school or doesn't that count. What do you think?

p.p.s. Write soon.

p.p.s.s. Can you wait for Christmas???? I can't.

p.p.p.s.s. Jon and Cheryl are really working on their house a lot.

Chapter 8

COME TO A SLUMBER PARTY
DECEMBER 15   SIX O'CLOCK
AT MARIKATE'S
                         Bring sleeping bags

Tanner took the invitation out of her pocket and waved it across the dinner table.

"Hey, look everybody. Marikate's having a slumber party and I'm invited and it's Friday night."

"Oh lord, slumber parties," said Courtney loftily, as she reached for a piece of bread. "I guess sixth grade is the year for slumber parties. Boy, will you be tired.

"I remember the year I was in sixth grade. I'll bet I went to at least eight. I was tired forever that year. You probably won't even like it, Tanner. It's just something you have to go through I guess—like getting your first bra or something."

Tanner looked up in time to see her mother and father exchanging glances across the table the way they did sometimes when the "zilch" was acting terribly old and sophisticated. Tanner liked the way her mother and father looked at each other—almost as though they reached out to touch hands—as though no one else were around. Suddenly she felt lonely.

"I will too like it. We're going to have subs and pizzas and Christmas cookies and make popcorn and stay up as long as we want and . . ."

"And you'll all probably throw up and . . ."

"Oh shut up, Courtney. You think you're so big. Anyway, we're going to play records and everything."

"Oh lord—top forty, I'll bet. Teeney bopper—my sister the teeney bopper."

"Cut it out, Courtney," said their father. "Of course Tanner will enjoy it. Why shouldn't she? You did at her age."

"Even if everyone else goes to sleep, I'm going to stay up and so's Jody. We made a pact. We're going to sleep in the family room and can I borrow your sleeping bag Walter, huh?"

"That's dumb," said Walter, taking his dishes into the kitchen. "Sleeping bags are for sleeping outside—for camping and stuff—not for staying up all night in someone's family room. When Scott and I went with his family last year—boy—now that's really camping, and at night it got so cold and . . ."

"But Walter, your sister wants to know if she may borrow your bag or not," said his mother, forestalling one of Walter's extended stories.

"I don't care. I just think it's dumb is all. And she better not get any smelly stuff on it—yuk," he said as he left the room, jumping up to touch the wall over the door frame.

Tanner scotchtaped the invitation over her desk and looked at it all through her homework. There was a funny nagging fear somewhere deep inside of her; a vague, shapeless I-don't-want-to-go kind of feeling that made her stomach hurt. When she tried to really take hold of it, she got a hot-all-over feeling —the kind of feeling you got in school when you started the second verse of the national anthem and no one else did.

Leaving her books on the desk, Tanner peeled the invitation off the wall and headed downstairs to her parents' study.

Her parents' study: where they all went if there was something to be talked over, even if the "something" couldn't be actually talked about. Just being there seemed to help. Tanner stood in the doorway and looked around. Her mother sat at her desk under a spill of yellow light, leaning on one elbow with her hand pushed up into her hair. Tanner watched as she wrote quickly, pausing occasionally to check something in a book. She seemed oblivious to her daughter standing there.

Her father's desk was dark and cluttered, and Tanner remembered at dinner that he had said he was going back to the university library. Dr. McClean's bagpipe leaned in the corner in its case, and the wall behind the desk was floor-to-ceiling books.

Alice McClean picked up her coffee mug and took a swallow.

"Oh, it's cold," she said, looking up and seeing Tanner.

"Hi, Tan. Come on in. There's nothing worse than cold coffee."

Tanner watched her mother swing around and fill her cup from the Pyrex pot on the hot plate by the window. She sat down in the vinyl rocker and leaned back. The plastic arms had begun to peel and crackle, and someone had patched the holes with masking tape. She picked at the curled up edge of tape and waited while her mother put sugar in her coffee and pushed her papers deeper into the mess on the top of her desk.

"Okay Beast, what's up?" Tanner chewed on the invitation for a minute. That's the thing about names, she thought. I mean when Mom says Beast, it sounds like a hug, but let the "zilch" say it, and I want to spit in her face. And Jon—it used to didn't matter *what* he called me, but now I'm not so sure.

"Tanner?" Her mother's voice prodded her. "What's up?"

"Oh, I don't know, nothing I guess. I mean Marikate's having this stupid slumber party and all and . . . well . . . I don't know, maybe I shouldn't go," she said all in a rush.

"Not go? But why? Look, Tanner, I hope you're not paying any attention to Courtney. Back in the days when she was going to slumber parties she loved them and . . ."

"It's not Courtney-smourtney," said Tanner, pulling off a wide chunk of masking tape and digging her finger down into a crack in the plastic.

"It's well . . . I don't know . . . all kinds of things." Tanner tried to sort our her churning thoughts. Thoughts about having to get ready for bed in front of all those girls—and what she was going to do with Fenhagen—how she could get into a sleeping bag and if she got in how could she get out anyway—"Oh, like, well with a sleeping bag and all that . . ." Tanner pulled stuffing out of the chair and tore it into little bits. "And besides, all my pajamas are all raggedy, and I'll look terrible."

Courtney and Cheryl came into the room and after a quick look at Tanner, Courtney broke in. "Mom, where's *Catcher in the Rye?* Can you believe, but Cheryl's never read it."

Alice McClean waved vaguely toward the bookcase by the door. "Over there, Courtney, Tanner was

[87]

talking." Turning back to her younger daughter she said, "If it's pajamas that's worrying you, I'll pick you up a new pair at lunchtime tomorrow. That's no problem."

"Not pajamas," wailed Tanner. "I can't possibly wear pajamas at a slumber party."

"What do you mean you can't wear pajamas at a slumber party?" asked Courtney, turning from the bookcase. "What do you plan to wear for heavens sake?"

"Oh shut up, Court. You think you're so smart." Tanner pushed herself out of the chair and went to stand by the big globe in the corner.

"I mean . . . don't you see? I—I can't wear pajamas cause they won't go over Fenhagen . . . I mean the pants and all."

"Over Fenhagen? Just take it off and put on your pajamas and then use your crutches." Her mother rearranged some papers on her desk.

"Honestly Tanner," said Courtney, "stop making such a production out of everything. Were you *really* going to sleep in Fenhagen? For pete's sake, I'd rather be a fakir on a bed of nails. Just go to the party and have fun. Hey Mom, can I borrow your stapler? I have this paper . . ."

All of a sudden things seemed to be going on without her. Courtney and her mother together at the desk. Tanner moved further back into the shadows. She felt Cheryl watching her and looked up. Tanner's eyes met Cheryl's and were held there for a

[88]

minute—a minute where time seemed to look all the way down into her deepest insides.

"Wait right there, Tanner. Don't go away." And Cheryl ran out of the room. Tanner could hear her running all the way to the third floor, and then back down again.

"Oh," she gasped, coming back into the den, "those steps." She seemed enveloped in red and white stripes which she pushed into Tanner's arms.

"Here, I made this for you for Christmas, but you may as well have it now. I mean, well, maybe . . ."

Tanner shook out the folds of material, holding a red and white striped granny gown up to herself. The nightgown was made of flannel and had a high neck and long sleeves trimmed with eyelet, and it reached all the way to Tanner's feet.

"Why, Cheryl, how lovely." Alice McClean came out from behind her desk.

"Is that what you do up there all the time?" asked Courtney. "That's neat."

Tanner held the soft flannel next to her face. It smelled new and clean. She looked up at Cheryl's yellow eyes then down again quickly. "Thanks a lot," she mumbled, as she hurried out of the room. She went quickly before Cheryl's eyes could see any deeper.

Little bits of flat gray morning were starting to push in around the edges of the picture window in Marikate's family room. Tanner jammed her fists

[89]

down into the couch and tried to rearrange herself so that everything would stop aching. She arched her back and stretched her good leg, then lifted Fenhagen off the couch and out in front of her. She shook her cobwebby head. Across the room her sleeping bag lay in a heap by the fireplace.

"What's everybody going to bed for? Party poop, party poop. I'm going to stay up forever." Tanner had kept up her steady war chant until one by one the girls had curled up in their sleeping bags and gone to sleep, leaving Tanner free to collapse on the sofa.

Tanner swooshed spit around in her mouth trying to get rid of the sour last night taste. She thought about the difference in houses: hers and Marikate's. How Marikate's house didn't seem to have any personality—no peopleness, no books or clutter. Nothing to tell you it wasn't a window in a furniture store.

"Well, it's cluttered now," thought Tanner, reaching down to take off her right shoe and wriggling her toes. One shoe off is better than none, she thought, looking at her other brown oxford, ugly and built up and clunky, that was hooked onto Fenhagen and sticking out from under the bottom of her nightgown.

"It's sure a mess now," said Tanner in a whisper, looking around at the clutter of the family room. All around the room the girls slept on the floor. Popcorn and Fritos littered the shag rug, and empty soda cans dotted the furniture. The record player, which had throbbed long into the night, was strangely quiet; jeans, shirts, bikini pants, and knee socks draped the furniture.

One Hallmark fold-out Christmas bell hung from the ceiling.

As the room lightened, Tanner reached absently for a bowl of M & M's on the coffee table and began popping them into her mouth. Across the room Jody sighed and rolled over, snoring lightly.

Tanner looked down at the large grape stain on her nightgown. She traced the edges with her fingers —little spikey lines and one fat purple blob—and tried to decide what it looked like. A bat? A clump of seaweed? A purple jellyfish? She looked further down at the zigzag rip in the gown, trying to piece it together, all the while wondering how even a card table in Marikate's picture-perfect house could have a nail sticking out. And guess who had to sit there, thought Tanner.

She put the sleeve of her nightgown up to her nose and sniffed, but it didn't even smell new anymore, or clean either. Tanner dropped the handful of M & M's back into the bowl, and for a minute she felt slightly sick.

Cheryl came to pick her up. She let Tanner stash her sleeping bag in the back and clump into the car before she said anything.

"I hope I'm not late. I went the wrong way on the beltway, and then I had to get off and on again, and . . . well, I had to come because everybody else went to Courtney's school to the father-daughter basketball game except Jon and he's studying."

Tanner put her head back and let the words run over her. She felt Cheryl pull up the car in front of the house, felt her put on the emergency brake.

"Okay, here we are. At least I didn't get lost coming home. You grab the sleeping bag, Tanner, and I'll take the crutches."

Tanner stood on the sidewalk and watched Cheryl root around on the backseat. Watched her rumble around looking for the crutches that weren't there.

"Oh, you must have left them at Marikate's. Oh dear, I guess . . . well, I mean we'll just have to go back for them. I mean you'll need them and all."

Tanner turned and walked towards the house, dragging Walter's sleeping bag along the sidewalk. "Come on, Cheryl. They're not at Marikate's. They're not at Marikate's at all."

Cheryl followed her up the steps and into the vestibule. They stood between the outside door and the inside door, and Cheryl looked at her with those yellow cat eyes again.

"But Tanner honey, I don't understand. I mean, if your crutches aren't at Marikate's and they aren't in the car . . . inside . . . and you never even took them. . . ."

Tanner felt tears edge out of the corners of her eyes. Big, angry tears. Tired tears.

[92]

If she touches me I'll scream, thought Tanner, swallowing hard. I'll scream and kick and spit right in the middle of those yellow eyes.

Cheryl ducked her head and shoved the key into the lock. All she said was "You must be pretty tired."

When Tanner woke up in the late afternoon, sun shadowed her room. For a minute she blinked her eyes and tried to think what day it was; should she get into her school uniform, and if so, why didn't the day have that bright new morning look. She rolled over, leaning on her elbow. On the foot of her bed, washed and dried, hung the red and white nightgown —the purple stain just a dusky shadow across the front, and the rip mended into a neat fold in the material.

Dear Jessie Lee,

I honestly truly believe that New Year's day is the most boring day of the whole year. How about you? I mean Christmas is Christmas and you know, sort of special. Thank you for the puzzle. I've done a really lot but not all. IT'S HARD. Did you ever try to do a thousand-piece puzzle of marbles where everything looks the same? Thanks a lot even if it does take till Easter. I hope you like the diary I sent. It even has a key.

Last night on New Year's Eve most everybody was home. My parents never go out that night, and even Courtney who had a date came home early and ate ham sandwiches in the kitchen. Walter and I went outside with pots and pans. How about you?

What did you get for Christmas? I got a tape recorder (neat) and a pair of pants and a shirt and games and stuff, and Cheryl made me a nightgown (red and white).

Did I tell you about Marikate's slumber party??? It was so much fun. There were ten girls and we all slept in sleeping bags, except we didn't really (sleep, I mean). We all stayed up all night, and nobody was even tired—not at all. We danced and ran around the outside of the house till her mother stopped us. And I'm going to have one, too, (slumber party) in the spring. It was neat.

Boy—you should see what Jon and Cheryl have done to their dollar house. They're working on the bricks in the fireplace and cleaning them and all, and the mantle is white just like the walls. When it's not so cold, they'll paint the outside trim light blue. I help them a lot.

love,
Tanner

p.s. write soon.

Chapter 9

Walter played the glockenspiel, and Tanner stuffed her fingers in her ears and tried to think. Even though he was a whole floor away and the walls were thick and she had her fingers all the way in her ears as far as they would go, Tanner could still hear the sharp bell sounds. "When Irish Eyes are Smiling" played over and over. Except that she never heard it all the way through because everytime Walter got as far as "morn in spring," he hit a sour note.

"Oh for pete's sake, shut up," Tanner called out loud. "A person can't even have a good think around here." She unplugged her ears and held a pillow over her head like a giant pair of earmuffs.

"How can anybody even think in this zoo?" she yelled at the empty room. "And everytime I complain about Walter and the glock Dad just laughs and says 'be glad it's not a trumpet.' But what do you expect from a father who plays the bagpipe." Tanner shouted the last word just as Walter hit a clinker again.

For a minute she held her breath, waiting to see if the silence was going to last; just as she was about to let her breath wisp out around her teeth and just as she was about to take the pillow-ear-muffs off her head, Walter started in again. With gusto.

"Walter McClean you shut up this minute because I have a very important think to think, and I don't care how smart you are and what a good athlete and all, you're a lousy glockenspiel player, and you can't even get past 'morn in spring' and besides . . ." Somewhere in the far back corners of her mind Tanner heard the absence of the bells and her brother thudding down the steps, but she couldn't stop. ". . . besides when you're not playing then Dad is, or the "zilch" has her stereo on, or Mom the radio, and nobody in this house ever shuts up long enough to let a person think, so SHUT UP."

With that her door burst open, and Walter poked his head into the room.

"Hey Tanner, what're you yelling for? A person can hardly think with all that racket. Hey, what's that?" he said, coming closer to the bed.

Tanner tried unsuccessfully to throw herself across the yellow fur ball on the foot of her bed.

"What's what?"

"That 'what' that looks like a cat, that's what,"

said Walter, jumping up and tossing an imaginary ball at the ceiling light as though it were a basket. "Hey, that's pretty good—that 'what' that looks . . ."

"Oh be quiet," said Tanner, hunching herself further over the foot of the bed, "and don't come in my room without knocking—ever."

"Okay, but where'd the cat come from, and you'd better get up or you're going to squash it."

"That's what I was trying to think about except you were making so much noise. A woman brought it to the door—it's pumpkin."

"You really ought to work on your powers of concentration," said Walter, taking Tanner's crutches from the side of the bed and stooping down to fit them as he swung around the room. "Doesn't seem like a little music ought to keep you from thinking. What woman?" he said as he swung the length of the room in four swoops.

"You call that music? Hah! And get off my crutches. You probably have BO, and you'll make the armpit part all smelly. And close the door, I have to think about poor pumpkin."

Walter kicked the door shut, then stood hanging onto the crutches and looking at his sister.

"How come? I mean, how come she came back? Hey, I like that too. How come she . . ."

"Oh Walter, shut up," wailed Tanner. "She was so awful—all mean and grouchy, and she had that poor little kid with her, and he had on the same funny red hat and runny nose and . . ."

[98]

"Couldn't have been the same runny nose. It'd have been all run out by now." Walter leaned the crutches on the bed and sat down, poking the kitten with his index finger.

"How come she brought her back?"

"Cause she said he was allergic—the kid, I mean —the one with the runny nose. And she said he got all red and splotchy and sneezed a lot, and she had to take him to the doctor, and she acted like it was all my fault—about her having to take him to the doctor, I mean. When all along I'll just bet you the kid is allergic to his mother, and he'll probably go on sneezing till he grows up. Now poor pumpkin doesn't have a home and . . ."

"What do you mean she doesn't have a home?" asked Walter, rubbing the kitten behind the ear. "Looks to me as if she's got a perfectly good home right here. You know Mom won't care."

"But the poor baby's been abandoned—thrown out into the alley in the cold and . . ." Tanner picked up the kitten and held it against her face.

"You're nuts," said Walter, heading for the door. "Positively nutty. That cat's in a perfectly warm house, and nobody threw it out into the cold. She brought him to the door and put it in your hands. But if you're really worried about pumpkin getting a complex or something, why don't you give her to Cheryl. She wanted her in the first place, except you were too mean and selfish to give it to her."

"I was not. I was not mean and selfish, and you

get out and stay out," screamed Tanner as she hurled a crutch towards the door. "And don't play that stupid glockenspiel again. You stink."

"What about it pumpkin pie," said Tanner, coaxing the kitten awake with the fringe on the end of her bedspread. "Do you want to go live with Cherylsmeryl? Actually, you might feel right at home. I mean, old Cheryl's all red and blotchy half the time anyway, but that's because she's a creep. I mean she's not allergic or anything. You could run up and down stairs all you wanted and play with Amber, and Cheryl could work on your damaged psyche and play nursemaid all she wants."

She settled the kitten on her shoulder and started out of the room. "And she's not quite as repulsive as she used to be, and sometimes she's not even half way repulsive, except I still can't see why Jon married her, even if she did make me a nightgown and sew up the hole and all that junk."

Tanner went up the stairs slowly, taking care that Fenhagen didn't clang against the risers. "And I'll make you into a surprise. When Cheryl comes up after dinner, there you'll be."

Settling the kitten on the studio couch, Tanner closed the door firmly behind her. Then she went down to dinner.

Tanner thought that dinner was never going to end. It seemed as though the meatloaf went on forever; the mashed potatoes and salad were endless.

[100]

Her mother and father discussed the city budget, and Walter gave a long detailed account of his basketball game and how the other team was really good but his team was better on defense. By then Courtney was off talking about colleges again, and Jon settled down to explain to her why he thought Southern colleges gave you a better value for your money. Courtney said she wanted to go to NYU, and both her mother and father said they couldn't afford it.

Tanner watched the grease on the meatloaf plate congeal into grayish yellow lumps. She shredded her paper napkin and wondered if dinner would ever end and what Cheryl would say when she saw pumpkin.

Finally, Jon jumped up from the table and looked at his watch. "I'm going to run upstairs and get my books so I can go to the library."

And Tanner held her breath. Held it as long as she could, then let it out slowly and started clearing the table. This wasn't the way it was supposed to happen, not Jon going upstairs first and finding pumpkin.

It was supposed to be Cheryl.

Cheryl finding the kitten: excited, happy. Cheryl saying "Oh, Tanner, what a wonderful surprise. Thank you. Thank you." And instead, there she sat, still at the dinner table drinking another cup of tea.

Tanner strained her ears. Any minute Jon would call Cheryl upstairs to show her the surprise. Maybe it would be better that way. Maybe . . .

"Tanner McClean, you get up here," yelled Jon. "On the double."

Tanner put the plate she was carrying on the stack already on the drain board and watched them slide slowly into the sink.

His voice doesn't sound excited, or even happy, she thought as she started clumsily up the stairs. Fenhagen seemed to be made of lead, seemed to be dragging her back as though she were trying to go up a down escalator. And she didn't want to go at all.

"Hurry up, Tanner, and for God's sake why can't you stay out of things." Jon's voice pounded down on her, and his face hanging over the third floor rail was red and angry.

And behind her on the stairs she was conscious of Cheryl, hovering there, not pushing on ahead but wanting to run. Wanting to see what was the matter.

Standing at the door, Tanner surveyed the wreckage. The Queen Elizabeth plate lay in pieces under the window; the spider plant was on the floor with the pot broken around it, the spattered dirt making a pattern on the tan rug. Several of the seashell girls had been dragged across the floor, their red net skirts torn off. As she stood and watched, pumpkin took a flying leap onto the bookcase sending the tiny plastic animals spinning across the room.

"It stinks in here," said Tanner.

"You're damn right it stinks," said Jon. "That animal thought my chair was a litter box, and look at Cheryl's pretty things. You apologize to her right this minute and I mean it."

Tanner heard Cheryl sniffing somewhere in the

corner, but she wouldn't look at her. She heard her sister-in-law saying through tears held-back, "Oh Jon . . . well, maybe . . . don't you think . . ."

She can't even get good and mad without being all namby pamby, thought Tanner. I hate her—I hate her, and it's all her fault.

·"Tanner, I'm waiting," said Jon.

Tanner felt as though she wanted to die, or throw up, or run away. She felt ashamed and angry and clumsy—and stupid. Everything I do turns out clunky, she thought. And why did pumpkin have to go to the bathroom on top of everything else?

Tanner wanted to cry. She wanted to fall right down on the rug and put her head in her arms and just cry and cry. But she couldn't. She wouldn't. She knew right then that she'd bite her tongue into a hundred pieces before she'd cry one tear.

"I won't," yelled Tanner. "I won't apologize to her ever—ever—ever. It was a present—pumpkin was— cause Cheryl wanted it and if she hadn't stayed downstairs so long . . . and it wasn't pumpkin's fault that she had to go. I'll never ever apologize to her—not as long as I live." Tanner started down the stairs, Fenhagen banging heavily against the wood. "And besides, all her stuff was ugly and cheap and tacky, and I'm glad it's broken, and Cheryl's nothing but a cry baby, and everybody knows McCleans don't cry in public."

Tanner took a deep breath and went on as she walked along the second floor hall, "Just try to do something nice for somebody around here and that's what happens. Well you just wait. You see if I ever . . ."

Tanner pushed her door open and ducked inside. She slammed the door behind her and burst into tears.

February 2

Dear Jessie Lee,

I haven't written in a really long time but this time of year is really blah. I mean everybody's sick of basketball and it won't, positively won't snow.

Mrs. Tyson (our teacher) says she has something planned for us to do. I don't know what but I hope it's some place to go—maybe the Planetarium or the Science Center would be neat.

Guess what? I'm really really sure that Cheryl's pregnant and guess what else—pumpkin (the kitten) came back. The little kid in the alley who wanted her was allergic so his mother brought pumpkin back, and that was all right because I gave her to Cheryl, and she was *so* happy. She was kind of surprised at first. I hid pumpkin in hers and Jon's living room, and when they went up after dinner—boy were they surprised—and there was pumpkin all curled up on the couch asleep. Tomorrow I'm going ice skating. I LOVE TO ICE SKATE. How about you?

love,
Tanner

p.s. write soon

p.p.s. the reason I think for sure that she's (Cheryl) pregnant is that she sings lullabys to pumpkin, and also she (Cheryl) said her pink skirt was too tight.

Chapter 10

"Wow! I thought we were really going to go someplace. I mean the way Mrs. Tyson went on—a real trip or something—but a yukky old hospital." Marikate jumped up and down on the playground, her pink ski coat bright against the grayness of the day.

"Even Fort McHenry would have been better, and we've been there hundreds of times—maybe thousands." Tanner pulled the hood of her parka close around her face and shoved her hands deep into her pockets. The cold pinched into her, making even her good leg feel heavy. She wondered for a minute what would happen if that leg froze and she was stuck there on the playground until spring, or until someone came and took her in and put her on the radiator to thaw.

"It stinks," said Jody, blowing her breath in big

puffs up in the air. "We could go to Washington to the Smithsonian, or to Mt. Vernon, but to a hospital?"

"And how about the floor bit—everybody all around as though we had something to say about it. 'Now girls, we have something to discuss.' I hate it when teachers do that, specially when you know they've already made up their minds anyhow."

Marikate hopped off, first on one foot and then the other, clapping her hands in front of her.

"Come on Tanner, let's get up against the building. I'm freezing."

The girls leaned against the brick side of the school. "Let's stare at her really hard—Mrs. Tyson, I mean. If we stare hard enough, maybe she'll ring that bell," said Tanner, wiggling the toes inside her shoe.

"Don't waste your stares. She won't ring it early. Even if we had a tornado and an earthquake all at once, she'd probably just say 'Fresh air is good for you girls.' Hey, about that hospital. Where we're going— Isn't that yours? I mean, wasn't it? I mean the one where you were?"

"Hn-huh," said Tanner, pushing herself away from the wall. "Hey, I'm going in for a minute. Tell Mrs. Tyson I went to the bathroom."

"Okay, but hurry up so I can be next, else I'll freeze to death."

Inside the building Tanner held up her hands against the radiator and sniffed the smell of soup from the cafeteria. She held the warm mittens up against her face and closed her eyes. Ever since Mrs. Tyson's class discussion that morning, Tanner had tried to keep the thoughts away, tried to pretend she hadn't heard the teacher's words.

". . . and so I thought it would be nice . . . the children would enjoy it so . . . around the holidays they're just swamped with offers . . . really appreciate a visit now . . . the crippled children . . . in the hospital . . ."

But now the thoughts crowded in. Thoughts and memories that she usually managed to keep away, but now they poked and prodded at Tanner as she stood in the hall and listened to the radiator hiss.

Awful, never-quite-forgotten memories: the white roughness of the sheets under her elbows and the way her back ached from lying on it, the smell of alcohol, and the hush of the nurses' shoes against the floors. The words "Wyman Hospital for Crippled Children and Adults" printed on the edge of the pillow cases. Her mother bringing clean nightgowns and sticky apples, and her father pulled up next to the bed with a second grade speller open between them. The rest of the family popping in and out, tangling her up into their lives and pulling her along with them.

Something deep down inside Tanner shuddered, and she put her hand down to touch Fenhagen. She remembered the doctors and the nurses, especially Miss Fenhagen with her awful sweetness that turned Tanner's spit sour inside her mouth; remembered the basement therapy room with fluorescent lights and ramps going up and down and steps that didn't go anyplace. And being fitted for the brace (later to be known as Fenhagen—the worst thing she could think to call it); and the cold pit-of-the-stomach horror when she knew in the middle of one night that her left leg was never going to work again. She remembered the doctor explaining it to her—how the growing portion of her leg had been damaged; and felt again the tears as they slithered down her face and into her ears.

And still the memories came: the cold humiliation of the bedpan; and the get-well cards taped on the door and then the walls and even up the window frame; the emptiness of the halls after the last visitor had left and the sounds of the television and the squeak of the juice cart were all that could be heard. And the times at night when the lights were turned down low and the shadows came back.

"I won't go," said Tanner out loud to the empty hall. "I won't go back there. I don't care what they say." She looked around quickly to see if anyone had heard.

Outside, the bell rang, and Tanner heard the children running to get into line. She ducked into the bathroom, managing to come out just as the sixth grade passed the door.

I'll throw up that day, or say I have a sore throat, or mononucleosis, or leprosy or both, or a combination—monolepriosis. But I won't go there again. I don't care what anybody says, thought Tanner as she hooked onto the end of the line and followed the class upstairs.

"Of course you're going, Tanner," said her mother, carrying dishes into the kitchen. "Remember when you were in the hospital how much you enjoyed visitors."

"But that was visitors—the kind you know. They were real people—that was different." Tanner scraped a plate into the garbage, then held the plate for Sandy to lick.

"Mo-ther, she's letting that dog lick off the plate. And who's real people anyway?" said Courtney, coming into the room.

"Sandy's clean as you are, and it's none of your business who's real and who's not."

"Touchy, touchy," said Courtney.

"Tanner's class is going to Wyman's hospital to visit the children there, and she doesn't want to go. A lovely idea, I think . . ." Tanner listened as her mother's voice drifted off, watched as she picked up the newspaper and jotted notes in the margin.

"What's a lovely idea?" asked Dr. McClean, heading for the coffee pot.

"Going to the hospital," said Courtney. "Not to be sick, but to visit. Tanner's class is going, but she's not interested."

"Zilch, zilchier, zilchiest," said Tanner as she slammed a plate into the dishwasher.

[111]

"I don't think it's a question of interest," said their father as he filled his cup and sat down at the table. "How about it Tan? Is it an optional trip, or do you feel that maybe . . ."

"Is what an optional trip and where's the scotch tape?" asked Walter as he tried to chin himself on the door frame.

"None of your business what's optional," said Tanner, looking around wildly. She saw Cheryl hovering over the dishwasher as though she were part of the scenery. Nosey old thing. I bet she's listening to every word, and it's none of her business either, thought Tanner.

Tanner pulled her baseball cap down over her eyes and wished she'd never opened her mouth. If she had never told her mother about the trip, she could have just gone ahead and gotten "monolepriosis." Or something.

Out loud, she said, "Boy, we could have a meeting or something, if only Jon were here . . ."

"Well, Jon's around someplace. Shall we call him?" said her father with a lopsided kind of grin. A grin that sometimes took away even Tanner's prickliest feelings. Tonight it didn't help.

"Seriously, Tanner," he went on over the sound of running water. "This trip would probably mean a lot to the kids at Wyman's . . ."

"What trip?" said Walter, working at the edge of the scotch tape with his teeth. "If I were a patient in the hospital and Tanner and her friends came to visit, I'd probably have a relapse."

Tanner felt her father's eyes on her, as though they were boring right through her. He ignored Walter and went on, "Unless you feel there might be a difficulty, having been . . ."

"What's a difficulty?" asked Courtney, coming back from the pantry.

"Oh for pete's sake," said Tanner, turning on the water as hard as she could and splattering the wall in back of the sink. She watched the water run in little dribbles down the tile. "Why does everything in this family have to be a federal case or something. I just said I didn't want to go. I mean, I'd rather . . ."

Alice McClean looked up from the paper. ". . . sometimes helps to put yourself in someone else's place . . ."

". . . if everyone else is going," added her father.

". . . still at that selfish age . . . In psychology we learned . . . the inner child . . ." Tanner heard the "zilch" going on.

"After our last trip the teacher said . . ." Walter jumped up to hit the wall over the door as he left the room.

"I think it's too much to expect that of Tanner . . . I mean, well, after all . . ." Tanner heard Cheryl's words fall on the noise of the kitchen. Heard the words reach out to the corners of the room and the corners of the conversation, bringing quiet the way

[113]

a knife on a water glass brings silence to a crowded room.

"You can't expect that of her," Cheryl's voice rushed on, thin and watery, almost as if it were against her will. "After all she went through—all that time in the hospital. I mean, I wasn't here, but from what Jon's said, it was a terrible time . . ."

Tanner watched Cheryl turn red and splotchy, but still she went on. "Of course she doesn't want to go back there. It's too much to expect. It's awful to go back there now . . ." Cheryl finished in a rush, like the last bit of air sputtering out of a balloon.

For a minute the kitchen was silent while everyone looked at Cheryl. They watched her twist the cuff of her sweater over and under, while her face went from white to red then back to white again.

Tanner could still hear Cheryl's words hanging there in the kitchen. "It would be awful to go back there now. It's too much to expect." And suddenly she wanted to run over and grab those words and hold them up like some kind of a banner. She's right, it would be awful, and I don't want to do it, and out of this whole super family dumb old spotty Cheryl's the only one who knows it, thought Tanner. She wanted to look at Cheryl right in the eye, and take hold of those words, and spit them right back out at everyone—her mother and father, the "zilch," even Walter. Wanted to yell, "I don't want to go back there even as a visitor. I've been there, and I'm scared to go back."

Then everyone started to talk. The words hanging over the kitchen faded and drifted away, and Tanner couldn't reach them anymore.

"... don't seem to understand ..."

"... a very brave girl ..."

"Typical McClean fashion ..."

"... no ill effects ..."

"all worked together ... to help her along ..."

"same as anyone else ..."

Tanner looked wildly around the kitchen, her fingers tight against a bowl of applesauce. She saw her mother starting to make the sandwiches for tomorrow, her father rinsing his coffee cup at the sink. She saw the "zilch" heading for the door, and Cheryl wiping off the counter, her hands shaking slightly. She stood for a moment, hesitating, waiting.

"I'm not afraid of anything. I can do anything I want to. Hospitals don't scare me. I'm not scared of anything." Her voice rose higher and higher. "It's just that something else would have been more fun—I mean a trip to someplace—not a stupid old hospital."

Then carefully, as if in slow motion, she let the bowl of applesauce slide out of her fingers and crash onto the floor.

Dear Jessie Lee,

It's okay (sort of) that you didn't write for so long cause I guess being in the play takes all your time even if you are just one of the Munchkins. Did your mother get your costume finished in time and what do Munchkins wear anyway? Last year the "zilch" was in "Fiddler on the Roof" at school and you'd have thought she was on Broadway the way she acted (and she was just in the chorus) but the play was good anyway.

At least you got to do something decent. Mrs. Tyson's idea of a field trip was pretty yuk. I mean we wanted to go someplace exciting, but she got this brilliant (ha-ha) idea that we should go to this hospital where they have a bunch of crippled children. It was sort of nice—I mean, talking to all the sick children made you feel sort of good inside (except there was this one girl who didn't want to go cause she had been sick there before as a patient, I mean, and she kept thinking she was going to faint or something. I guess she did cause that's the way she looked). Well, anyway, there was this one nurse named Miss Fenhagen who kept saying dumb things like "aren't *we* having fun" and "shall *we* have our ice cream." She sort of made everybody want to throw up. They (the nurses) had a lot of kids in this big room. I mean they were there in beds and wheelchairs and stuff, but some had to stay in their rooms so we walked all round and visited them, too. Then they (the nurses) served ice cream and we brought cupcakes and stuff to drink (Hawaiian punch) and everybody had a big party. It was fun sort of except I really felt sorry for those kids. I mean can you think of anything worse than being crippled and having to use wheelchairs and crutches and stuff, and some kids even have braces (not the kind on your teeth) but on their legs, and what would you do?

Write soon and tell me more about the play.

love,
Tanner

p.s. write soon
p.s.jr. did you get your hair cut?

Chapter 11

Tanner waited for the mailman to go through the vestibule and down the steps before she held the letter up to the light. The envelope looked more important than it felt: single-sheet thin and floppy, but crusted across the front with stamps. It was addressed to Cheryl in small spikey handwriting, with the words "special delivery" printed in purple.

The vestibule was shadowed, and Tanner stepped out onto the front steps, holding the envelope into the sunlight.

Don't see why people can't write so I can read it, she thought as she turned the letter sideways and upside down. She examined the back flap, picking at the corner, trying to pry it up. Why do people spit so much spit on an envelope, for pete's sake.

"Hi Tanner. Try steam, it works better. What do you have there?"

Tanner stepped back, catching herself on the black iron railing, as Jon came around the corner from the alley.

"Oh, oh nothing. I mean, it just came. I was just looking for her—Cheryl—it's special delivery."

"Don't worry about it, Super Spy," said Jon. "It's spring, almost, and for once I'm ahead in the studying and all's right with the world." He plucked the letter out of Tanner's hand. "It's from Cheryl's tenant in Virginia. Probably a leak in the kitchen faucet or something urgent. Come on. Let's go find her."

Tanner looked up at her brother, noticing the relaxed look around his eyes. For once he looked like Jon the way Jon used to be—not like the character in *Alice in Wonderland* who ran around carrying a pocket watch and worrying about being late.

She followed Jon into the house, back through the hall to the kitchen where the air was warm and smelled of coffee. All the way from the third floor came the sound of the glockenspiel.

It really must be spring, thought Tanner. Even Walter doesn't sound all bad today.

She heard the whine of the bagpipe coming from the den. Her father was practicing "Scotland the Brave," and the music made her want to step out across the floor, leaving Fenhagen behind—a metal heap on the floor.

[119]

"Oh Lord," said Jon, pouring a cup of coffee, "I forgot about the parade tomorrow. This might be a good afternoon to get lost what with those two practicing all day. How about it, Tanner? How about we go someplace this afternoon—you and Cheryl and I? What do you say? How about the zoo? I haven't been there in ages and Cheryl's never been."

"Could we? Go someplace, I mean? Would Cheryl, well . . ."

"Sure Tanner. You name it. Let me call her," he said, disappearing into the front of the house.

"Hey Jon," asked Tanner when her brother came back into the kitchen, "can we go any place? I mean, not the zoo, but someplace special?"

"We-ll, within reason. What did you have in mind?"

"The houses on Stirling Street. I mean, the dollar ones—you've never seen them and . . ."

"That's definitely not within reason. Besides I'm more in a peanuts-for-the-elephants mood today. Hey Cheryl, here's a letter for you—special delivery—and how about going somewhere with us this afternoon? You even get to pick the place. I'm for the zoo, and Tanner's still pushing those dollar houses. It's up to you," said Jon.

"I never could make a decision," said Cheryl. "The zoo seems so sort of . . . captive I guess, and the houses don't really interest me." Tanner felt the beginning prick of disappointment, then she heard Cheryl going on. "I know. How about the planetarium. I've never been there and Tanner loves it so. What do you say?"

"Good idea. Open your letter, then we'll get ready."

Cheryl took the letter and held it up to the light.

"Hey, what are you doing? You don't have to do that, it's your letter," said Jon.

"I know, but I always do. It makes a letter more exciting." She ripped open the envelope and caught her breath.

"Oh Jon, wait a minute. This is exciting."

Tanner watched Cheryl read the letter, then read it over again. And all of a sudden, without knowing anything at all, she felt as though any sign of spring was gone and bone cold winter was back. Walter hit a wrong note on the glock, and the wail of the bagpipe made her want to scream—the music suddenly almost sad.

"Jon, listen. The tenants in Aunt May's house —well, in our house—want to get out of the lease. He has a chance of an assistant professorship in Illinois someplace . . . to leave as soon as school's out down there . . . out West in June . . . even though the lease runs on . . . wonder if we could . . . find another tenant . . ."

Tanner watched as Cheryl laughed and waved the letter toward Jon. She heard her brother pick up the bits of conversation.

". . . fit in with our plans . . . force us to make a

decision . . . apply for next year at school down there
. . . a summer job . . ."

". . . be in our very own house . . . Aunt May's
garden . . . enroll for the September semester myself
. . . my job back part-time . . ."

". . . known all along what we've wanted . . .
settle in Virginia . . ."

Tanner watched Jon and Cheryl. She saw their
faces and heard their voices, but she couldn't reach
them. They were locked away like two dancing dolls
on the top of a music box, under a glass dome, turning and bowing while the music played. Tanner
reached out her hand. Jon and Cheryl turned away
without seeing her, their heads bowed over the piece
of paper. The bagpipe wailed, and Tanner felt her
world come crashing down.

After a while Jon looked up and caught her arm.
"Hey there, Tanner, I think you were just witness to
one of the quickest decisions ever made. It looks as
though we're moving to Virginia, but first, let's go
to the planetarium, how about it? The three of us are
going to the planetarium."

"No . . . no, I'm not. I mean, I can't. I have to
write a letter—to Jessie Lee. I mean, I absolutely promised to do it today. I—I . . ." she backed slowly out
of the room. It seemed to Tanner that all her screams
and yells were there waiting to be yelled, and she
couldn't use them. Her throat felt as numb as her leg;
the words were locked somewhere inside of her. As

she worked her way up the back steps, she heard Cheryl start to read the letter again.

Tanner was sitting at her desk in front of a blank piece of paper when her mother came in shortly before dinner. Alice McClean put her hand on her daughter's shoulder and gave her a quick hug.

"I know you're disappointed Tanner . . . how you feel about it . . . but Jon and Cheryl are so happy . . ."

"It's stinking rotten not fair," said Tanner, looking at her mother. "It's dumb. I mean all of a sudden, poof, they change their whole lives—just like that because of a dumb old letter from some dumb old . . ."

"I don't think it was all of a sudden, Tanner, Jon and Cheryl have talked about this very thing. But sometimes you don't listen. And when the letter came today and the tenant wanted to get out of the lease early, well, sometimes decisions made like that are the best kind. Of course you'll miss them. We all . . ."

"I won't miss them," said Tanner through clenched teeth. "I won't miss them one little bit and they'll hate it. I hope they hate it—all that country and fields and cows and . . ."

"Do you remember last fall—the day we spent together at Stirling Street and had lunch and all? Do you remember what I said to you that day, Tanner?" her mother asked.

Tanner pulled her baseball cap down over her eyes and folded her arms across her chest.

"I told you then Tanner McClean," her mother

[123]

went on, "not to put someone else in your own day-dreams, remember? Now how about coming down and helping me with dinner?"

"I can't." Tanner hunched her shoulders over the desk. "I can't. I *have* to write to Jessie Lee today. I couldn't even go to the planetarium because I had to write, and I have a whole bunch of really important stuff to tell her."

"Well, write quickly," said her mother, heading for the door. "I'll give you fifteen minutes, and then I really need you downstairs."

As Tanner heard the door click shut behind her mother, she picked up her pen and chewed on the blue plastic end. After a few minutes she began to write.

Dear Jessie Lee,

This is a really important letter cause I have a lot of stuff to tell you. It was so important I couldn't even go to the planetarium with Jon and Cheryl, and they begged and begged me.

1) Cheryl is really truly pregnant—she told everybody today (but I already knew) and that makes me an aunt (almost, in July) and if it's a girl, they might even name it Tanner.

2) all the yukky part of the work on the dollar house is finished, and now we're ready to start on the pretty part—the paint and all—and now there can even be a nursery.

3) Cheryl got a letter from the tenants in her house in Virginia (the one that looks like a mansion), and they (the tenants) want a new lease for ten years, and that's almost forever.

4) tomorrow is the St. Patrick's Day parade, and we're all going (we go every year) because my father and brother are both in it. My father plays the bagpipe (well), and Walter plays the glockenspiel (horribly). We always watch it downtown in front of the library a) because it gives my mother something to do before the parade—I'd rather eat hot dogs—and b) if you

really get freezing or have to go to the bathroom really bad, you can always go into the library.

5) we are studying outlining in school and I hate it.

6) now about baseball—oh yuk—my mother's calling me to set the table and she sounds really *mad* so I'll finish this later. See you . . .

Chapter 12

"Get out of my room. What are you doing here? That's mine, and you're a rotten lousy snoop, and I can't believe you're really doing that except I can believe it cause you stink, and you married Jon, and now you make him stink too."

Tanner's voice raged up and down as she stood in the doorway to her room watching her sister-in-law. Cheryl was leaning over the desk, half in shadow, half in the puddle of light spilling onto the desk. Her hand was on a piece of paper.

"Tanner, uh . . . I . . . well . . ."

"Uh-I-uh-well—that's what you sound like old spotty face, nosey old blotch head," yelled Tanner as she came into the room, grabbing the letter off the desk and stuffing it under her sweater. "How dare you read my letter? Nobody reads mail—not in this family at least—nobody. Not even Walter. Get out and don't come back. Ever, ever, ever."

"But Tanner, let me explain, I mean, well . . . I guess I can't explain but . . ." Cheryl moved out of the light, edging toward the door.

"I don't want you to explain, or, or anything, except go away." Tanner opened her bottom drawer and took out a looseleaf binder and a broken conch shell and a Kleenex box filled with letters. She took the letter out of her sweater and put it carefully in the drawer, then piled everything back in on top of it.

"There. I'll have to hide that letter. Really hide it, I mean," she said out loud. "Maybe even lock-and-key hide it."

"Tanner, wait a minute." Cheryl came across the room. "Let me try, well, if I can. We were sorry you didn't go with us today—Jon and I—to the planetarium. We brought you something. Stars that glow in the dark. You put them on your walls, or ceiling, or any place. I mean, if you want to." Cheryl stuffed at her shirt, pushing it down inside her skirt. She shifted from one foot to the other, then rubbed her hand over her forehead. Tanner stood looking at her. She stood with the desk chair between herself and Cheryl as if to protect herself.

"I don't care. I didn't want to go anyway, and I don't want your gloppy old stars all over my walls."

Cheryl reached out her hand, and Tanner stepped back, pulling the chair with her. "Don't touch me. Don't touch me you snooper-smopper. You . . ."

"You're right."

Tanner stopped and looked at Cheryl.

"Of course I'm right. About everything."

Cheryl wiped her hand down the side of her skirt. "You're not right about everything. Nobody is. But you're right about me being a snoop."

"I hate snoops."

"I hate them too."

Tanner wasn't sure exactly why, but she had the sudden overwhelming feeling that she was losing this fight. Not that it was exactly a fight. Not a real scream and yell all out war. And here was Cheryl with her meek-mouthed voice getting stronger and saying "I'm a snoop."

"And I'm sorry Tanner. I didn't mean to read your letter. I just came up here to leave these stars for you, and . . . well . . . and to tell you we missed you . . . and there was the letter. Well, I guess, well, I read it . . ."

"Well, I'm going to get a padlock—a great huge padlock with a key that goes on a chain around my neck, and nobody'll ever come here again. What's mine is mine and you just better stay out."

Cheryl started for the door. "You don't need a key, Tanner, but, about that letter, about the things you said, I mean, well, don't you think . . ."

"It's none of your business what I say in my letters. And besides, besides it wasn't a real letter. It was a joke. A great big fat stinking joke. Who'd ever mail anything like that anyway? That's just dumb— a dumb old stinking joke and dumb old Cheryl fell for it. And now I'm going to stand on my head so you can just get out of here."

Cheryl went out quietly, pulling the door closed behind her. Tanner waited until she heard Cheryl start up the stairs then she sat down at her desk, burying her head in her hands. Her face felt hot and crawly as she remembered the words Cheryl had read. She tried to push them back, but the words kept popping up all around the inside of her head, like lights in a pinball machine. Words in the letter to Jessie Lee, wonderful never-ever-wish-it-were-true words.

From upstairs came the sound of the glocken-spiel. Walter hit each note sharply and cleanly. "The Stars and Stripes Forever": through the floor; through the walls; through Tanner's thoughts.

Oh shut up, Walter McClean. I hate the glock-enspiel.

"I'll be in the Reference department if you want me, Tanner. Try and get a space by the reviewing stand, and get yourself a hot dog if you want. Okay, Cheryl, you coming? The parade won't be along for another half hour, and it's warmer in here."

Tanner turned away from her mother and sister-in-law and started back across the marble floor of the lobby. The library reminded her somewhat of a train station: people going in many directions, some hurrying, some straggling; in lines and out of lines, settling in at chairs and tables. She stood for a moment by the old brown card catalog and watched an old man dozing in a chair, his head lolling forward, his gray-brown overcoat blending into the grayness of his face. His hands fretted over a folded newspaper.

Tanner shivered. He looks empty, she thought. Empty and gray and never filled, as though he sits from one place to the next. Suddenly, she didn't want a hot dog anymore. For a minute she even thought of following her mother into the Reference room, of going up on the balcony and running her fingers over the books as she looked down on her mother poring over a report of some kind.

Oh yuk, *she's* there—Cheryl. I'll go see the goldfish, then, and Tanner started out of the Cathedral Street door to go around to the children's room. She edged her way in back of the reviewing stand along the tall library windows.

"Tanner, hey, wait a minute. I'm coming with you." Cheryl pushed her way through the crowd.

"You can't come with me cause I'm not going any place." She leaned back against the wall, folding her arms across her chest. "Go away. I'm going to get a hot dog after all. Alone." Tanner pushed away from the wall and worked her way back to the front of the library. She sensed, rather than heard, Cheryl following her.

"Go away," she called back over her shoulder.

"Go away." Her voice was lost as the first marching band came by, the trumpets stabbing the air, the voice from the loud speaker squawking over all.

Tanner stopped at a push cart and bought a hot dog and a grape soda. She stuffed the hot dog into her mouth as quickly as she could swallow it, all the while conscious of Cheryl standing next to her. She did not turn around.

"Tanner, I . . . uh . . ."

"I can't hear you. I don't want to hear you. Anyway, I'm going to watch the parade." She moved forward, snaking her way awkwardly through the crowd until she found a place behind a group of children sitting on the curb. A yellow balloon bobbed in front of her face, and she swatted it with her hand.

"It's not true, Tanner," said Cheryl. "None of it's true."

"What's not true?"

"The letter."

"That dumb old thing? Are you still talking about that dumb old letter? I told you last night that was a joke. Don't you know anything?"

The band stopped playing, and Tanner's last sentence rang out alone. "Don't you know anything?"

A man carrying a board covered back and front with souvenir shamrocks and green pom poms stopped in front of them. "How about it today? Only fifty cents?"

"No, no, not today," said Cheryl, quickly. The man went on. The band started up again, moving down in front of the reviewing stand. From over the hill came the sound of bagpipes.

"Here they come," called Tanner, stepping forward and losing her balance. She caught Cheryl's arm. "Here they are—the pipers—and there's Dad."

The pipers were slow and stately. They played "The Earl of Mansfield," the notes reaching out sad and happy at once, and Tanner heard the soft hush of their feet against the street. She scrunched her fingers together inside her pockets and shivered all the way through. Her father was in the third row across, looking straight ahead. He looks so beautiful, she thought. So tall and proud and as though the pipe were a part of him—not absentminded or busy or anything. Tanner watched even after the pipers had passed Mulberry Street and started down the hill. She strained her ears for the last note.

A drill team came along: marching and turning, in and out in front of her; criss crossing, opening ranks, closing ranks. Tanner looked along the curb for her mother. She found her next to the reviewing stand talking to the "zilch."

"There's Mom. I'm going down there." She turned away from Cheryl; away from the drill team; away from the man selling balloons.

"Wait a minute, Tanner. We're going to talk about this."

"Are not."

"Oh yes, we are." Tanner saw Cheryl's eyes, hard and determined. Saw her block the way. She felt something inside of herself begin to crumble. Still she didn't say anything. Turned to try and cross the street. Her way was blocked by the Mummers with their clinky clanky high-pitched sounds and their huge waving hats. She felt Cheryl take her hand.

"Let's move over here—away from the crowd."

Cheryl pulled, moving quickly, and Tanner stumbled.

"Hey, cut it out. What're you trying to do? Knock me down?"

Cheryl went on without looking back.

Over against the wall, which was getting grayer and colder as the March sun moved on leaving the west side of the street in shadow, over behind the pushcart with its steamy smell of hot dogs, Cheryl turned to face Tanner.

"Okay, we're going to talk, but first I have to spell a few things out . . ." Tanner pushed her hands further into her pockets and wondered where this new Cheryl had come from—this new non-splotchy, sure-voiced girl with her hair blowing back and her eyes wide and dark.

"First of all, I'm not pregnant, and you're not going to be an aunt. Second of all, we don't own a dollar house and we're not going to. And we're not fixing anything up . . ."

Tanner felt the something inside of her—the hard cold block that had started to crumble—begin to go even faster, as if her very innards were shattering

[134]

and splintering. She reached her hand up and held onto the side of the building, her woolen mittens sticking and pulling against the stone.

"And thirdly, my tenants in Virginia—tenants in a really tiny house, by the way—didn't renew their lease for ten years or nine years or eight seven six five—not even one. They want out, and we're going to let them because we can live there—Jon and I—and Jon will finish law school there, and . . ."

"It was a joke, I told you. It was a joke—a dumb old joke . . ."

"I don't care about the part about me," Cheryl's voice pushed on. "It doesn't matter to *me* that the things you told Jessie Lee weren't true, but it matters to me about *you*."

Tanner turned away toward the man with the cart, fumbling in her pocket for a quarter to get a box of buttered popcorn. She heard Cheryl's words, pushing on in back of her: sharp and clear.

"You don't have to lie."

"It's not a lie. I mean . . . I told you . . . a joke." Tanner ripped at the top of the box and stuffed popcorn into her mouth, letting the butter dribble down her chin. Well, I might choke to death right here in front of the Pratt Library, she thought, but at least she can't expect me to talk with my mouth full.

"That's what worries me," said Cheryl, dabbing at Tanner's chin with a Kleenex. "I think to you it's not a lie. I think it's so much the way you want things to be . . . playing baseball and . . . well, it must be hard in this family and all, but Tanner," Cheryl's voice was firm again, "you don't have to do it."

"Do what? You want me to stop writing to my friend?" She rubbed at her chin, leaving little flecks of red wool caught in the grease around her mouth.

"You know I don't mean that—not stop writing. I mean you don't have to, well, make things . . . different. It's just that, well, you're okay the way you are. Don't try to change . . ."

"It was a joke, and now you say I'm a liar, and you're . . . you're a . . . what do I care what you say . . ."

The little bit of spring was gone. The wind picked up, jerking at balloons, snapping flags, scudding trash along the street.

The sound of the glockenspiel pierced Tanner's thoughts: her jumbled, crumbled, angry thoughts.

"See. See what you made us do. You made us miss Walter, and he had a solo in 'Stars and Stripes Forever' and now they're all the way down by the reviewing stand, and . . . and that's all—the end of the parade I mean. It's over."

All around them the crowd began to break up: children running out onto the street to follow the end of the parade; souvenir sellers making one last try, "50 cents, just 50 cents—get your souvenir of the St. Patrick's Day parade here." Old women folded aluminum chairs and moved away. A policeman blew his whistle to let the cars across.

March 17

Hi, I'm back. I didn't get to finish this letter last night cause I got doing other stuff (like homework, ugh)—but back to 5) baseball—we're having tryouts at school next week (I want to play third base or else catcher) but we won't start tryouts till after Easter.

6) today was the parade and it was really neat—even Walter and the glockenspiel. And after it was over (the parade I mean) I sort of hooked onto the end of it and so did a lot of other kids and marched all the way to the end (down by City Hall).

7) after the parade we all went out to dinner (McDonald's) except first my father went home to change his clothes cause he wouldn't go out in his kilt.

8) and now we're home and I'm writing to you except I have to stop and go to bed and take a bath and find my tennis shoes because of tryouts.

9) pumpkin is so big she looks more like a cat than a kitten.

10) good night.

love,
Tanner

11) p.s. write soon.

[137]

Chapter 13

There was no one else.

No one but Cheryl.

Tanner took the letter out of the envelope and looked at it again. Already there were fuzzy worn lines on the page from being opened and closed so much; and there was Jessie Lee's slanty writing sprawling across the page. Tanner quickly stuffed the letter back in the envelope and shoved it down in her pocket.

There was only Cheryl.

She took the letter out and spread it on the table in front of her, yanking her hands away as if from something hot. Tanner closed her eyes and leaned against the table, not wanting to see the jumping-out words.

I've got to ask someone or I'll explode, and Cheryl knows—but *her?* I . . . I . . .

Tanner opened her eyes, looking down at the miserable piece of paper in front of her. Words and phrases leapt up at her, jabbing, stabbing, poking at her.

". . . so excited . . . to Washington over Easter . . . to see my married sister . . . my parents' big surprise . . . over to Baltimore to meet you . . . the day after Easter . . . really, really, really coming . . ."

Tanner shook her head, trying to clear it, but the words only rearranged themselves like pieces in a kaleidoscope; ". . . over to Baltimore . . . so excited . . . really coming . . . big surprise . . ."

I won't let her come, thought Tanner. I'll write and tell her not to. I'll tell her I'm sick, that we've moved, we're quarantined—anything, everything, nothing. I'll say my mother won't let me have company, that we hate people, that we're going to the South Sea Islands, have a vicious dog. Who wants to meet a dumb old pen pal anyway?

Tanner turned away from the letter, then back again, hoping it would be gone. The letter still lay on the table, but it looked as though it were growing: bigger and bigger. Spreading out across the table, across the room. She slammed both hands down flat on it, tearing a jagged rip down the center.

She thought about showing the letter to her parents; thought about settling down in the crackled brown vinyl chair in the den and . . . could almost hear their excited voices. Welcoming. Planning plans for Jessie Lee, for her. And then she'd have to tell them what she'd done; tell them the things she'd told Jessie Lee; the things she hadn't told her.

Standing by the tall front window, Tanner looked out at the street. She watched a green delivery truck stop, then start and stop again. She felt squirmy inside when she thought of telling her mother and father the truth. Or the "zilch"—the way she'd laugh. Or Jon.

Tanner felt hot all over, and her hands shook as she picked up the letter. There was only Cheryl who already knew; who had tried the day of the parade . . . Cheryl, Tanner was somehow sure, wouldn't laugh.

Cheryl read the letter through once. Then once again.

"Wow! You do have a problem, don't you?" she said.

Tanner picked at the pine needle cushion on the day bed. The needles felt prickly through the satin cover. She held it close to her face and it smelled of forest.

"I—I—I don't know what to do. I mean, well, if I tell my mother and father they'll know I lied, and the "zilch" will think it's dumb, and Walter . . . and Jon. Jon'll hate me and . . ." Tanner hiccoughed.

"Nobody's going to hate you, and when Jessie Lee comes . . ."

"What do you mean when Jessie Lee comes? She's not coming here—never, ever. I'll tell her I have the plague—the black plague, or the bubonic, or both, or . . . or . . . What good are you anyway?" Tanner screeched. "What do you mean when Jessie Lee comes?" Cheryl picked pumpkin off the window-sill and held the kitten on her lap.

"I mean after you write and tell her the truth. After she comes . . ."

"The truth?" Tanner struggled up off the couch. "What do you mean the truth? I can't tell her the truth. If I could tell her the truth, I wouldn't have had to write her all that stuff in the first place."

"But you did write it."

"Well, it was a joke. I told you that, and now, well, I'll tell her I'm busy—really busy, or . . ."

"For a friend? Too busy for that?"

"She's not my friend." Tanner pulled her base-ball cap down over her eyes.

"Not yet," Cheryl went on, "because she doesn't know you."

"What do you mean she doesn't know me?" asked Tanner, flopping back down on the couch, her left leg in the brace clanging against Cheryl's coffee table trunk. "Of course she knows me. We've written letters for ages—more than a whole year—tons of let-ters. We tell each other everything. We . . ."

"You know Jessie Lee, but she only knows some make-believe baseball-playing girl who . . ."

"I hate you," screamed Tanner, throwing the cushion across the room. "First you tell me that Jessie Lee's still coming, then you tell me to tell her the

[141]

truth, then you say my best friend doesn't even know me, and I . . ."

"You haven't given her a chance." Cheryl went on as though Tanner had never spoken. "What does Jessie Lee know about Mary Tanner McClean . . ."

"Tanner Mary."

"Okay, about Tanner Mary McClean and about Fenhagen and all your spunk and about how you love the city and how someday you'll do something really big—not through Jon or me or your mother or father, but on your own—you, yourself—not because you're a McClean, but because you're Tanner McClean."

"You expect me to tell her that? I mean, about Fenhagen . . . and . . . and how I can't run or play baseball or, or anything—and the lies, I mean, you know, the joke and all . . ."

"Well, it's up to you," said Cheryl, dropping pumpkin on the floor and getting up. "But if you don't tell her, you'll have to come up with something better than the bubonic plague. I don't think people get that anymore." Cheryl started toward the door. "I have to go to work now, but think about it. We all think the real Tanner's sort of special, and Jessie Lee deserves that. And by the way, if you run out of things to tell her, you might say that Jon and I are expecting you down to Virginia for a visit this summer, okay?"

March 25

Dear Jessie Lee,
    Ha—ha—ha—did I fool you . . .

March 25

Dear Jessie Lee,
    It was all a big dumb old joke and boy did you fall for it . . .

March 25

Dear Jessie Lee,
    I guess you'll think I'm really awful but . . .

March 25

Dear Jessie Lee,
    Cheryl says to tell you . . .

[143]

Dear Jessie Lee,

    I bet you think I'm a rotten stinking louse . . .

Dear Jessie Lee,

    I guess I really am a rotten stinking louse, but, well, a lot of the stuff I told you wasn't exactly true. I mean, I wasn't lying, but I guess I better say it right out and get it over with.

    I have this thing on my leg—well, it's really a brace named Fenhagen, and the reason it's there is cause I was hit by a car once when we were visiting my Aunt Milly, and then I spent a whole bunch of time in the hospital, and my leg is paralyzed so the only way I can walk on it is with the brace (Fenhagen) or with crutches so you can see that I can't really do a lot of stuff like play basketball or baseball or junk like that (but I can do just about EVERYTHING else), and I guess I was afraid you'd think I was dull so I made up a lot of stuff so you wouldn't (think I was dull).

    And there are some other things too—like Cheryl —she's not even really pregnant, and I'm not going to be an aunt, and they (Jon and Cheryl) didn't buy a dollar house (but I wish they had) and Cheryl doesn't own a mansion in Virginia, but a little tiny house, and

she and Jon are going to go back and live there AND
I WISH THEY WOULDN'T. And Cheryl found out
all the stuff I'd told you cause she read my letter, and
I hated her for it. But then when you said you were
coming here I got really scared, and she (Cheryl) was
really nice and told me (well, she didn't really tell me
but that's what she meant) to write you the truth—so
I am. Another thing—I have this kind of family where
everybody does something, but Cheryl says I will, too,
someday, and she said a lot of other stuff too, and I
think I like her now even if she did marry Jon and
sometimes gets all splotchy when she talks and I guess
I'll mail this before I get too scared to.

love,
Tanner Mary McClean

p.s. Cheryl and Jon invited me to come for a visit ~~and~~
~~stay the whole summer.~~

p.p.s. write soon.

Chapter 14

Dear Tanner Mary McClean,

You really are a rotten stinking louse for not telling me the truth. That was dumb and now I have to start all over getting to know you. I have about a ton of questions—is there really a "zilch" and did Amber have a kitten and did you give it to Cheryl and does Walter play the glockenspiel and most of all why did you name your brace Fenhagen? When I see you on Easter Monday I bet we'll have to spend about a whole half hour sorting everything out.

I can't wait to go to Washington. We're going to the Washington Monument and the Smithsonian and maybe the White House. My mother is writing to your mother to see if it's all right for us to come that day and to get directions to your house. She (my mother) also said I could invite you down this summer. You could come on the Trailways bus and we would meet you here. What do you do with Fenhagen when you go to the beach? My father said swimming is good for people with paralyzed legs and he can carry you out to the raft. Do you like to fish? I love it.

I have to go help my mother go through my clothes. You'd think we were going to Timbuktu instead of just Washington and Baltimore.

I still don't know why you made all that stuff up. I don't think I would have (but maybe I would). See you on the day after Easter.

love,
Jessie Lee

p.s. write soon.

"Cheryl, hey Cheryl, where are you? I have something to show you." Tanner stood at the bottom of the steps and yelled up.

"I'm on the third floor. Come on up."

Tanner started up the stairs as fast as she could. One step up, then swing Fenhagen alongside—one step up, then swing, one step up.

"Hey, guess what? I have a letter and . . . I'm going for a visit . . . and Jessie Lee's still coming here . . . and . . ."

Suddenly Tanner felt as though she were running out ahead of herself. Leaping and bounding. Jumping in and out of Fenhagen. Over and under and upside down.

"Cheryl," called Tanner from halfway up the third floor stairs. "Hey, Cheryl, I'm running," she said as she pulled her way up the steps.

"I see you Tanner."

Tanner looked up. Cheryl was leaning over the railing watching her. Her face was upside down, her hair hanging down. "I see you running," said Cheryl. And they both laughed out loud—Cheryl upside down and red in the face, Tanner starting up the last half flight of stairs.

"And Tanner, you're running on the inside. Everybody knows that's better than outside running any day. What's your letter say?"

April 2

Dear Jessie Lee,

I'm glad you're really coming. My mother wrote your mother and sent her a map. Guess what—She says I can come this summer on the bus. Fenhagen is because of a really yukky nurse I had in the hospital. I'll tell you about her someday (ugh). I love to swim and fish too (I guess. I never did—fish, I mean).

love,
Tanner

p.s. write soon
p.s. see you soon.

About the author

Colby Rodowsky's first novel, *What About Me?*, received wide critical acclaim. The *School Library Journal* said, "...the strains put upon a family by a retarded child are portrayed with compassion and realism...." And ALA *Booklist* wrote, "...Rodowsky's development of plot and character gathers real force, and her family dynamics are intuitively skillful...."

The author and her husband, a lawyer, live in Baltimore, Maryland and have a large family of six children.